KURSK

The Stackpole Military History Series

THE AMERICAN CIVIL WAR

Cavalry Raids of the Civil War
Ghost, Thunderbolt, and Wizard
Pickett's Charge
Witness to Gettysburg

WORLD WAR II

Armor Battles of the Waffen-SS, 1943–45
Army of the West
Australian Commandos
The B-24 in China
Backwater War
The Battle of Sicily
Beyond the Beachhead
The Brandenburger Commandos
The Brigade
Bringing the Thunder
Coast Watching in World War II
Colossal Cracks
A Dangerous Assignment
D-Day to Berlin
Dive Bomber!
A Drop Too Many
Eagles of the Third Reich
Exit Rommel
Fist from the Sky
Flying American Combat Aircraft of WorldWar II
Forging the Thunderbolt
Fortress France
The German Defeat in the East, 1944–45
German Order of Battle, Vol. 1
German Order of Battle, Vol. 2
German Order of Battle, Vol. 3
The Germans in Normandy
Germany's Panzer Arm in World War II
GI Ingenuity
The Great Ships
Grenadiers
Infantry Aces
Iron Arm
Iron Knights
Kampfgruppe Peiper at the Battle of the Bulge
Kursk
Luftwaffe Aces
Massacre at Tobruk
Mechanized Juggernaut or Military Anachronism?

Messerschmitts over Sicily
Michael Wittmann, Vol. 1
Michael Wittmann, Vol. 2
Mountain Warriors
The Nazi Rocketeers
On the Canal
Operation Mercury
Packs On!
Panzer Aces
Panzer Aces II
Panzer Commanders of the Western Front
The Panzer Legions
Panzers in Winter
The Path to Blitzkrieg
Retreat to the Reich
Rommel's Desert Commanders
Rommel's Desert War
The Savage Sky
A Soldier in the Cockpit
Soviet Blitzkrieg
Stalin's Keys to Victory
Surviving Bataan and Beyond
T-34 in Action
Tigers in the Mud
The 12th SS, Vol. 1
The 12th SS, Vol. 2
The War against Rommel's Supply Lines
War in the Aegean

THE COLD WAR / VIETNAM

Cyclops in the Jungle
Flying American Combat Aircraft: The Cold War
Here There Are Tigers
Land with No Sun
Street without Joy
Through the Valley

WARS OF THE MIDDLE EAST

Never-Ending Conflict

GENERAL MILITARY HISTORY

Carriers in Combat
Desert Battles
Guerrilla Warfare

KURSK

Hitlers Gamble, 1943

Walter S. Dunn, Jr.

STACKPOLE
BOOKS

Copyright © 1997 by Walter S. Dunn, Jr.

Published in paperback in 2008 by
STACKPOLE BOOKS
5067 Ritter Road
Mechanicsburg, PA 17055
www.stackpolebooks.com

Cover design by Tracy Patterson
Cover photo courtesy of Private Collection

Printed in the United States of America

10 9 8 7 6 5 4 3 2 1

ISBN 0-8117-3502-8 (Stackpole paperback)
ISBN 978-0-8117-3502-5 (Stackpole paperback)

Library of Congress Cataloging-in-Publication Data

Dunn, Walter S. (Walter Scott), 1928–
    Kursk : Hitler's gamble, 1943 / Walter S. Dunn, Jr.
        p. cm. — (Stackpole military history series)
    Originally published: Westport, Conn. : Praeger, 1997.
    Includes bibliographical references and index.
    ISBN 978-0-8117-3502-5
    1. Kursk, Battle of, Russia, 1943. 2. World War, 1939–1945—Germany. I. Title.
    D764.3.K8D86 2008
    940.54'21735—dc22

                                                                        2008004399

Contents

Preface

The justification for another study of Kursk has a wide span from "who cares" to an interesting compilation of data for war games, to an esoteric exercise of historic methodology. The late Professor H. S. Offler lectured me as an undergraduate in one of our first meetings at Durham University in 1949 on the primary importance of determining the motivation and bias of the creator of any historical document. The most dangerous sources, he warned, were those created by authors who claimed to be impartial or unbiased because the detection of their bias would be extremely difficult when they admittedly had gone to some pains to conceal it. Every attorney recognizes that witnesses usually are biased and have a motive in presenting their testimony; therefore, determining their motive is often a major part of the legal process. My bias is a cynical attitude toward most of the policymakers (politicians, generals, and admirals) of World War II, whose major concern was the role their country or their arm of service would play in the post-war world regardless of the loss of life in meaningless campaigns and the needless prolongation of the war for political purposes. While war was an extension of politics, politics was an extension of war.

All of us are constantly exposed to half-truths, distortions, and outright lies from the media and individuals who could benefit in some way from our acceptance of their interpretation of the facts. With the help of research in publications and information from other sources, we can often test the validity of claims about products and the truthfulness of statements. Given this broad exposure to deception, the persistence of accepted and untested interpretations of the Battle of Kursk is surprising. Distortions of the facts made by participants in the events are comparatively easy to detect because the motive is usually quite obvious. The German officers' motive in blaming Hitler for much of what went wrong with the German Army in World War II was to preserve their reputations. The Russians credited their forces with incredible feats and denigrated the role of Lend Lease because of the perceived need to reinforce the reputation of the Red Army during the Cold War.

The motivation of British and American historians is more difficult to assess. American historians have tended to follow both the German and British lead concerning the battle of Kursk, blaming the German defeat on a combination of Hitler's personal interference and the Allied invasion of Sicily that diverted German divisions from Kursk.

The focus of the book is the presentation of a factual account of the battle of Kursk and related events and the placement of the battle in a historical perspective. The objective is to examine the facts in detail to see if they reveal something that approaches a rational explanation of what occurred and the consequences. Rather than assuming that an event occurred based on one or two quotations from contemporary sources, a determined effort has been made to compare quantitative data from numerous sources, and on that basis to present rational interpretations of events. In some instances, the individuals involved were not aware of all of the facts at the time.

While historians should be concerned with, in the words of Sergeant Joe Friday, "just the facts ma'am," they should also provide some interpretation of those facts, over and above placement in either chronological or subject order, leaving it to the reader to make his or her own interpretation. To some the writing of history is the meticulous, carefully documented organization of details based on archival evidence, usually the contemporary written statements of the individuals directly involved in the events.

In Britain the ultimate test was caricatured in a vaudeville routine that began with one comedian describing an event in vivid detail to another comedian. The second comedian invariably interrupted at some point and asked, "But vas you dere Charlie?" The first comedian replied, "Nooo, but a fella told me about it." Many believed that personal participation in World War II was a prerequisite to writing about the war. With the passage of time and the death of most participants, this school of thought was faced with the alternative of either ending the study of World War II or admitting nonparticipants into the field.

The emphasis on documents produced by participants, however, continues the "participants only" school of thought. The only admissible facts are those found in public speeches, diplomatic correspondences, official reports, memoirs, and similar material even though in some instances the contemporary documents are incorrect or distorted for one reason or another. In other instances, untrue statements were made for purposes of deception. Some of the deceptions that were employed were embodied in the most respected documents and continue to be accepted as facts presented by contemporary witnesses.

In brief, it may not be sufficient proof to quote a document produced at the time of an event or a memoir by a participant. One must question the qualifications of the creator of the document, the presence of any bias or objective that would lead to the distortion of the facts, and the reason why the document was created. A diary entry is usually intended to place the author in a favorable light, while a memorandum from a staff officer is more likely to provide the most accurate information given to the commander. Public pronouncements by political leaders rarely indicate the true beliefs of the speaker, while transcripts or private minutes of meetings more often reflect the actual opinions of the participants.

An authorized lie can survive despite the existence of contradictory fact. As a youth in the 1930s, I heard a widely circulated story of the German worker employed in a factory supposedly making parts for baby carriages before Hitler openly renounced arms limitations imposed by the Treaty of Versailles. The worker's wife was pregnant and being a clever lad, the worker decided to steal parts and assemble a carriage for the expected baby. With great cunning, he was able to steal examples of every part made by the factory, but every time he tried to assemble a baby carriage, it turned out to be a machine gun. The story remains with me not only because it satirized the thinly veiled German violations of the treaty but also because it revealed that no matter how deceptive the camouflage, if one assembles the facts, the truth will emerge; and the challenge is to recognize the truth despite the authorized lies. Unfortunately, even the factory worker believed that he was still making parts for baby carriages.

In any study of a battle, one of the first priorities is to determine who participated. The previous dearth of information concerning the Red Army has been alleviated by the release of some information. Details concerning the orders of battle of the Red Army and the German Army have been compiled by the author over the past forty years—the former in a computer database and the latter in more conventional hard copy. To document each mention of a Soviet or German unit would have resulted in at least 200 additional pages of footnotes of limited interest to most readers. The Soviet order of battle information came from German intelligence records based on information from spies, prisoners of war, intercepts of radio transmissions by units, Soviet publications and broadcasts, and captured documents. This material was combined in a computer database with the published Soviet order of battle data. When the German information was compared to the Soviet data, remarkably few irregularities surfaced. Reinhard Gehlen, the chief of the *Fremde Heer Ost* (Foreign Armies East) used the data during World War II to develop forecasts of Russian intentions and potential strength, presenting conclusions that were often ignored. The German order of battle information came from hundreds of published sources, the most notable the series by Georg Tessin.[1]

Many individuals deserve recognition for contributions in completing this work. The consultations with Colonel David Glantz and Robert Volz were invaluable. William H. Robins, a fellow student at Durham University, read the manuscript and made many helpful suggestions. James VanDe Bogert, Calvin Wittmus, David McNamara, David Schmidt, and many others provided information, support, and encouragement.

No scholarly work could succeed without resources. The librarians of the Memorial Library of the University of Wisconsin were unstinting in their support. No one contributed as much as my wife, Jean, who read the manuscript many times and helped turn the mass of detail into a readable piece.

Introduction

The closing statement in Hitler's order concerning the German preparations for the Battle of Kursk was that winning the battle would be a *fanal* to the world that Germany was still a great military power able to defeat communist hordes. The German word *fanal*, usually translated as beacon, has a passive meaning in English representing a warning light, such as a lighthouse. The Russians translated the word as torch. The German *fanal* refers to a powerful light used in signaling, for example, the system used in Europe in the mid-nineteenth century before the telegraph. The blinking code of the lights was used to transmit messages from beacon to beacon for hundreds of miles. Similarly, the Battle of Kursk would send a message loud and clear to the world that Germany was not beaten. Hitler was correct in anticipating the monumental significance of the outcome of the Battle of Kursk, and that a victory would broadcast a message.

Ironically the defeat informed the leaders in the West that the Eastern Front was no longer a seesaw with Soviet victories in the winter and German victories in the summer. Instead the Soviets had established a dominant position in the East by the time of Kursk, and the German Army was no longer able to defeat the Red Army during the summer. Prior to Kursk, the assumption in the West was that the war on the Eastern Front would be indecisive with one side winning battles at first, and then the other. The resulting bloody stalemate was expected to weaken both nations in the same fashion that the young men of Britain, France, and Germany had been slaughtered on the Western Front in World War I. Just as the United States was able to end World War I with fresh divisions, so, it was assumed, the Western Allies would tip the balance in World War II after both Russia and Germany were exhausted. And, the slaughter would leave both Germany and Russia weak in the post-war world.

Kursk demonstrated that the Red Army could drive the German Army back to Berlin with no outside assistance. The danger to the free world was that with no Western presence in Germany at the end of the war, the Russians could dictate the terms of surrender and determine the occupation policy and reparations. Instead of merely stripping the relatively undeveloped eastern provinces of Germany, as in 1945, the Russians would have been able to loot all of Germany. Russian domination of Germany would have disrupted the balance of power in post-war Europe as American occupation of Japan changed the Far East. Realizing the need to be involved in the kill, Roosevelt was ready to give Stalin a firm commitment for a second front in the conference at Teheran in November 1943, despite Churchill's lack of enthusiasm.

This book will describe why the battle was fought, where and when it took place, who fought in the battle, how well the protagonists performed, as well as the implications of the Battle of Kursk on the war and on the post-war world.

The Battle of Kursk has suffered from two conflicting interpretations: the official Soviet version and the German version. In the former, the Soviets emerged as victors after grinding down the German forces in a complex defensive system "held to the last man." The 2nd SS Panzer Corps, a "powerful rolling armada of steel," was defeated in a Trafalgar-like tank battle by a wild charge of hundreds of tanks of the 5th Guards Tank Army.

In the German version, the heroic SS units had driven through the Soviet defenses in the south and had destroyed the Soviet tank units on a piecemeal basis, culminating with the destruction of the 5th Guards Tank Army at Prokorovka, only to have victory snatched from their hands by Hitler, who refused to release the Viking SS Division and the 23rd Panzer Division. He then called off the offensive and sent the SS to Italy in response to the threat posed by the Western Allies invasion of Sicily.

The principal proponent of the German version was Field Marshal Erich von Manstein, who believed that the Soviets had committed all of their available reserves by July 12 and that the battle could be won with the commitment of the 24th Panzer Corps standing by near Kharkov. In the original German edition of Manstein's book, *Lost Victories*, nineteen pages were devoted to Kursk, and most of them detailed the discussions made with Hitler on strategy before the battle. In contrast, Manstein devoted over seventy pages to the German counteroffensive that he led in the spring of 1943.[1]

An analysis of the details concerning the Battle of Kursk leads to a third interpretation. Operation *Citadel* was in fact four distinct battles: the first was the drive south by the 9th German Army that was held at the second line of defense by the 2nd Tank Army without drawing on either the Steppe Front or Stavka reserves. The second battle was the push of the 48th Panzer Corps on the west side of the advance in the south toward Oboyan, which was halted by the 1st Tank Army far short of Oboyan. The third and most successful was the drive by the 2nd SS Panzer Corps that ran into the 5th Guards Tank Army at Prokorovka. The final battle was the broad front offensive of Army Detachment Kempf that bogged down in the early days. Army Detachment Kempf made progress after the 3rd Panzer Corps turned north away from the objective of Korotscha.

Much of the fighting took place, not in the defensive zones, but in the intervening territory between the first and second zones in the north and the second and third zones in the south. None of these engagements involved a thousand tanks in one huge swirling battle. The major battle at Prokorovka on July 12 was fought in mud rather than clouds of swirling dust. The action resulted from the collision between the tank regiments of the Adolf Hitler and Reich Divisions, about 200 tanks, astride the Prokorovka road versus three tank brigades and a mechanized brigade (about 200 tanks) of the 5th Guards Tank Army striking south on the same road. Although there were 1,500 German and Soviet tanks "in the area," these were divided into three separate engagements: the engagement at Prokorovka, another south of Prokorovka between the 3rd Panzer Corps and the 69th Army, and a third north of Prokorovka, between the Death Head Division and the 10th Soviet Tank Corps.

Few, if any, land battles during World War II were strictly accidental. Intelligence resources had escalated to the point of virtually eliminating the encounter battle, with two armies colliding at some unexpected location at an unforeseen time, neither army being prepared for defense or offense. Information concerning enemy movements and capabilities gave one or both commanders the ability to select or at least influence the location, timing, and magnitude of a battle. In World War II commanders selected points at which to launch massive offensives and then concentrated men and material to carry out detailed, planned movements that had been orchestrated days in advance. Other commanders chose to defend, preparing elaborate fortified positions to repel the attacker, after discovering the location of a planned attack. Although the outcome of a battle was always in doubt, preparation and planning reduced considerably the element of chance.

The elements that influenced a decision to launch a major offensive or fight a decisive battle were exceedingly complex. Too often the observer misjudges or even ignores the factors that led to a battle or oversimplifies the causation. The Axis powers were not doing well in mid-1943. The Japanese had passed their zenith in the Pacific, and the struggle for North Africa had ended with the German collapse in Tunisia. The Allied air war against Germany was gathering momentum. The single major German victory had been the counteroffensive in the Ukraine orchestrated by Manstein in the spring, and Hitler needed a follow-up victory.

The German planning for the battle of Kursk began in March, 1943, four months before the event, and was strongly influenced by events that had taken place in November 1942. The invasion of North Africa by Britain and the United States in November 1942 signaled Hitler that the likelihood of an invasion of France in 1943 was slim. The plans made at Casablanca by Churchill and Roosevelt in January 1943, soon revealed to Hitler, confirmed that fact.

Even before the Casablanca Conference, the German General Staff began stripping the armies in Western Europe of their best divisions to restore the balance on the Eastern Front after the defeat at Stalingrad. The divisions from France were replaced with worn out shells of divisions often with only a division commander and a bakery company. Other divisions consisted of older men with a minimum of support weapons and no transport. These static divisions formed a thin, brittle shell along the coast of France and the low countries, while the battered remnants of divisions from the Eastern Front were reformed from recruits in the interior. By the late summer of 1943, the German 38th Infantry Division was the only German division capable of mobile warfare in Western Europe.

Even considering the enormous appetite of the Eastern Front for German divisions, the sudden availability of a strategic reserve of over twenty divisions gave Hitler a unique opportunity to seize the initiative once again and deal the Soviets a devastating blow. The vanguard of these Western divisions was sufficient to reverse the balance in the Ukraine in February 1943, providing Field Marshal Manstein the means to perform his miracle: forcing back the advancing Red Army and retaking Kharkov. The German intelligence leader, General Reinhard Gehlen, attempted to convince Hitler that the balance had not been reversed in the long run, but his pessimistic advice was rejected by Hitler. In one instance, Hitler scrawled the word "garbage" across the first page of one of Gehlen's reports, indicating a rapid expansion of the Red Army.

Therefore, we have one factor in Hitler's decision to fight in the summer of 1943—the availability of a large strategic reserve as a result of the Allied decision not to invade France in 1943. The decision when to fight the battle was complicated by several factors. In March the spring thaw reduced the dirt roads and the fields to quagmires. In 1940 of the 400,000 km of roads in the Soviet Union, only 7,100 km were either asphalt or concrete. Of the rest, only 136,000 km were surfaced with gravel, and the remaining 250,000 km were scraped dirt trails.[2] After a few vehicles churned the sparse coat of gravel on the roads, horses would sink into the mud up to their bellies. The steel treads of one tank could literally destroy a Soviet dirt road during the muddy period. The battle had to be postponed until the roads dried in April. Manstein advised Hitler that the attack had to be made as soon as possible after the spring muddy season. Manstein believed that a mobile defense was the only chance for Germany to utilize its superiority in leadership and fighting ability. Therefore Germany could make a preemptive strike at Kursk before the Russians could make up their losses and then turn south and roll up the Soviet Front in the Ukraine. However Manstein preferred that Germany wait for the Russians to attack, give ground, and then attack the north flank of the Soviet spearheads when they overextended themselves. The German forces could then drive south into the Ukraine and cut off large numbers of Russians.

Hitler, however, refused the second alternative because it involved the surrender of the Donets basin and delayed the attack on Kursk, which would give German industry more time to produce additional Tiger and Panther tanks. The Germans did increase their tank strength significantly in April, May, and June, but Hitler's decision to wait until more tanks were available also gave the Soviets the opportunity to build tanks at a faster rate than the Germans. Given the mechanical problems of the early production models of the Tiger and Panther, the Germans lost ground in the comparable tank numbers by delaying from April to July 1943.[3] Hitler's error was compounded when one compares German intelligence estimates of Soviet tank production with the official figures now available. German intelligence knew that they would lose, not gain, ground with tank forces by delaying the battle. Weather had determined the earliest and best time for the battle to take place, but the optimum date was sacrificed by Hitler's concern for more Tigers and Panthers.

Another factor in Hitler's decision to delay was the desire to give German divisions, worn down in previous battles, the opportunity to absorb replacements and obtain new weapons. Again the problem was that the delay gave the Russians time to make similar restorations and to rebuild their own worn units. In addition, the Soviets had a larger population and a larger pool of incoming recruits. About half of the annual class of new recruits trained in the spring and were sent to the front in late spring and early summer. The other half were trained in the fall. As a result the Red Army had enough men to both restore worn divisions and to create new units, including self-propelled tank destroyer regiments and tank destroyer brigades that would play a major role in the battle at Kursk. In April 1943, Hitler had a strategic reserve provided by the divisions from France that the Red Army could not match. However, in July, while the German reserves had grown slightly, the Russians had an entire army group (the Steppe Front) in reserve behind the Kursk salient. The Germans were not able to make a significant increase in the number of units in the three-month interval, although individual units had improved in quality.

According to Zhukov and others, Hitler's miscalculation was almost rescued by a compensating misjudgment on the part of Stalin. Stalin argued that a preemptive strike, similar to the disastrous attack at Izium in the spring of 1942, would catch the Germans off guard and ward off the attack. Stalin's position had considerable validity. By the time the roads dried in April, the Red Army had recovered some of its strength and was far superior to the German forces in manpower and tanks. Traditionally the numerically superior force usually attacks the numerically inferior force. However, the level of Russian training was low and engaging the experienced German divisions would have been a risky ploy. Stalin deferred to his generals and waited for the German attack.

The final factor, the battle location, was dictated by the presence of the bulge at Kursk that presented the Germans with an ideal opportunity to encircle a large number of Russians with minimal effort. The Russians were faced with strong German forces on the north, west, and south. A quick drive from both sides would close the pocket. Eliminating the bulge would restore direct rail links between Army Groups South and Center. The Russians, on the other hand, lacked rail capacity in the area with only a single line that was in poor condition leading into Kursk from the east. The Russians also were short of the rolling stock to move the hundreds of thousands of troops and mountains of supplies and equipment from Stalingrad and Moscow.

The primary reasons for the battle at Kursk can be briefly summarized: first, because the resources were available to show the world that Germany was still strong; second, German panzer forces were in a time frame that afforded technical superiority over their Russian opponents; and third, the Kursk salient offered Hitler the opportunity to destroy two Soviet fronts and open a gaping hole in the Russian line. Why Hitler's gamble failed will be examined in detail in the chapters that follow.

CHAPTER 1

The Strategic Position, April 1943

In April 1943 military action in Russia was halted by the spring muddy season. The Red Army was recovering from the setback in the Ukraine where Manstein had used the divisions transferred from France to stop the Soviet offensive and retake Kharkov. Although the Western Allies were still bogged down in Tunisia, Hitler was aware of their plans to attack somewhere in the Mediterranean, rather than France. Stalin wanted to resume the attack as soon as possible; however, the Soviet General Staff, learning of the German plan to attack Kursk, advised him to let the Germans strike first.

The Battle of Kursk had its origins in the offensives ordered by Stalin in late January 1943 to drive the German and satellite armies back to the Dnieper River. However, the German Sixth Army was still holding out in Stalingrad, diverting several Soviet armies. The final phase of the destruction of that pocket began on January 22, 1943. Four days later the pocket was split into two segments as the Soviet armies exerted maximum pressure to finish off the Germans. On January 31, 1943, the recently promoted German Field Marshal Friedrich von Paulus surrendered, and the Soviets claimed 91,000 prisoners of war. The prisoners were marched out of Stalingrad and placed on trains at Saratov and sent to Tashkent. Only half of those that reached Saratov survived the train trip. Most of the prisoners suffered from symptoms of an enlarged heart and respiratory disease, brought on by the fear of death or capture, and malnutrition during the two months in the pocket. About 5,000 survived captivity and return to Germany after the war.[1] In the Stalingrad area, over 209,000 men were killed or went into captivity during the period November 23, 1942, to February 2, 1943.[2] When the losses outside of the pocket are added, the total casualties at Stalingrad were 300,000 men.

In addition, the Germans lost prestige and the Nazi reputation of invincibility. Although the defeat at Moscow in December 1941 had marked the first defeat experienced by the Wermacht in World War II, the Germans had stopped the Red Army and retained most of the ground taken in 1941. The summer of the 1942 campaign, following the Soviet disaster at Izium, had restored German stature and influence over the satellite nations. That stature was reversed by Stalingrad and entailed not only numerous casualties but the loss of most of the territory gained by the Germans during the summer.

As Hitler suffered a momentary loss of confidence and agreed to major withdrawals from the Caucasus in an attempt to restore the military situation in the Ukraine, Stalin was emboldened to order ambitious offensives. Using three fronts, the Voronezh, the Southwest, and the Southern, the Stavka planned to destroy seventy-five German divisions in the Ukraine. The Voronezh Front was to retake Kharkov and Kursk and drive the Germans back to a line west of Kursk and Kharkov. The Southwest and Southern Fronts were to cut off the Germans in the south by driving to the coast of the Sea of Azov at Mariupol with a final objective of forcing the Germans back across the Dnieper River.[3] Farther north the Bryansk Front and the new Central Front, formed on February 15, 1943, from the units of the Don Front and transferred from the Stalingrad pocket, were ordered to drive west through Bryansk to Smolensk. The Kalinin and Western Fronts were to attack the German Army Group Center while the Northwest Front was to pinch off the salient at Demyansk and attempt to cut off the Germans surrounding Leningrad.[4] These grandiose Russian plans were reminiscent of the Russian dispersed buckshot approach that had failed in the previous winter.

The Soviet strategy was dictated by the need to prevent the Nazis from shifting divisions from the center and north in order to restore the situation in the south. The Germans had one great advantage in the game of shifting forces—the Russian railway system. The farther east one moved in Russia, the fewer the railroads. To supply Kursk, the Soviets had use of only one railroad leading south from Moscow through Yelets and on to Stalingrad. The line was under German fire from a bulge held by the German 2nd Army as it passed through Voronezh. An alternate route led east of the Donets with a branch line into Lisk, south of Voronezh. The rail line north from Rostov was blocked north of Kantemirovka about halfway between Voronezh and Rostov. These limited rail facilities were severely damaged as they had been taken recently from the Germans.

In contrast behind the German lines the railroads were in excellent condition. The rails had been refitted to the European gauge in the year and a half after the Germans occupied the Ukraine. The Nazis enjoyed at least five north-south lines and nine east-west lines between the Moscow area and the Sea of Azov. The number of lines was important because of the inflexibility of rail traffic. The maximum number of trains in one direction on a double rail line was forty-eight per day, and only twenty-four per day on a single line track as time was lost shunting an oncoming train onto a siding while the first train passed. These numbers were predicated on excellent block signal equipment that was not always available to the Russians. A German infantry division at full strength required forty trains if the vehicles moved by road. If the vehicles were also placed on trains, the most common practice, the total trains required was sixty-six. The Red Army divisions, smaller and with less organic transport, required about thirty trains. Therefore while the Russians could move one and a half divisions per day, the Germans had the rail capacity to move each day more than five divisions north-south and over nine east-west. The major delay for the Germans was loading the trains, not the capacity of the railroad. Obviously in a contest to move divisions south, the Germans could move five times as many divisions as the Russians. Therefore the Red Army had to tie down the German Center and North Army Groups with attacks, even though there was little hope of local success, in order to maintain the Red Army superiority in the south.

The Soviet offensive began on January 28, 1943, when the Soviet 40th Army launched an offensive through a gap in the German line hitting the open flank of the 7th Corps of the 2nd German Army. The hole in the front had developed as a result of the encirclement and virtual annihilation of the 2nd Hungarian Army early in January. On the north flank of the German 2nd Army the 13th Soviet Army of the Bryansk Front struck south against the German 13th Corps. These two attacks in the final days of January 1943 opened a series of offensives designed to drive the Germans back to the Dnieper River.[5]

The 13th Soviet Army was a substantial army that had seen little action in the past three months, and its units were in good condition. The army had nine rifle divisions (8th, 15th, 74th, 81st, 132nd, 148th, 211th, 280th, and 307th), three tank brigades (79th, 118th, and 129th), and three tank regiments (42nd, 43rd, and 193rd). Of there, the only new unit was the 193rd Tank Regiment that had come from the Stavka Reserve in November 1942. The army's very ample artillery support included the 5th and 12th Artillery Divisions plus three tank destroyer regiments (130th, 543rd, and 874th), the 1287th Antiaircraft Regiment, the 19th Guards Artillery Regiment, the 65th Guards Mortar Regiment, and four mortar regiments (131st, 476th, 477th, and 479th). All of the supporting units had been with the Bryansk Front for three months or more, with the exception of three of the mortar regiments, that were added in November from the Stavka Reserve, and the 12th Artillery Division that came from the Ural Military District in November. The 13th Army was strong in supporting units and probably utilized the front reserves in the offensive.

The Bryansk Front also included the 2nd Tank Army that had been refitted in the Volga District in December 1942 and sent to the Bryansk Front in January 1943, with only one tank corps (the 16th), the 6th Guards Rifle Division, the 37th Guards Mortar Regiment, and the 51st Motorcycle Battalion. The Bryansk Front reserve had the 11th Tank Corps, the 19th Tank Corps, the 11th Guards

Tank Brigade, and the 29th Guards Tank Regiment with a total of over 550 tanks in the tank army and the reserve. The reserve also had the 137th Rifle Division, two tank destroyer regiments (563rd and 567th), the 16th Antiaircraft Division, the 461st Antiaircraft Regiment, the 5th Guards Mortar Division with two brigades and two regiments, and the 286th Guards Mortar Battalion.

To the south the Soviet Voronezh Front consisted of the 60th Army on the right with Kursk as its objective; the 38th Army with Oboyan as its objective; and the 40th, 69th, and 3rd Tank Armies with Kharkov as their objective. The Voronezh Front had a strong reserve directly under front control: the 4th Tank Corps with three refitted tank brigades, which had arrived from the Volga District after having fought with the 21st Army in the Don Front at Stalingrad in November 1942. The tank corps had none of the usual supporting troops, only the three tank brigades and the 4th Mechanized Brigade. The Voronezh Front also had six independent tank brigades (14th, 86th, 96th, 173rd, 192nd, and 201st) all of which had been with the front for some time. The 6th Guards Cavalry Corps (redesignated from the 7th Cavalry Corps in January) came from the Bryansk Front. The Voronezh Front reserve had a total of nine tank brigades plus the tank regiments in the mechanized brigade and the cavalry corps, with a total of about 600 tanks. The front reserve had some elite infantry units including two ski brigades (4th and 8th) from the Moscow Military District and two sled battalions (43rd and 50th) formed in the Ural and Archangel Districts in November 1942. The sled battalions were equipped with sleds powered by aircraft propellers and engines that were very useful when the ground was covered with snow and the lakes and rivers were frozen.

The Voronezh Front reserve also included a powerful artillery component. In December 1942, the 10th Artillery Division came from the Moscow District where it had been formed in November. The 4th Guards Mortar Division and the 5th Antiaircraft Division came from the Stavka Reserve in January 1943. The front reserve also had two antiaircraft regiments (1281st and 1289th), two artillery regiments (875th and 1109th), and the 1240th Tank Destroyer Regiment.

The Voronezh Front had a total of over 1,000 tanks and ample artillery support provided by the two artillery divisions plus independent regiments. The tank corps, the cavalry corps, and the six tank brigades in the front reserve provided the commander with the equivalent of an additional tank army.

Opposing the Soviet 13th Army and three armies of the Voronezh Front were the German 7th and 13th Corps of the 2nd Army with seven weak divisions. The 7th Corps had been part of the 2nd Army for over eight months. Included were the 57th, 75th, and 323rd Infantry Divisions that had been assigned to the corps on an essentially quiet front since August 1942. The 13th Corps included the 82nd, 68th, 340th, and 377th Infantry Divisions that formed the 13th Corps since September 1942. All of these divisions had probably been reduced to six or seven infantry battalions in 1942 providing a total of no more than fifty rifle battalions to resist the combined offensive power of nine rifle divisions of the 13th Soviet Army and thirty rifle divisions and 1,600 tanks of the Voronezh Front.

The Voronezh Front attacked the Germans on a line from Kursk to Belgorod to Kharkov in late January 1943. The most northerly of the Voronezh Front armies was the 60th that drove directly toward Kursk along the Kastornoie-Kursk railroad. The 60th Army had only five rifle formations. The 121st and 141st Rifle Divisions and the 104th and 248th Rifle Brigades had been with the Voronezh Front for some time. The 322nd Rifle Division had been added to the 60th Army in January 1943 from the 16th Army in the Western Front. The army also had two antiaircraft regiments (217th and 235th), three artillery regiments (522nd, 1148th, and 1156th), two tank destroyer regiments (694th and 1178th), two destroyer brigades (8th and 14th), each with two antitank gun regiments and other antitank battalions. The 60th Army also had the 150th Tank Brigade (with fifty tanks), the 98th Guards Mortar Regiment, the 326th Guards Mortar Battalion, and four mortar regiments. Two regiments (128th and 138th) had been with the army and two others (495th and 496th) were new regiments formed in December 1942. The army, with about thirty-five rifle battalions, was strong in antitank and antiaircraft defense, but weak in artillery and tanks.

To the south of the 60th Army, the 38th Soviet Army in February 1943 had as its objective Oboyan, south of Kursk. Again it was a small army with only five rifle divisions (167th, 206th, 232nd, 237th, and 240th). The 206th and 232nd had been added recently along with the 180th Tank Brigade. The army also had the 7th Destroyer Brigade, two tank destroyer regiments (611th and 1244th), the 1112th Artillery Regiment, and the 66th Guards Mortar Regiment. The 491st and 492nd Mortar Regiments were two new regiments added in December 1942. The 125th Artillery Regiment, detached from the 12th Artillery Division, had come from the Bryansk Front, and the 21st Guards Mortar Brigade of the 4th Guards Mortar Division had come from the Stavka Reserve. With forty-five rifle battalions, the 38th Army had ample artillery, but only fifty tanks.

The Soviet 40th Army launched its attack on February 3, 1943, with Kharkov as its objective. The 40th Army was much stronger and had been heavily reinforced.[6] The army had eleven rifle formations. Nine had been with the army (25th Guards, 100th, 107th, 303rd, 305th, 309th and 340th Rifle Divisions, and 129th and 253rd Rifle Brigades), and two were recent additions. The 183rd Rifle Division transferred in January 1943 from the 3rd Reserve Army in the Stavka Reserve, and the 37th Rifle Brigade in December 1942 from the

30th Army in the Western Front. The 37th Rifle Brigade and 305th Rifle Division were transferred to the new 69th Army in early February, reducing the army from eighty-four rifle battalions to seventy-one. The 40th Army had the 116th Tank Brigade and received the 68th Tank Brigade from the 61st Army in the Western Front in January. The army also had the 332nd Antiaircraft Battalion, two tank destroyer regiments (4th Guards and 595th), the 16th Destroyer Brigade, the 76th Guards Artillery Regiment, and the 36th Guards Mortar Regiment. The 493rd and 494th Mortar were new regiments added in December along with the 512th Artillery Regiment. The 40th Army had comparatively few supporting units for eleven (later nine) rifle formations, and was especially weak in artillery and tanks. The 40th Army moved past the south flank of the German 2nd Army and then turned some units north to link up with the 13th Army from the Bryansk Front but it was short of fuel and ammunition.

Two German corps were encircled in February 1943 as the two Soviet armies met at Kastornoie. However the bitter cold, heavy snow, and icy roads prevented the formation of a firm pocket, and many of the Germans escaped leaving their equipment behind.[7] The Russians opened another gap in the German line and pursued the remnants of the German 2nd Army, taking Kursk along the way. The 13th Army of the Bryansk Front and the 60th and 38th Armies of the Voronezh Front drove the Germans back to a point over 350 km west of Voronezh on March 3, 1943. The Germans moved in divisions from the 2nd Panzer Army on the north of the salient, reinforced the 2nd Army in the south, and drove the Soviet spearhead back about 40 km to a line north and south of Rylsk 75 km west of Kursk. The offensive by the 13th, 60th, and 38th Armies had carved out the Kursk bulge.[8]

Meanwhile the Germans had taken steps to make divisions available to shore up the gaps in the south opened by the Soviet offensive. The German General Staff proposed the abandonment of the Rzhev salient, a huge bulge that pointed toward Moscow. The protrusion had resulted from the Soviet winter offensive of 1941–42 that had cut deeply into the German Front from the north and south of Rzhev. Rzhev had held out, and German counterattacks had broadened the base of the salient. The German position had remained stable since the spring of 1942, but to shorten the line and free up divisions for use in the south, Hitler agreed to the withdrawal on February 6, 1943. Preparations began with the destruction of facilities that might have aided the Russians and the evacuation of Russians of military age. On March 1, 1943, the withdrawal began and was complete by March 25, 1943. The 544 km line was reduced to 176 km, releasing both German and Russian units for use elsewhere. The Germans pulled out the 9th Army headquarters and shifted it south to the northern shoulder of the Kursk salient where it assumed command of the units that would launch the attack in July 1943.

Farther north the Germans decided to liquidate another salient at Demyansk for the same purpose of shortening the line to make divisions available at Leningrad and in the south. The withdrawal began on February 20, 1943, and was completed by March 18. The Russians also withdrew units from the Demyansk area. The 11th and 27th Army headquarters, along with many divisions that would appear at Kursk, were removed from the line and transferred to the reserve east of the Kursk bulge. The two German withdrawals were based on the assumption that they would be able to make good use of their released divisions before the Russians could move divisions south because the Germans had a better railroad network. Whereas the released German divisions were in action elsewhere in March, turning back Soviet offensives, the Russians transferred most of the divisions from the Rzhev salient to the reserve.

The Soviets, aware of the Germans thinning out the line in the Rzhev salient, had begun withdrawing units at the same time. In addition to the units sent along with the 65th Army to the Central Front, the 61st Army with three rifle divisions, four rifle brigades, and the 16th Artillery Division went to the Bryansk Front. The Western Front released the 18th Artillery Division to the Leningrad Front and the 13th Guards Mortar Brigade and the 6th Tank Corps to the Northwest Front. Two divisions were sent to the 21st Army in the Central Front (325th and 375th); the 149th Division went to the Central Front 2nd Tank Army; three divisions went to the Southwest Front (19th, 50th, and 53rd); and two divisions went to the Stavka Reserve (20th Guards and 113th). This scattering of resources was probably the product of available rail capacity rather than overall strategy. Extensive rail connections were available to the north of the two abandoned salients, while very limited capacity was available to the south, even though the need was greater there.

The Kalinin Front, which held the northern face of the Rzhev salient, also gave up substantial units. The 3rd Mechanized Corps was given to the 1st Tank Army of the Northwest Front along with the 6th Tank Corps from the Western Front. The 74th Rifle Brigade went to the Leningrad Front, and the 28th Guards Tank Brigade went to the 2nd Tank Army in the Central Front. Many units went back to the Stavka Reserve and the Moscow Military District for refitting. Included in the movement from the Kalinin Front were the 184th Tank Brigade, five tank regiments (13th Guards, 34th, 39th, 45th, and 229th), the 11th Guards Mortar Brigade, and the 61st Guards Mortar Regiment. Again available rail capacity was a major factor in the movements.

The Germans, on the other hand, had been able to move their divisions swiftly. The combination of the skillful use of their forces and the overextension of the Red Army (350 km from the supply depots at Voronezh) provided the Germans with the opportunity to nip off the tip of the offensive west of Kursk and drive the Russians back.

On February 15, 1943, the Don Front headquarters, from the Stalingrad pocket, was inserted between the Bryansk Front and the Voronezh Front and given the title of Central Front. To reinforce the Soviet forces in the Kursk bulge, Stalin ordered the transfer of divisions from the Stalingrad pocket in February. The troops had to come by rail over a limited network. Two rail lines led to the Kursk area, one leading south from Moscow through Yelets, and an alternate route leading east of the Donets with a branch line into Lisk, south of Voronezh. There was no line between Lisk and Rostov, which meant that all troops, equipment, and supplies from the Stalingrad area took long round-about routes to reach the new front. Most of the units from Stalingrad moved to the rail junction at Yelets northeast of Kursk and then came south on the Yelets Kastornoie line.

The last leg of the trip was 130 km of single-track line from Kastornoie to Kursk, and the final 50 km was not open until the end of February. The track, in poor condition at certain points, could not sustain the weight and stress of a working locomotive. The trains were disassembled and individual cars were pulled by teams of horses. The severe winter added to the difficulty with drifts of snow blocking part of the track and the roads.[9]

General Konstantin Rokossovsky described the difficulties in moving two armies from the Don Front to the Kursk area in February. The move, which began on February 15, 1943, used a single-track railway and was soon behind schedule because requests for troop trains were not met. Railway cars to move supplies and weapons were not always the correct type needed. Major problems developed in loading troops and weapons and also in unloading at the destination. Units arrived in the Kursk area in disarray. Artillery pieces arrived with no tractors or horses to draw them. Weapons and troops were unloaded in the wrong area, far from the planned area of concentration. For many weeks 169 service units remained in Stalingrad because of the lack of troop trains to move them.[10]

Lack of good rail connections created an incredible handicap for the Red Army that eased later in 1943 with the enormous flow of the American 2.5-ton trucks beginning in the summer of 1943. The trucks provided the Red Army with the mobility to carry out far-reaching offensives from late 1943 to the end of the war. But until the arrival of the American trucks, the Russians had to rely on a relatively short supply of Soviet made GAZ trucks, which were copies of Ford Model A trucks with a two-wheel drive and small engines. Given the primitive state of Russian roads, these trucks were of little use except under ideal weather conditions—hard front or dry summer. During the rainy season supplies moved on horse-drawn carts or on the backs of men. The troops walked and tanks wore out their tracks on 100-km road marches. In the buildup for Kursk the heavy snow added to the problems. Trucks and horses were in short supply, so the troops not only marched but also carried heavy loads of weapons and supplies. The local population was drafted into the operation. The people of one village relayed a load of supplies to the next village, and the people of that village carried it on to the next one.

Moving the armies of the Don Front to Kursk required an enormous number of trains. A single motorized brigade needed seven trains with 449 cars. A tank corps required twenty trains; a cavalry division, eighteen; and a rifle division, fifteen. The maximum number of trains that a single-track line could accommodate was only twenty-four per day, and the trains were moving about 150 km per day.[11] Less than two divisions could move per day, and to reach Kursk from Stalingrad under the best conditions was a week's trip. Moving the divisions of the 6th and 7th Guards Armies demanded a considerable effort, while the same limited rail network continued to supply the Southwest and Southern Fronts. Needless to say the operation that began on February 15 was not completed by February 25, when the Soviets launched an attack to stabilize the situation on the south shoulder of the bulge. The 21st Army was in transit from Stalingrad, and the 70th Army had not completed its move from the east.[12] In February, the Central Front consisted of the 65th, 70th, 13th, and 48th Armies and formed the northern rim of the Kursk bulge. The 48th and 13th Armies were taken from the Bryansk Front; the 70th Army had come from the Stavka Reserve; and the 65th Army had shifted from the Western Front opposite the Rzhev salient to the tip of the Kursk bulge, facing the right flank of the 2nd Panzer Army.

At the end of February the 65th Army consisted of seven rifle divisions (37th Guards, 69th, 149th, 173rd, 193rd, 246th, and 354th). The 37th Guards and 193rd Divisions came from the Volga Military District. The 173rd came from Stalingrad where it had fought with the 21st Army of the Don Front. The 69th, 149th, 246th, and 354th came from the Western Front along with the 65th Army headquarters. All of the divisions were experienced, and four had come from quiet sectors. The 65th Army had three tank regiments (40th, 84th, and 255th), two from the Moscow Military District and one from the Volga Military District with a total of about 100 tanks. The 1st Guards Artillery Division, six mortar regiments (114th, 136th, 143rd, 210th, 218th, and 226th), and the 1180th Tank Destroyer Regiment provided the army with abundant artillery support. Three of the mortar regiments and the tank destroyer regiment had been with the Don Front, while the remaining three mortar regiments were newly formed.

On February 25, 1943, the Central Front launched an attack even though some of the units of the 70th Army had not yet arrived. Three armies, from left to right, the 2nd Tank, the 65th, and the 70th, advanced quickly beyond Svesk, but the Bryansk Front to the north failed to keep pace, and a bulge extended westward.[13] Advance units of the 2nd Tank Army reached the Desna River on March 10, but the Germans were being reinforced with divisions from the Rzhev salient. On March 7 the Stavka ordered the Central Front with the 65th, 70th, and 21st Armies to turn north toward Orel. [14] The 21st Army had finally arrived from Stalingrad and was introduced to the fighting after the Germans had stopped the 65th and 70th Armies. However a crisis was looming south of Kursk so the 21st Army was pulled out and sent to Oboyan. On March 15 the Central Front went on the defensive forming the north shoulder of the Kursk pocket.[15]

The German elements facing the Central Front on the north of the Kursk salient on March 4, 1943, were three corps of the German 2nd Panzer Army, the 50th Corps with the 216th, 383rd Infantry, and 18th Panzer Divisions; the 46th Corps with the 258th and 78th Infantry Divisions and 12th and 20th Panzer Divisions; and the 47th Corps with the 707th and 137th Infantry Divisions. In army reserve were the 442nd, 45th, 3rd Mountain, 72nd, and 251st Infantry Divisions. These divisions had been transferred from other armies in Army Group Center. The 216th, 12th Panzer, 20th Panzer, 72nd, 78th, and 251st Divisions came from the 9th Army in the Rzhev salient and the 258th and 137th Divisions came from the 4th Army. The 383rd and 45th Divisions came from the 55th Corps of the 2nd Panzer Army, the 18th Panzer Division came from the 35th Corps, and the 442nd and 707th Divisions came from the reserve of the same army. The 3rd Mountain Division came from the Fretter Pico battle group in the south. To close the gap the Germans had taken seven divisions from the 4th and 9th Armies and five divisions from the left flank of the 2nd Panzer Army, seriously weakening the forces facing the Western and Bryansk Front. Most of the divisions from the 4th and 9th Army were made available from the Rzhev salient. Here was an excellent example of the advantages provided to the Germans in possessing the superior rail network. The Germans were able to transfer twelve divisions within a few weeks to close the gap in front of the Central and Voronezh Fronts.

On March 4, 1943, the German 2nd Army facing the Voronezh Front on the south side of the Kursk bulge consisted of the 13th Corps with the 340th, 88th, 327th, 82nd, and 26th Infantry Divisions; the 7th Corps with the 68th, 75th, 255th, 57th Infantry, and the 4th Panzer Divisions; with the 332nd, 323rd, and 377th Divisions under army control. The army also controlled an occupation force of the 205th and 105th Hungarian Infantry Divisions and the 1st Hungarian Security Division.[16] Eight of these divisions (57th, 68th, 75th, 82nd, 88th, 323rd, 340th, and 377th) were battered remnants of units that had been driven back in February. Two (4th Panzer and 26th Infantry Division) came from the 2nd Army reserve, the 255th Division from the 4th Army of Army Group Center, and two infantry divisions (327th and 332nd) arrived from France in late February. Again the better rail facilities enabled the Germans to bring in two infantry divisions from France and another from the 4th Army in Army Group Center, while the Russians were having great difficulty supplying the existing units.

While the 60th and 38th Soviet Armies of the Voronezh Front had been working with the Bryansk and Central Fronts creating the Kursk salient, farther to the south the remainder of the Voronezh Front drove toward Kharkov. On February 3, 1943, the 3rd Tank Army reached the Donets River but was held there by the Adolf Hitler SS Division that had recently arrived from France. However the 3rd Tank Army took Pechengi on February 10, 1943, and the 40th Army occupied Belgorod.

The 69th Army took Volchansk in early February shortly after being formed from the 18th Rifle Corps. The 69th Army included three rifle divisions (161st, 180th, and 270th) of the 18th Rifle Corps previously attached directly to the Voronezh Front, the 305th Rifle Division from the 40th Army, and the 37th Rifle Brigade. The 6th Ski Brigade, 262nd Tank Regiment, two antiaircraft regiments (1288th and 1289th), the 16th Guards Mortar Brigade and the 496th Mortar Regiment were added to the 69th Army from the front reserve. A provisional mortar regiment was formed for the army. An unusually strong antitank defense was provided by the 1st Destroyer Division consisting of four destroyer brigades, each with two antitank regiments. The makeup of the new Soviet army indicated that like the 18th Corps before, it had limited offensive capability.

On February 11, 1943, the 69th Army entered Kharkov with the 6th Guards Cavalry Corps and came up against the SS Panzer Corps.[17] By February 15, 1943, the Russians had nearly surrounded Kharkov, and the German SS corps evacuated the city, opening a 160-km gap between the 2nd German Army near Sumy and Army Group South. The 69th Army was finally stopped west of Kharkov by the German Army Detachment Lanz.

To the south, the Soviet 3rd Tank Army passed south of Kharkov but was stopped shortly by Army Detachment Lanz and the SS divisions. The 3rd Tank Army was an extremely powerful formation with a much larger infantry component than tank armies later in the war. The 3rd Tank Army had been transferred to the Voronezh Front from the Stavka Reserve in December 1942. The army included the 12th Tank Corps and the 15th Tank Corps—both with three tank brigades, a mechanized brigade, and supporting units—the 48th Guards Rifle Division, the 179th Tank Brigade, the 39th Armored Car Battalion, three antiaircraft regiments (71st, 319th, and 470th), two tank destroyer regiments (1112th and 1245th), and the 97th Guards Mortar Regiment. The 184th Rifle Division from the Volga Military District was added to the army in December.

In January 1943 the army received further reinforcements: the 62nd Guards Rifle Division, the 160th Rifle Division, and the 8th Artillery Division from the Southwest Front 6th Army, the 111th Rifle Division from the Western Front, the 15th Guards Mortar Brigade and 97th Guards Mortar Regiment from the Voronezh Front reserve, and the 315th Guards Mortar Regiment from the Moscow Military District. By February 1, 1943, the 3rd Tank Army had seven tank brigades (over 350 tanks), two mechanized brigades, an artillery division, and five rifle divisions. The infantry component was almost equal to a field army. All of the tank brigades had come from the Stavka Reserve, and therefore, were fresh and at full strength in January 1943. However, the army had been in action since January 13, 1943, and had advanced 270 km by the time it halted, far too great a distance from supply depots for reliable delivery of fuel and ammunition.

On February 3, 1943, the Germans had gathered remnants into Army Detachment Lanz holding a line west of Kharkov. The detachment at first included only the 24th Corps with the 385th and 387th Divisions and 320th and 298th Divisions. The 298th, 385th, and 387th Divisions had been assigned to the 2nd Hungarian and 8th Italian Armies. When those armies collapsed in January 1943, the remnants of the three German divisions formed the thin screen west of Kharkov in February along with the 320th Division that has just arrived from France. Later Corps Kramer was formed with the Gross Deutschland Panzer Grenadier Division, two regiments from the 168th Division, and remnants from six other divisions.

By the end of February 1943, the group was renamed Army Detachment Kempf and included Corps Raus with the 168th, 167th, and 320th Infantry Divisions, and the Gross Deutschland Divisions. The 167th Division had arrived from France, and the 168th Infantry Division and the Gross Deutschland Panzer Grenadier Divisions came from the Rzhev salient. The remnants of the 298th, 385th, and 387th were withdrawn from the front and later joined to form a new 387th Division. Detachment Lanz, later Kempf, was not a strong force, even though the two divisions from France and the Gross Deutschland were fresh. The latter division had the same organization as an SS panzer grenadier division but was not part of the SS organization. However this thin screen linked with the right flank of the 2nd German Army, delaying the 69th Soviet Army and permitting the SS panzer grenadier divisions to concentrate at Poltava and Krasnodar.

The SS panzer divisions were the elite of the German Army. The SS Panzer Corps included the Adolf Hitler and the Das Reich Divisions that had been refitting in France and had arrived in early February at full strength. The SS panzer grenadier divisions had two tank battalions in their tank regiment (instead of the single battalion in other panzer grenadier divisions), an assault gun battalion, and six panzer grenadier battalions. After surrendering Kharkov, the SS corps concentrated in the Krasnodar area.

Stalin, misreading intelligence reports of German movements, ordered an all-out pursuit of what appeared to be the fleeing Nazis, regardless of supply considerations and the condition of the Red Army units. Stalin ordered the 6th Soviet Army, the 1st Guards Army and Group Popov to pursue the Germans. On the left of the 3rd Tank Army at Kupyansk, the 6th Soviet Army drove west across the Donets, south of Kharkov.[18] The Soviet Sixth Army had five rifle divisions, the former 153rd, now the 57th Guards, 6th, 267th, 172nd, and 350th), and the 106th Rifle Brigade. All of these units had been in action for three months except the 6th Rifle Division, which had been part of the 10th Reserve Army in the Stavka Reserve and then the Volga District in December 1942 and joined the 6th Army in January. The army had the 115th Tank Brigade and the 212th Tank Regiment, both weary from battle, two tank destroyer regiments (150th and 462nd), two antiaircraft regiments (1290th and 1474th), the 126th Antiaircraft Battalion, two guards mortar regiments (45th and 87th), and a single artillery regiment, the 870th. All of the supporting units had been at the front for three months and had moved long distances. The single fresh division was not sufficient to restore the weary army. Passing south of Kharkov through Balakleya, the 6th Soviet Army bypassed the SS panzer grenadier divisions at Krasnograd and sent advance forces that approached within 30 km west of Dnepropetrovsk.

To the left of the 6th Army, the 1st Guards Army crossed the Donets on January 23, 1943, west of Voroshilovgrad. The temperature was below freezing, and there was a heavy snow storm on January 27, 1943.[19] The 1st Guards Army with nine rifle divisions (52nd, 78th, 244nd, 35th Guards, 41st Guards, 195th, 38th Guards, 44th Guards, and 58th Guards) took Izium on February 5, 1943. Two of the Soviet divisions had arrived from the Western Front in January (52nd and 78th), and the 244th had come from the Moscow Military Zone. The other six had been in combat for three months and were probably exhausted despite their guards designation. The army had the 9th Artillery Division and the 4th Antiaircraft Division that had come from the Stavka Reserve in November but had been in action ever since. In addition the army had the 40th Guards Artillery Regiment, the 42nd Guards Tank Destroyer Regiment, the 302nd and 303rd Guards Mortar Regiments, the 115th Guards Mortar Battalion, and 139th Antiaircraft Battalion. The army was lacking in armor with only the 127th Tank Regiment which had been assigned in November 1942 and in action since then. Despite the number of units, the 1st Guards Army was a tired group, and the three new rifle divisions had been added for that reason.

On February 1, 1943, Group Popov was ordered to drive southwest over the Donets to Slavyansk through a gap northwest of Army Detachment Fretter

Pico. Group Popov included four tank corps (4th Guards, 3rd, 10th, and 18th), which had been in action since December 1942 and were battle weary. The tanks had probably exhausted both their track and engine life expectancy because they had fought in difficult engagements and traveled long distances. None of the tank corps had supporting combat units but consisted of three tank brigades and a mechanized brigade. The service units probably were insufficient. Group Popov also included the 6th Guards Rifle Corps (with 38th Guards, 57th Guards, and 52nd Rifle Divisions) which had been in combat for the past three months, below strength, and battle weary. Two fresh units were the 9th Guards Tank Brigade and the 7th Ski Brigade transferred from the Stavka Reserve in January 1943. Two additional ski brigades (5th and 10th) arrived on February 18, 1943.

Most of the Popov Group units had been reduced by battle and travel and were probably 300 km from their supply depots. Given the state of the roads, the shortage of trucks, and the slow delivery rate of horse-drawn wagons (30 km per day), very few supplies reached Group Popov as it advanced. The troops were tired and the units were not at full strength.[20] The number of tanks ready for combat dropped from 212 on January 25, 1943; to 180 on January 30; 140 on February 7; 145 on February 16; and 25 on February 21. By February 26 the number had increased to 50; however, this was a shadow of formations that should have had over 600 tanks in operating condition.[21]

The demise of Group Popov and the two other Soviet armies began on January 27, 1943, when Hitler ordered the headquarters of 1st Panzer Army, two corps headquarters, and four divisions to move from Rostov to the left of Army Detachment Fretter Pico. The Russian tanks fell victim to mechanical failure through lack of maintenance, and they also had exhausted their fuel. Meanwhile, divisions from the 1st and 4th Panzer passed through Rostov and were gathering to the south, despite the heavy snow that delayed the move through Rostov. The 3rd and 11th Panzer Divisions were stopped by the snow north of Rostov on February 1, 1943.[22]

By February 11, 1943, 1st Panzer Army included the 30th Army Corps (the 335th Division, the 3rd Mountain Division, and a regiment of the 304th Division); the 3rd Panzer Corps (the 3rd and 17th Panzer Divisions); Group Schmidt (the 19th Panzer Division, a regiment of 7th Panzer Division, and the 901st School Regiment); and the 40th Panzer Corps (the 7th and 11th Panzer Divisions, the Viking SS Panzer Grenadier Division, and the 333rd Infantry Division). The 4th Panzer Army included the 5th Corps (the 444th Security Division and a Cossack regiment); the 57th Panzer Corps (the 16th Panzer Grenadier and 23rd Panzer Division, the 15th Luftwaffe Field Division, and the 111th Infantry Division); and the 29th Corps (two battle groups).

Of the twelve divisions in the 1st and 4th Panzer Armies, five were comparatively fresh, although the combat value of the Luftwaffe division, with only five rifle battalions, was questionable. Three divisions had come from France in December and January (7th Panzer, 304th, and 335th), the 15th Luftwaffe Division had been formed in Russia in December 1942 from airfield defense units, and the 19th Panzer came from the reserve of Army Group Center to support the Italian 8th Army in December. The remaining seven had been in combat since December. The two armies gathered west of the penetration made by Group Popov in early February.

On February 7, 1943, Manstein withdrew the 4th Panzer Army and Army Detachment Hollidt from Rostov to the Mius River line with Hitler's permission. The 160-km withdrawal was completed in nine days. Army Detachment Hollidt occupied defensive positions on February 16, 1943, with Group Mieth (384th and 336th Infantry Divisions), 17th Corps (62nd and 294th Infantry Divisions and 8th Luftwaffe Division), and 48th Panzer Corps (6th Panzer, 302nd, 304th, 306th Infantry Divisions, and Group Schuldt, which contained three battered battalions of the 79th Division). Of the nine divisions in the army detachment, four had come from France in December and January (6th Panzer, 302nd, 304th, and 306th); the 8th Luftwaffe had been formed in Germany in October, 1942, and joined the detachment in January; the 384th Division consisted of the headquarters and five miscellaneous battalions not part of the division that was in the Stalingrad pocket, and the remaining three (62nd, 294th, and 336th) had been with the Don Army Group since December.

This comparatively weak force, both in numbers and in combat condition, managed to delay the Soviet Southern Front on the Mius River line while Manstein turned most of his divisions to strike at the flank of the advancing armies of the Southwest Front. The Soviet Southwest Front included the 3rd Guards Army, the 5th Tank Army, the 5th Shock Army, the 2nd Guards Army, and the 28th Army. Two additional armies, the 44th and 51st, were left behind as the Germans retreated. Although the Russians had overwhelming forces, the lack of roads and the shrinking length of the front line as the Germans pulled their flank back to the Sea of Azov prevented the Red Army from making full use of their resources. A week later on February 18, 1943, the Southern Front had only the 5th Shock Army, the 2nd Guards Army, the 51st Army, and the 44th Army facing Army Detachment Hollidt. By then Manstein had moved three divisions (23rd Panzer, 111th Infantry, and 444th Security) from the 4th Panzer Army and the 454th Security Division from the rear to shore up the line, which held firm.

The remainder of the German and Rumanian troops from the Caucasus retreated into a bridgehead in the Kuban opposite Kerch in the Crimea. The Russians made some effort to disrupt this movement but were unsuccessful,

and position lapsed into inactivity. While the Germans held, the Russians
made the effort to dislodge them. Meanwhile, the Russians moved their divisions to active fronts as quickly as the rail lines would accommodate, while the
Germans made similar withdrawals through the Crimea.

The final act of the drama began on February 20, 1943, with simultaneous
German advances against the Soviet probes from the north, south, and east.
The SS panzer corps struck the right flank of the Soviet 6th Army; the 48th
Panzer Corps of the 4th Panzer Army struck the left flank of the 6th Army at
Pavlograd; and the 1st Panzer Army attacked the Popov Group at Kras-
noarmeiskoie. After mauling the two Red Army forces, the Germans extended
the attack. Army Detachment Hollidt and the 4th Panzer Army continued to
advance northward driving the 40th and 69th Soviet Armies out of Kharkov
and Belgorod, leaving the Kursk bulge protruding into the German line. The
rainy season halted operations on March 18, but Manstein had restored the situation in the south to a defensible line.

The activity on the southern end of the Russian Front from late January to
March can be divided into four areas. The outcome in each area can be ana-
lyzed, and some conclusions can be drawn. In the Bryansk Front area that
became the Kursk bulge, the Russians encircled two corps and then threw back
the German Second Army about 300 km. However the Red Army overextended
itself, and the Germans transferred two fresh divisions from France and some
divisions released by abandoning the Rzhev salient to the north shoulder of the
Kursk bulge, while the SS Panzer Corps held the south shoulder. These new
forces were able to nip off the Soviet advance, but the Red Army was able to stabilize its position in the Kursk salient. This salient, protruding into the German
line, would become the focus of the campaign in July 1943. The Soviet offensive
in this area was successful, and the Red Army remained in a strong position.

Farther south, the second area centered on Kharkov and Poltava, where
the Red Army succeeded initially in breaching the German line and driving
close to Dnepropetrovsk. However by misreading the German movements as a
headlong retreat, the 6th Soviet Army and the Popov Group outran their supplies and continued advancing, even though their divisions and tank brigades
were battle weary. Using the SS Panzer Corps from the north and the 1st and
4th Panzer Army divisions transferred through Rostov from the Caucasus,
Manstein was able to cut off the 6th Army and the Popov Group and inflict
considerable losses. In this area, the Red Army was forced to return to its late
January starting line considerably weakened. This action was called "Manstein's
Miracle" which provided Hitler with his greatest encouragement during the
spring of 1943.

Around Rostov, the third area, the Red Army could not close the noose
and failed to take Rostov in time to prevent the escape of the 1st and 4th

Panzer Army. Rostov was surrendered as a result of Hitler's decision, not by overwhelming pressure. The Germans withdrew in an orderly fashion to previously prepared positions behind the Mius River where the front stabilized at a point of Germany's choosing. The Russians and Germans had a draw in this area, with the Germans in the better position.

In the fourth area, the Caucasus, the 17th German Army withdrew into the Kuban Peninsula providing protection for the Kerch Strait and the Crimea, despite Soviet attempts to disrupt the withdrawal. Although the Germans succeeded in saving the Rumanian divisions as well as their own, the Germans were left in an awkward position which made the movement of troops to more active fronts difficult. On the other hand, the Russians were able to move their divisions using rail connections through Rostov to reinforce more significant fronts. The Red Army made little effort to dislodge the 17th Army, and it eventually withdrew voluntarily to supply divisions to more important areas.

Summarizing the February events, the Russians were the definite winners at Kursk, the losers at Kharkov, and drew even at Rostov and the Kuban. The stalemate created by the rainy season was a mixed blessing to both the Germans and Russians. The pause allowed the Germans to move more divisions from France and gave German industry time to produce more tanks and other weapons. More manpower for the German Army, recruits, returning wounded, men combed out of service units, and Russian volunteers to replace German service personnel in the infantry divisions restored much of the combat power of the German divisions on the Eastern Front.

The transfer of German divisions from France had played a major role in stabilizing the German defense. Most of the divisions defending southern Russia in February had come from France, from the Rzhev salient, or from the Caucasus. These sources were drained to provide the maximum buildup for the major offensive at Kursk. However, while the Germans rebuilt their divisions, the Red Army was regenerated into a far more formidable foe with improved leadership, better weapons, and better trained men that would meet the challenge of the summer.

CHAPTER 2

Rebuilding the Red Army

After the repulse in the Ukraine, the Soviet General Staff set about reconstructing the Red Army. Major improvement, in fact a rebirth, of the Red Army took place in the first half of 1943. The Soviet military potential was renovated in four areas: leadership, organization, logistics, and weapons production. Improvements in all of these areas produced an army that was capable of meeting the Germans at any time or place and inflicting a crushing defeat that would deny the Germans the initiative for the remainder of the war. The gunners no longer belonged to the Germans; the Soviet offensives rolled on twelve months of the year, halted only by the need to move the logistical tail forward, rather than through any effort made by the Nazis and their satellites.

Improved leadership resulted for the most part from the experience of two years of combat. Inept generals were weeded out, talented junior commanders were promoted to higher commands, and officer schools turned out thousands of junior grade officers to command the new companies and battalions. Over 250,000 wounded officers returned to duty in 1943. The extension of officer training courses and the increase from one to two years of military academy courses indicated that the officer shortage that had plagued the Red Army in 1942 had ended.[1] Zhukov in his memoirs stated that the Russians had 93,500 officers in reserve in 1943.[2]

At the division and army level, generals had more experience and a better understanding of their roles. Even in the setback in the Ukraine, the local commanders were aware of the overextension of their forces, and they requested time to rehabilitate their troops and equipment before advancing farther into the Nazi trap. But their caution was overridden by Stalin. In the prelude to Kursk, Stalin deferred to the opinion of his generals to wait for the Germans to attack first. In the previous year, Stalin had opposed his advisors and insisted that they go ahead with the abortive attack at Izyum in the spring of 1942. Therefore, from the very top to the platoon level, the leadership of the Red Army was enhanced in 1943.

In the all-important area of logistics, the reoccupation of the territory that was lost during the summer of 1942 restored the economy and the infrastructure. Two major logistical crises in 1942 were the oil supply and poor rail connections. The severe shortages of fuel in 1942 were caused by inadequate distribution rather than lack of production. The German invasion of the Caucasus had cut the major routes that brought oil to the rest of the Soviet Union. In 1941, 33 million tons of oil were produced (86 percent in the Caucasus) with 15.7 million produced in the fast six months. In the first six months of 1942, 11.7 million tons were produced, and a total of 22 million tons in the entire year. The 1942 production was lower but still adequate for the demand.

Before the war most of the oil was moved from the refineries in Baku (on the west coast of the Caspian Sea) via pipeline across the Caucasus either to Rostov for rail shipment or to the Black Sea and then by ship to Odessa, Sevastopol, and other Black Sea ports. About 9 million tons moved by barge up the Volga River. Only limited supplies were sent by the Caspian Sea to Astrakhan for a tortuous round-about rail trip to the north. The Black Sea, the rail routes, and the Volga route were cut by the summer 1942 campaign.

The Russians destroyed the oil producing facilities before the Germans occupied the Grozny wells. As a result the Germans were unable to return the wells to production, despite vigorous attempts by technicians to do so. When the Germans evacuated the Grozny area, they too made every effort to prevent the Russians from reopening the oil fields. Not surprisingly, Soviet production of oil by the end of the war in 1945 had not returned to the 1941 level of 33 million tons. Production rose slowly from 18 million tons in 1943 to 18.3 million tons in 1944 and to 19.4 million tons in 1945. However, the amount produced was adequate for the Soviet war effort. With the reopening of the Volga route and the availability of the rail route through Rostov after the winter of 1942–43, distribution improved immensely. The Soviet shortage of fuel had ended by the spring of 1943.[3]

In early 1943, the all-important railroads were repaired quickly in the reoccupied areas, and the supply depots were moved forward. The newly won territory provided at least one additional north-south and east-west rail line for each front. These new lines ended the long detours to the east that had previously required traveling northwest to Moscow and then southeast to the battle area. The line through Novy Oskol and Valuiki with branches to Kastornoie-Kursk, Kupyansk-Lisitschansk, and Starobelsk-Voroshilovgrad was an important asset, providing direct rail access to the Kursk salient from Moscow and Stalingrad. The Red Army was able to create vast reserves of supplies in and about the Kursk salient, sufficient not only for the defensive phase, but for the support of the counteroffensives that followed. In contrast the February offensives had failed because of the lack of fuel and because of supply problems generated by the lack of operating rail lines.

The third area of rebirth was in the Red Army. Exhausted divisions were restored, and new units were created to provide resources for defense and future offensives, requiring a huge intake of fresh manpower. The Soviet Union had a population of about 194 million in 1941. About 40 percent of the population lived in the area under German control after the first six months of the war, but an undetermined number of refugees fled east before the Germans arrived. Many of those that chose to remain under German control were unsympathetic to the Communist regime (Latvians, Lithuanians, Estonians, and some White Russians and Ukrainians) and were not a true loss in terms of the military manpower.

There remained at least 120 million people under Soviet control.

The Germans estimated that the Soviet Union had 50.4 million men of military age in June 1942, representing those born between 1888 and 1927. According to the German estimate, each year an additional 1,700,000 men fit for the service would reach military age.[4] Gehlen, chief of *Fremde Heer Ost*, charged with gathering intelligence on the Soviet Union, estimated that the Class of 1926 would include only 1.5 million men.[5] Gehlen may have underestimated as the real number was much higher. Males born in the Soviet Union in 1926 would reach the age of seventeen years in 1943 and would then be eligible for military service. This group of males was referred to as the "Class of 1926." The Russian birth rate in 1926 was 43.6 per thousand or 6,409,000 births based on a total of 147 million, the estimated population of the Soviet Union in 1926. Births in the newly acquired territory are ignored because the Germans occupied the provinces in 1941. The division between male and female births was approximately equal, amounting to a total of 3,200,000 males in the Class of 1926. Some would have died before their seventeenth birthday, but not many. The Civil War was over by 1926 and, though there were shortages of food and many children died of starvation in the 1920s, there were far more survivors than the Germans had estimated.[6] Rather than adding only 1.5 million recruits to the Red Army in 1943, the total was over 3 million, which included men picked up in liberated areas and women.

Although the Russians lost 1,977,000 troops (male and female) in 1943 and 5,506,000 were hospitalized, most of the losses occurred in the first half of the year. The Red Army lost 656,000 men in the first quarter of 1943, and 1.4 million were hospitalized (a total of 2 million). The loss rate dropped precipitously in the second quarter, only 125,000 lost and 471,000 hospitalized (a total of fewer than 700,000). The much heralded victory of Manstein in the Ukraine cost the Voronezh and Southwest Fronts only 45,219 losses and 41,250 hospitalized from March 4 to March 25, 1943, a total of fewer than 90,000, a trivial loss in manpower in Eastern Front terms.[7] The total strength of the field forces of the Red Army grew from 5.3 million on January 1, 1943, to 6.4 million on January 1, 1944, a gain of 1.1 million men, despite the heavy losses inflicted by the Germans. Of the 5.5 million hospitalized, 73 percent would return to duty in 60 days, and more would come later, leading to a net loss of fewer than 800,000. Many of the invalids were assigned to the replacement regiments, releasing able bodied men for combat. One can only conclude that given the loss of nearly 2 million killed and perhaps a half million invalids, and the net gain of 1 million in the field army, the number of recruits added to the Red Army during 1943 must have been about 3.5 million men and women! This total supports the estimate based on the birth rate.[8]

Unfortunately Russian statistics do not provide much information concerning the participation of women in the war effort. Over and above the enormous contribution made by women in industry, where they replaced the men called to military service, many women served in a wide range of tasks. Women provided a large portion of personnel in the medical units, the communications units, and in traffic control. Rifle companies had at least one or two women. The divisional signal company had ten women, and at the army level, the signal regiment had up to 200 women radio and telegraph operators. Women were part of the rifle regiment medical unit, which placed them directly on the battlefield.[9]

Women also assumed combat roles. The major contribution by women was manning the antiaircraft guns that defended Russian cities and factories. In March 1942, 100,000 women were serving in the home air defense organization (PVO); 20,000 in Moscow, 9,000 in Leningrad, 8,000 in Stalingrad, and 6,000 in Baku.[10] By the end of the war 74 percent of the PVO was staffed by women. They also flew transport and combat aircraft and drove trucks and tanks. In March 1943 the artillery division had an entire battalion of trucks with women drivers.[11] Women tank drivers were especially valuable to the armored force, because with prior experience in operating tractors on collective farms, women could quickly learn to drive a tank. Training time for a tank driver, longer than any other position in a tank crew, was reduced considerably if the student had prior experience with tractors. The need for over 20,000 tank drivers each year to replace losses was a staggering training burden. Women also served as military police, directing traffic and guarding prisoners and installations.

A unique role that women played in the Red Army was sniping. Sniping was as much a psychological weapon as a means of killing Germans. Every soldier who served in the front line in World War II shared a fear and intense hatred for enemy snipers. The Soviet snipers caused severe emotional pressure on the German front line soldier who knew that momentarily raising his head above the ground would induce Soviet sniper fire at him. Sniping demanded enormous patience, remaining motionless for hours and waiting for a German to show himself. Any movement would reveal the Soviet sniper's position to German counter snipers. Sniping also called for the emotional intensity to kill deliberately an unsuspecting person, as opposed to killing an enemy threatening one's life, firing a howitzer that might kill someone miles away, or dropping a bomb. Women, especially those who had been raped or abused by Germans, were among the most successful snipers in the Red Army. In 1943 there were 1,061 women snipers and 407 sniper instructors. During the war, women snipers were credited with killing 12,000 German.[12]

The Germans estimated that there were 2 million women in the Russian armed services by 1945, 400,000 in the PVO, and 1,600,000 in the army and the NKVD (the security service).[13] The availability of millions of women for service in the Red Army was an additional source of personnel to restore battle-worn units and create new units in 1943.

The timing of replacements was of considerable concern to the outcome of the battle of Kursk. The Soviets called up about half of the class of recruits in the spring and the other half in the fall of each year. Roughly 1.5 million men would have been added in the spring of 1943 to complete their training by the end of June. Prisoner interrogation at Kursk revealed that many replacements arrived in June 1943. At the same time over a million wounded men would have been returning to their units. The total number available in the replacement streams was about 2.5 million. The replacement regiments sent 2,857,000 troops to the front line from January 1, 1943, to July 15, 1943. This number probably includes returning wounded and men combed from the service units and retrained as riflemen.[14] Over 1.3 million men were combed from service units between May 1943 and December 1943.[15]

Fremde Heer Ost made an analysis of intelligence data gathered at the front concerning replacements in 1943. In the Kursk area, divisions in the Central Front armies received about a thousand replacements during 1943, with individual divisions receiving from 200 to 1,600. Many of these divisions had seen little combat compared to the divisions that fought with the fronts farther south. Most of these replacements (92.3 percent) were from the Class of 1926; 6.5 percent were returning wounded; and 1.2 percent were men transferred from the rear services.[16]

The recruits had from one to six months training in replacement regiments under the replacement command. Most infantry replacements received from two to four months of training, while tanks crews required eight to twelve months. On completion of their training, recruits were formed into march companies of 200 men and were sent to field replacement regiments attached to each field army. Training continued in the field replacement regiment, where attempts were made to give the new recruits training in the operation of the group or squad, platoon, company, and battalion. The army field replacement regiment then sent replacements to the divisional replacement schools that provided combat experience and training for snipers, scouts, and other specialties.

Noncommissioned officers were trained in NCO schools in the front and in army replacement regiments and in divisional schools. Front- and army-replacement training regiments also conducted officer classes lasting from two to six months with emphasis on front line experience.[17]

The army field replacement regiment also administered to the returning wounded, limited service men, and men being transferred from service organizations. When a territory was liberated, all military-age, combat-fit men were immediately drafted and assigned to units except for the youngest men who had received no prewar training. In October 1943 untrained men inducted in newly acquired territory were sent to replacement regiments for instruction before being assigned to rifle divisions.[18]

The replacement process was illustrated by the experience of two prisoners captured by the Germans. A lieutenant was captured in October 1944 and gave minute details on his military service. He was inducted on November 9, 1942, at the age of nineteen and sent to an antiaircraft replacement brigade at Tifflis in the Caucasus. After one month of training, he was sent to the 20th Antiaircraft Division near Tuapse. In January 1944 he was reassigned to the infantry and, after twenty days of infantry training in the 180th Replacement Regiment, he was sent to officer training school for three months. In May 1944 he was assigned to the 318th Rifle Division.[19]

Another example was a private who was born in 1925 and drafted on August 30, 1943, from the newly liberated area around Orel. He was trained in the 72nd Replacement Regiment and on December 24, 1943, was assigned to the machine pistol company of the 508th Rifle Regiment of the 174th Rifle Division. The machine pistol companies usually had the best soldiers in a regiment.[20]

In summary in the first half of 1943, the Red Army lost 781,000 men and women and 1.9 million were hospitalized, a total of nearly 2.7 million troops. Returning wounded probably exceeded the number hospitalized in that period, providing 2 million experienced soldiers. The 1.5 million new recruits increased the total to 3.5 million, for a calculated net gain of 800,000. In fact, the total manpower of the Red Army increased from 5.3 million on January 1, 1943, to 6.46 million on June 30, 1943.[21] The Red Army gained over a million men in the first six months of 1943. The additional half million could have resulted from more hospital returnees, as well as a larger percentage of recruits taken in the first six months, and a combing of service units. There are repeated references in prisoner of war interrogations at Kursk of men being drafted in the newly liberated areas that would have boosted the number of recruits in the first six months of 1943. Regardless of the source, the Soviets had an enormous pool of over 3.5 million men with which to restore battered divisions, to increase the table of organization of existing units, and to create new units.

In late 1942 and early 1943, the tables of organization of units were changed, and additional artillery units were formed to give the infantry and the armored forces more firepower and support. Large numbers of SU regiments, a generic Soviet term that included mechanized artillery, assault guns, and self-propelled tank destroyers, were formed to counter the increasing power of the new German tanks.

The primary building block of the Red Army was the rifle division. The authorized size of the division had been reduced in 1942 to 9,435 men in three rifle regiments, an artillery regiment, and other support units. In June 1943 the division organization again was reduced, dropping to 9,380 men, but retaining the 32 76mm guns, 12 122mm howitzers, 160 mortars, 48 57mm anti-tank guns, 212 antitank rifles, 434 light machine guns, 111 heavy machine guns, 124 vehicles, and 1,700 horses. However, the number of rifles was reduced by 200 and replaced by an increase of machine pistols from 727 to 1,048. The latter change was a major improvement in the fire power of the rifle companies. One out of seven men was armed with an automatic weapon.[22]

A German report estimated that Soviet rifle divisions on the Leningrad Front had 8,000 men with 1,900 men in each of the three rifle regiments. The rifle company had 120 men, and the rifle battalion had 513 men. The total for nine battalions was 4,617 men. The remainder were in the supporting units.[23] Rifle divisions in the Voronezh Front were increased to between 8,000 and 9,000 men in the first half of 1943, while the Central Front divisions were raised to between 7,000 and 7,500 men. In May 1943, for example, three thousand men from the 15th, 19th, and 23rd Replacement Training Regiments in Chelyabinsk were transported by rail to the 42nd Guards Rifle Division in the Kursk area. Additional smaller replacement groups with from thirty to fifty men continued to arrive in June.[24] After the heavy fighting in July and August of 1943, divisional strength dropped to below 6,000 as the Soviets diverted much of the available manpower to combat support units, tank brigades, artillery regiments, and tank destroyer brigades.

The number of Soviet rifle divisions increased sharply in the first six months of 1943. On January 1, 1943, there were 369 rifle divisions at the front, 8 in reserve, and 30 in the military districts and the Far East, for a total of 407. On July 1, 1943, there were 376 at the front, 58 in reserve (an increase of 50!), 28 in the districts and the Far East, for a total of 462—an increase of 55. Part of the increase came from combining two rifle brigades to form a new division or using a rifle brigade as cadre for a new division. The number of rifle brigades declined from 177 on January 1, 1943, to only 98 on July 1, 1943. The number of brigades at the front declined from 134 to only 66. Two of the four-battalion brigades were roughly equal to one nine-battalion division, so the loss of seventy-nine brigades (equal to 39.5 divisions) reduced the impact of the gain of fifty-five divisions. However, in the reorganization, many understrength rifle brigades emerged as rehabilitated rifle divisions with 9,000 men. Of the seventy-nine brigades lost, sixty-eight brigades were from the front. This was a positive indication that worn out brigades were taken from the front lines, rebuilt into first line divisions, and returned to the front or placed in the Stavka reserve.

The new divisions were of high quality with young men. An example was the 226th Rifle Division. The third division to bear this number was formed in Lgov in July 1943 using the 129th Rifle Brigade as cadre. Lgov is located directly west of Kursk on the Seim River, a little more than twenty miles from the front line, so this reformation occurred just behind the front. The previous 226th Rifle Division had been redesignated the 95th Guards Rifle Division in May 1943.

The men in the new 226th Division ranged in age from twenty-one to forty-six, but 70 percent were from twenty-one to twenty-seven. Russians made up 90 percent of the men. Based on the age and nationality of the men, the 129th Brigade received an influx of young men when the division was formed. Apparently the four rifle battalions of the brigade were divided to form cadres for the nine battalions of the division, and new recruits came in to fill out the new battalions. The transition happened very quickly as the cadre 129th Brigade still appeared in the 60th Army in the Soviet order of battle on July 1, 1943, and the new division appeared on August 1, 1943, in the 24th Corps of the 60th Army. The Germans continued to identify the unit as the 129th Brigade in the 24th Corps in early July. The 24th Corps was in the 60th Army reserve in July 1943, located at the tip of the Kursk bulge where little activity was expected.[25]

While the rifle divisions were being reinforced and rifle brigades were transformed into divisions, major increases also were made in the combat support units. The tendency to reinforce the combat support units was evident in early 1943, as units assigned to the field armies increased dramatically. In 1942 the number of artillery, mortar, and antitank regiments assigned to army commands had been more or less arbitrary, depending on the mission of the army. In 1943 the armies received a minimum assignment of supporting units to be supplemented from Stavka reserves as the role of the army in a particular operation dictated.

In 1943 each field army was assigned an antiaircraft regiment, a gun artillery regiment with 152mm guns, a mortar regiment with thirty-six 120mm mortars, and a tank destroyer regiment with twenty-four 76mm antitank guns. In April 1943, each army was authorized an additional 37mm antiaircraft regiment. The field army in 1943 had over 2,000 guns and mortars.

The artillery was reorganized in 1943. The artillery divisions, formed in October 1942 to provide centralized control for the large numbers of guns to break through the German defenses, had proved successful in the Stalingrad operation. However, the eight independent regiments with 168 guns were difficult to control because the different types of regiments had different roles in a battle. In December 1942 the regiments were divided into brigades by type and in April 1943 the artillery division was reinforced with additional brigades.

The April 1943 organization called for a light artillery brigade with three 76mm gun regiments, a howitzer brigade with three 122mm howitzer regiments. A heavy howitzer brigade with three 152mm howitzer regiments, a gun brigade with three 152mm gun regiments, a long-range howitzer brigade with four 203mm howitzer battalions, and a mortar brigade with three 120mm mortar regiments. The 1943 artillery division had 72 76mm guns, 84 122mm howitzers, 32 152mm howitzers, 36 152mm guns, 24 203mm howitzers, and 108 120mm mortars, for a total of 256 guns and mortars compared to 168 in the 1942 division. The addition of heavier gun regiments practically doubled the firepower of the division.

The number of artillery divisions increased from twenty-five on January 1, 1943, to twenty-eight on April 1, 1943, and then declined to twenty-five on July 1, 1943. The guards mortar divisions remained at seven. Seventeen new independent artillery brigades were formed, but the number of independent artillery regiments declined from 271 on January 1, 1943, to 234 on July 1, 1943, as a result of converting many artillery regiments to tank destroyer units and other roles or joining them into the new brigades.

One artillery role that was completely overhauled was the tank destroyer function. In 1942 the antitank guns were formed into destroyer brigades with two or three mixed regiments of 76mm, 45mm, and 37mm guns plus a rifle battalion armed with antitank rifles. Three of these brigades were sometimes joined to form a destroyer division. The division was too large to control, and the mixture of guns in the regiments was a challenge to the regimental commander. In April 1943 the destroyer division was eliminated, and some destroyer brigades were reorganized as tank destroyer brigades containing two 76mm gun regiments and one 57mm or 45mm gun regiment.

The most crucial factor in the defense at Kursk was the distribution of the antitank guns. In his proposal to Stalin on April 8, 1943, Zhukov stressed the need to "strengthen the antitank defence of the Central and Voronezh Fronts" by moving units from other sectors.[26] The Red Army high command was well informed by intelligence sources of both the area and the forces that would launch concentrated armored attacks on very limited frontages.

The Russians used a formula for the assignment of antitank guns based on the number of tanks expected, the number of rounds required to stop one enemy tank, the number of rounds a gun could fire per minute, the maximum distance at which each type of tank could be destroyed, and the distance a tank could move in one minute. This calculation indicated the number of guns required.[27] Assuming that fifty Mk IV tanks would attack on a 1km front, the formula determined that fifteen 76mm guns would be required per km. The heavier armor on the Panther, Tiger, and Ferdinand probably doubled the number of guns required because of the shorter range at which the 76mm gun would be effective. Using the 85mm gun as an antitank gun would lengthen the effective range and reduce the number of guns needed.

To provide the required density of antitank guns, the new tank destroyer brigades were activated, providing central control of from sixty to seventy-two guns. By July 1, 1943, twenty-seven of the brigades (including eighty-one regiments) had been formed, and twenty-four were at the front. A few of the old type destroyer brigades continued in action at Kursk.[28]

The tank destroyer brigades played an incredibly significant role in the battle of Kursk. The brigade commander controlled the antitank defense of a sector, creating antitank strong points with four or more guns and with interlocking fire with other strong points. The brigade commander also held a reserve that could move swiftly (the guns were drawn by trucks, not horses) to any threatened point. The front commander could also hold a brigade or more in reserve to counter any tank penetration of the first line of defense. A brigade with sixty guns was sufficient to stop a panzer division, though it might lose most of its guns in the process if the Germans used Tiger tanks to combat the antitank guns.

Independent tank destroyer regiments with twenty or twenty-four 76mm or 45mm guns were held in front reserve or assigned to army reserves.[29] The number of independent tank destroyer regiments remained static with 171 in January and 163 in July of 1943 despite the rapid increase in the number of regiments assigned to tank destroyer brigades.

In reaction to the Tiger tank, the Soviets began formation of thirty antitank battalions to be assigned to the tank and mechanized corps, beginning in April 1943. The battalions were armed with 85mm antiaircraft guns on special mounts with crews trained as antitank gunners. The 85mm gun was a match for the 88mm gun on the Tiger. Many, although not all, of the tank and mechanized corps at Kursk had been reinforced with 85mm antitank battalions. Other battalions were still in training in the Moscow Military District.

The Russians continued to have faith in the antitank rifle, a long heavy barrelled high velocity weapon firing a 14.5mm projectile. The Degtyarev antitank rifle had a muzzle velocity of 1,010 meters per second and could inflict damage on the Panzer III or on the tracks of the heavier German tanks.[30] An example of the antitank rifle organizations was the 121st Independent Antitank Battalion established in March 1943 near Moscow. The men had been inducted in the winter of 1942–43 and were from the Classes of 1923, 1924, and 1925: eighteen to twenty years old. The men came through the 131st

Replacement Regiment and the officers from a school at Pokrov near Moscow. The battalion had three companies each with seventy men and eighteen to twenty antitank rifles. On April 5, 1943, less than a month after being formed, the battalion was sent by rail to Staryi Oskol, and from there they marched to Korotscha. Later the battalion was assigned to the 69th Army.[31]

The antiaircraft forces with the field army increased in number in the first six months of 1943, probably as a result of the heavy losses to air attack in early 1943. The number of antiaircraft divisions with the field armies and training in the districts increased from twenty-seven on January 1, 1943, to forty-eight on July 1, 1943. These antiaircraft divisions had three regiments of 37mm guns and one regiment of 85mm guns that also could serve as heavy antitank guns in the same way that the Germans used their 88mm antiaircraft guns. The Russian 85mm gun was a close relative of the German 88mm gun with many common design characteristics. The antiaircraft division had a total of forty-eight 37mm guns and sixteen 85mm guns.[32]

The number of independent antiaircraft regiments increased from 123 on January 1, 1943, to 183 on July 1, 1943, including 24 in the PVO, the home defense organization. The total of 109 independent antiaircraft battalions remained stable with more than half the battalions at the front. Each cavalry tank, and mechanized corps had an antiaircraft battalion with four batteries of 37mm guns and a company of machine guns. An antiaircraft company was added to the armored brigades to protect against German ground attack aircraft. Each of these companies had nine heavy machine guns. The cavalry divisions were given a two-company battalion of eighteen machine guns to protect the valuable horsemen.[33]

Fifteen new antiaircraft divisions were formed in June 1943 in the PVO. Over a hundred new battalions and regiments were organized in that month to fill the divisions. Three-fourths of the personnel of these new units were women. This remarkable expansion reflected the increased availability of antiaircraft guns, available personnel, and the recognition that the factories and communications system needed protection from Luftwaffe attacks. Although antiaircraft guns did not destroy a large percentage of attacking aircraft, the presence of the guns prevented the attackers from flying low and making accurate bomb runs. Even if the guns only damaged the German aircraft, the planes required repairs or were sometimes scrapped. The antiaircraft guns were a powerful deterrent to air attacks on Russian cities and railroads.

The increase in artillery, tank destroyer, and antiaircraft units in the first six months of 1943 radically altered the fire power of the Red Army, especially the creation of the twenty-seven tank destroyer brigades and thirty-six antiaircraft divisions. Both of these units were essentially defensive formations to protect the troops from German tank and air attack. The lessons of 1942 had been well learned. The troops could not be left defenseless in the face of German tanks and aircraft, as happened in the Ukraine in the summer of 1942. The Soviet high command saw the problem and applied solutions.

In the armored force, the Russians did not subscribe to the theory that the best antitank weapon was another tank, but they did make major changes in the spring and summer of 1943. The changes were in the composition and strength of the units rather than the number. The concept of the tank army was revived in early 1943 with a radical change in doctrine, organization, and strength. Previous tank armies had included both tank formations and marching infantry. The new tank armies were completely motorized. Rifle divisions were seldom attached to the tank armies, which gained complete mobility. The 1943 tank army usually had two tank corps, one mechanized corps, a motorcycle regiment, an antiaircraft division (four regiments), a tank destroyer regiment, a howitzer regiment, and a Guards mortar regiment of rocket launchers. In support the tank army had a service regiment, an engineer battalion, a motor transport regiment, two tank repair battalions, and medical and other service units. A special unit for the evacuation of captured tanks was included. The tank army had over 600 tanks and twenty-two battalions of motorized infantry.[34]

The 1943 tank corps had three tank brigades, each with two tank battalions and a motorized rifle battalion, a mechanized brigade with three motorized battalions and a tank regiment especially fitted to carry riflemen, three SU regiments, a mortar regiment, a light artillery regiment, a Guards mortar battalion, an armored car battalion, an engineer battalion, and a service battalion. The tank corps had a total of 10,977 men (an increase from 7,800 men in the 1942 corps), 208 T34 tanks (increased from 98 medium and 70 light tanks in 1942), 49 SUs, 60 guns and mortars, and 8 rocket launchers in the Guards mortar battalion.[35] In comparison German panzer divisions had only about 150 tanks and assault guns.

The mechanized corps of 1943 was an even more powerful unit. The corps had three mechanized brigades each with three motorized battalions and a tank regiment modified to carry riflemen, a tank brigade with two tank battalions and a motorized battalion, three tank regiments, three SU regiments, a mortar regiment, a light artillery regiment, a Guards mortar battalion, an armored car battalion, an engineer battalion, and a service battalion. The corps had 15,018 men, 229 tanks and assault guns (including 162 T34s, 42 light tanks, and 25 assault guns), 108 guns and mortars, and 8 rocket launchers.[36]

Independent tank brigades were also brought up to the new tables of organization when possible, but often light tanks and Lend Lease tanks were issued to the independent brigades. The independent tank brigades were more often used for infantry support along with the assault guns. Independent tank regiments were also formed for use with the infantry, and in 1943 a new type of tank regiment equipped with specially modified T34s to clear mine fields was introduced. The mine clearing tank regiment had twenty-two T34s and eighteen mine clearing vehicles.[37]

Four additional tank corps were created in the first six month of 1943, increasing the number to twenty-four. The number of mechanized corps increased from eight to thirteen. The number of tank brigades declined from 114 to 101 on July 1, 1943, while the number of independent tank regiments increased from 77 to 110. These changes reflected a continuing Soviet allocation of substantial numbers of tanks to direct support of the infantry. At Kursk half of the available tanks were in tank brigades and regiments assigned to the field armies. There were 211 tank brigades and regiments available to support 462 rifle divisions and 98 rifle brigades on July 1, 1943.

The major change in the armored force was the reorganization of the assault gun or SU regiments in early 1943. The SU regiments used the newly developed SU76 mounted on a light tank chassis, the SU 122 mounted a 122mm howitzer on a T34 chassis, and the SU 152 mounted a 152mm howitzer on the KV chassis. By mid-1943 the Russians had formed three types of SU regiments after trying unsuccessfully to combine several types in a single regiment. The SU76 regiment had four batteries of five guns and a total of twenty-one in the regiment. The SU122 regiment had four batteries of four guns with a total of sixteen guns and one T34 tank. The SU152s were organized in regiments with four batteries of three guns each for a total of twelve guns and a KV tank.[38] The cadres for the new SU regiments probably came from disbanded tank brigades. Nearly twenty tank brigades disappeared from the Soviet order of battle in May and June 1943. The SU regiments were designed to counter the heavy tanks being developed by the Germans. The Soviets first encountered the Tiger in the Leningrad area in November 1942 and immediately moved to find an antidote. By eliminating the turret, and in most cases the overhead armor, a chassis could carry a much heavier gun than would otherwise be possible. Theoretically the SU would use its larger gun to destroy its opponent while remaining beyond the range of the gun mounted on the enemy tank. The Russians had formed forty-one of the new SU regiments by April 1, 1943, but only nine were at the front and four in reserve, with the remaining twenty-eight still training in the military districts. By July 1, twenty-one were at the front and three in reserve with only seventeen still in training. These regiments were concentrated in the Kursk area and played a vital role in the battle.

The cavalry organization was standardized in early 1943. The role of the cavalry was then clearly defined to work in cooperation with the armored force. There were seven cavalry corps in 1943, each with three divisions, a tank destroyer regiment (twenty-four 76mm guns), an SU regiment (twenty SU76s), an antiaircraft regiment, a guards mortar regiment, a heavy tank destroyer battalion, and service units. Each division had a tank regiment with twenty-nine T34s and sixteen T70 light tanks. The cavalry corps had a total of 117 tanks, approximately equal to the number in a German panzer division of that time. The corps had 21,000 men and 19,000 horses.[39]

Many of the cavalry divisions had been disbanded earlier because of the shortage of horses. In the first six months of 1943 four more divisions were disbanded, leaving twenty-one in the seven corps on the German front and six in the Far East. On July 1, 1943, five of the cavalry corps were held in reserve waiting for the counteroffensives to be used to exploit the breakthroughs. After November 1942 the cavalry corps were usually joined with a tank corps to form horse mechanized groups to exploit breakthroughs. The cavalry was more mobile than the truck mounted infantry in the mechanized corps across country and in mud and snow, making the horse mechanized group preferable in bad terrain.

The airborne forces also witnessed a major expansion. The number of divisions remained stable at ten, all being retained in the Stavka reserve, but twenty new Guards airborne brigades were formed in April and May and held in the Stavka reserve. The men in the airborne divisions were the elite of the Red Army and formed a strong reserve force in the Moscow area to ensure the safety of the capital. The diversion of so many (probably 60,000) excellent troops to the new brigades that performed a reserve activity was another indication of the plentiful supply of manpower in the spring of the 1943.[40]

Some of the airborne divisions were used at Kursk. The 9th Guards Parachute Division had been moved by rail from Gorki to Staryi Oskol in May 1943 and on July 9 was ordered to move to Prokorovka as part of the 5th Guards Tank Army. The division was parachute in name only; the men had no jump training or parachute equipment.[41]

During the first half of 1943 the home defense antiaircraft command (PVO) was expanded and reorganized. The previous organization was replaced by two fronts (East and West) and three zones (Far East, Transbaikal, and Central Asia). Corps areas and division areas were named after the cities they defended, usually significant military targets, for example, the oil fields at Grozny and the tank plants at Saratov and Yaroslavl. The corps and division areas had varying numbers of regiments and battalions, with the Moscow area having the largest contingent. Most PVO antiaircraft divisions had have regiments of twenty 85mm guns each, a battalion of 37mm guns, and a searchlight regiment.

The rapid expansion of the total number of units in the Red Army in early 1943 occurred at the same time as battle-worn rifle divisions were being restored to full strength in men and equipment. By July 1943 the Red Army had absorbed millions of new recruits, replaced losses in existing units, and formed hundreds

of new battalions, regiments, brigades, and divisions. All of this activity compelled the Russian economy to provide enormous quantities of equipment and
weapons.

Soviet factories were turning out ample supplies of all kinds of weapons to
equip the new troops. After the disaster of 1941 and the hurried evacuation of
many factories, Soviet industry was back in stride by mid-1942, but in 1943 production reached a point at which available stocks exceeded demand, and in
1944 production of some weapons either leveled off or was reduced.

Beginning with the basic weapon, the rifle or carbine issued most widely
to troops, production in 1942 reached 4 million. In 1943 production was
reduced to 3.4 million and further reduced to 2.4 million in 1944.[42] The Red
Army lost only 198,000 rifles and carbines in the Voronezh and Kharkov operations in March 1943 compared to 1,764,000 in the Kiev disaster in 1941.[43]
The downward trend in rifle production reflected not only fewer losses, but
also a movement toward more automatic weapons in the rifle company. The
number of machine pistols in the rifle regiment increased from 216 in 1942 to
450 in the summer of 1943. One-fourth of the men in the rifle companies had
machine pistols.[44] Production of machine pistols increased from 1,560,000 in
1942 to 2,060,000 in 1943. The stock on hand increased from 100,000 on January 1, 1942, to 2,640,000 on January 1, 1944. The ratio of rifles to machine
pistols changed from 37:1 in January 1942 to 5:1 in January 1943. Providing
the rifle company with an ample supply of machine pistols increased the firepower of the company both on defense and offense.[45]

The rifle companies also received more light machine guns, the most
effective weapon in delivering a high volume of fire, both in defense and
offense. Light machine gun production increased from 173,000 in 1942 to
250,000 in 1943, increasing the number on hand for use at the end of 1943 to
344,000 from 177,000 at the beginning of the year. By July 1943 there were
ample stocks to fill the needs of the infantry. A similar increase took place in
heavy machine guns; production increased from 58,000 in 1942 to 90,500 in
1943, and in 1943 the stock increased from 63,500 to 133,000, more than dou-
bling. This immense outpouring of weapons from Soviet factories provided
the new and rebuilt units with ample supplies. All of the prisoners taken at
Kursk reported that the rifle companies were fully equipped.

The story was the same with artillery—the stocks grew rapidly in 1943. Production of antiaircraft guns increased from 6,800 in 1942 to 12,200 in 1943, and
the stocks on hand increased from 13,100 in January to 24,600 in December,
providing the weapons for the explosive growth in the number of antiaircraft
units. Field artillery production declined from 30,100 in 1942 to 22,100 in 1943
as production facilities were diverted to tank guns, antiaircraft, and antitank gun
production. Losses were minuscule (only 5,700 guns in 1943), and the number

of pieces on hand increased in 1943 from 36,700 in January to 53,100 in December. Production was reduced because supply had outrun demands.[46]

Tank and SU deliveries leveled off in 1943 with only 22,900 received compared to 27,900 in 1942. Total Soviet tank and SU receipts included both production and Lend Lease tanks, with no breakdown in the Soviet sources. About 4,000 tanks came from the United States and Great Britain in 1943. The decline in production resulted from the beginning of SU production which increased from less than 100 in 1942 to 4,400 in 1943. Production was also shifted to heavier tanks. The receipts of light tanks declined from 11,900 to 5,700 in this period as production was diverted to produce the SU76. Lend Lease provided more medium tanks in place of the light tanks provided in 1942.

Receipts of medium tanks increased from 13,400 to 16,300 as more T34s were built and the West delivered more medium tanks. Production of the KV dropped from 2,600 to only 900 as the Russian engineers sought ways to produce a more effective heavy tank. The total stock of tanks and SUs on hand decreased slightly from 28,000 at the beginning of the year to 27,300 at the end of 1943, despite the loss of 23,500 tanks.[47]

Soviet statistics published prior to 1995 vary considerably from these totals because only the authorized number of tanks in units at the front were included. Tanks in depots, in training schools, and in units in the military districts were omitted. Red Army tank units after June 1943 often went into battle with large numbers of replacement tanks and crews in front and army replacement regiments. These tanks were able to replace losses quickly, while the tank replacement regiments were refilled from tank depots located at the major tank factories.

The expansion of the Red Army in early 1943 also benefitted from increased deliveries of Lend Lease supplies. The improvement of port facilities and railroads in Iran made major Lend Lease deliveries possible, especially trucks so necessary to improve the Red Army supply system. In 1942 the United States delivered 2,740,000 tons of Lend Lease supplies to the Soviet Union, but only 790,000 came through Iran. Over a million tons came through Murmansk and Archangel as the Germans did not block the northern route until June 1942. The remaining million tons of supplies in 1942 were delivered to Vladivostok. In 1943 1,800,000 tons came by way of Iran, while only 760,000 tons came on six convoys to Murmansk, which slipped through the Nazi blockade in the winter months when the Arctic route had the benefit of almost total darkness.[48] By July 31, 1943, 120,000 motor vehicles and 2,411 American tanks had been delivered by the three routes. Total Russian additions to their supply of motor vehicles in 1943 was 158,500, and losses were 67,000 leaving a total on hand at the end of the year of 496,000 vehicles. Russian official figures do not specify Lend Lease contributions to their war effort, and the 158,500 additional trucks included Lend Lease vehicles.[49] The trucks and jeeps transformed Soviet logistics and increased the combat value of the artillery as the American 2.5 truck became the vehicle of choice to tow Soviet guns. At least one-quarter of the motor vehicles in use by mid-1943 were of American origin.

Other American supplies were arriving in substantial amounts by mid-1943. American boots and rations arrived in considerable numbers, improving the life of the individual soldier. Prisoners at Kursk frequently referred to American canned rations. Pictures of Russian soldiers generally show well-fed individuals from 1943 on. When deliveries were delayed in the early part of 1943, Stalin in his note to Churchill on April 2, 1943, stated that the cancellation of the northern convoys in March 1943 represented "a catastrophic diminution of supplies and arms" indicating the value of the aid that had arrived.[50]

In summary, the Red Army was rebuilt in the first half of 1943, restoring the combat value of the divisions that had been worn down in the Stalingrad operation and the offensives that followed. The number of units was increased with special emphasis on support units that would cope with the German panzers. These great strides were made possible by the 1.5 million new soldiers and millions of returning wounded. The outpouring of weapons from Soviet factories and the arrival of millions of tons of Lend Lease provided the trucks, weapons, and supplies for the new and renewed forces. Not the least of the improvements was the accumulated battle experience and a gain in competence in the leadership of the Red Army from the Supreme Commander to the platoon leaders. The Red Army of July 1943 was far more formidable foe than the army that melted before the Nazis in the summers of 1941 and 1942.

CHAPTER 3

The Germans Rebuild

During the lull beginning with the muddy season in the spring of 1943 to July 1943, Hitler engaged in a massive program to rebuild the German Army. From the beginning of *Barbarossa* in June 1941 to July 1, 1943, the Wermacht on all fronts lost 3,950,000 men (killed, wounded, and missing). Only 2,970,000 additions (new recruits and returning wounded) were made during those two years, a net loss of nearly one million.[1] During the same two years, the German Navy gained over 200,000 men and the air force 556,000, but some of the air force men fought as infantry with the army, and the total does not include the SS. Still by July 1, 1943, the 243 German divisions were short an average of 2,500 men from their table of organization.[2]

The vigorous program of rebuilding began in January 1943 after the disastrous winter of 1942–43. Not only had the Wermacht lost the entire 6th Army at Stalingrad, but also the Rumanian 3rd and 4th Armies, the Italian 8th Army, and the Hungarian 2nd Army had been removed from the order of battle by the Soviet offensives following one another east to west from November 1942 until February 1943. At Stalingrad the Germans lost thirteen infantry divisions (44th, 71st, 76th, 79th, 94th, 113th, 295th, 297th, 305th, 371st, 376th, 384th, and 389th), the 100th Mountain Division, three motorized divisions (3rd, 29th, and 60th), and three panzer divisions (14th, 16th, and 24th).[3] In the battles that followed six more divisions were lost (298th, 385th, 7th Luftwaffe, 8th Luftwaffe, 22nd Panzer, and 27th Panzer).[4] Six divisions (334th Infantry, 90th Motorized, 164th Light, 10th, 15th, and 21st Panzer) were lost in Tunisia.[5] The three operations cost the German the loss of thirty-two divisions including twenty at Stalingrad, six in southern Russia in early 1943, and six in Tunisia.

The Germans withdrew from the salients at Demyansk and Rzhev to free up divisions to hall the Soviet offensives in February and March. Twenty-two divisions (fifteen infantry, three motorized, three panzer, one cavalry) were released from the Rzhev salient alone. The divisions from Rzhev played an essential role in halting the Red Army advance west of Kursk.[6]

The alarming losses and the fear of growing Soviet power led to a fundamental change in Nazi strategy. Prior to 1943 the German civilian population had not been unduly stressed by the war, other than by the British air raids.

German industry, working only on day shifts, continued to make consumer goods. Military service was limited more or less to the annual group of young men reaching military age. On January 13, 1943, Hitler announced that henceforth the German nation would devote itself to total war. On February 18, 1943, Joseph Goebbels detailed some of the changes. The work week would be lengthened to sixty hours; student exemptions would be reduced; more women were to be employed; and the German Labor Service would enroll young men at seventeen, two years before entering the armed forces instead of one.[7]

The German High Command estimated that 800,000 men would be required to replace the losses of the winter of 1942–43 exclusive of the returning wounded. In comparison, the Russians added 1.5 million recruits in the first half of 1943. Hitler's orders of January 8 and 22, 1943, set forth the measures to provide the 800,000 troops. The 1925 Class of men (eighteen years old) were to be inducted in early 1943 producing 400,000 new soldiers. The Russians were inducting the Class of 1926. An additional 200,000 would come from previously deferred men from the domestic economy, industry, and coal mining. The men taken from industry were replaced by foreigners, women, and youngsters.

Still more men were needed to make up the total need of 800,000. Therefore, another 200,000 older men had to be inducted, half from the age group twenty-one to thirty-seven years of age, and half from the thirty-eight to forty-two age group. The number was still short so additional men were taken from the forty-three to forty-six age group. Two months later, 112,000 men were sought from the fifty years plus group to replace younger men in antiaircraft, service, and occupation units.[8] All of these measures produced a total of 800,000 trained men by July 1, 1943.

During 1943 the Wermacht reached its highest point, 9.5 million men on May 30, 1943. Of these 4,250,000 were in the army, 450,000 in the SS, 1,700,000 in the air force, 810,000 in the navy, and 2,300,000 in the replacement system, plus 100,000 in foreign units. There were 15.5 million men working in the civilian economy along with 14.8 million women, far more than one would assume, but still far short of the contribution of Soviet women. In addition there were 6.3 million foreigners working in Germany. That number was 50 percent higher than the previous year and increased to 7.5 million on September 30, 1944.[9]

The German prisoner of war camps, containing millions of Soviet prisoners, were a potential source of manpower. Faced with bad treatment and starvation and a distinct possibility of dying, an increasing number of Russian prisoners volunteered to work for the Germans in exchange for better food and conditions. Volunteers were called *hiwis*, a contraction of the German term for volunteer helper. They were widely used in the Replacement Army and railroad construction units for service duties to free men for the front. On February 6, 1943, the Luftwaffe had 100,000 hiwis in construction and antiaircraft units, replacing Germans.[10]

Hiwis became part of the official table of organization of army units. The infantry division was assigned more than a thousand to perform supply duties, or for horses, and other noncombatant roles. In early 1943 the army replaced Germans with 200,000 hiwis and later an additional 500,000. Other ethnic groups were also used as hiwis. On March 18, 1943, the 715th Division in France used 800 black French prisoners, who volunteered to fill 800 vacancies as wagon drivers, grooms, laborers, and other noncombat positions.[11]

In January 1943, the 9th German Army of Army Group Center included 39,400 Russians, either volunteers or conscripted. The infantry divisions in the 9th Army had a total of 7,700 hiwis assigned plus an additional group of 6,000 attached laborers. When the 9th Army evacuated the Rzhev salient, 21,800 more Russians were seized to prevent their working for the Red Army when it reoccupied the territory, and on March 20, 1943, many were assigned to construction battalions to work on fortifications and roads. The Russians made up one-quarter of the manpower for the 9th German Army. On the Eastern Front in 1943 nearly a million Russians were working or fighting for the German Army. Another 900,000 were employed in Germany to work in factories and on the farms.[12]

The Soviet prisoners were also formed into Ost battalions, equipped with captured Russian weapons, and used to fight the partisans. In early 1943 the Germans had 176 Ost battalions, many formed by anti-Communist ethnic minorities from the Caucasus. In May 1943 there were thirty-two Turkestan battalions, twelve Georgian battalions, eleven Armenian battalions, eight North Caucasus battalions, sixteen Muslim and Azerbaijan battalions, and ten Volga Tarlar battalions.[13] By June 1943 there were 320,000 Ost troops.[14]

Ost battalions also replaced Germans in the occupation divisions in France. On January 27, 1943, the German High Command ordered the German divisions in France to send one of their infantry battalions to Russia and in exchange received an Ost battalion. The Ost battalion had German uniforms, but Russian weapons.[15] The first ten battalions were quickly followed at a rate of three Ost battalions in exchange for a single German battalion.[16]

Another source of manpower were individuals in the occupied territories who had some German ancestry. These quasi-foreigners were categorized in four classes of Volksdeutsch, ranging from Class I, who were active Nazis; Class II, who were passive Nazis, but preserved their German identity; Class III who were Germans that had acquired Polish or another culture, spoke very little German but were amenable to German orientation; and Class IV who had German blood, but were hostile to the Nazis. Class I and II were inducted into the army without reservation as German citizens. The Volksdeutsch Class III were given ten years probationary citizenship and then inducted into the army. Because of their doubtful loyalty, they could not be promoted beyond private first class.[17] In 1943 in the search for manpower, more Polish-Germans were reclassified as Volksdeutsch III and inducted. On March 31, 1943, there were so many Poles in the German Army that their use was limited on the Eastern Front. No more than percent of the total strength of a company unit on the Eastern Front or in North Africa were allowed to come from this group, as they were not considered completely trustworthy.[18]

Interrogation of Polish Volksdeutsch III prisoners in North Africa in 1943 revealed much information about the German replacement problems in early 1943. In training, some of the replacement companies were completely Polish. Because the Poles spoke little or no German, their training had to be conducted in Polish. Many Slovenians from Yugoslavia, most of whom did not speak German, also were called up in this period. Most of the foreign recruits received only from three to eight weeks of basic training in the replacement battalions, depending on the amount of their prior military experience. Rifles were scarce, and very little weapons training was given. The foreigners were shipped out as soon as they were considered ready by the training personnel, and very few went on the advanced training battalions where most German youths acquired more experience before entering combat. The foreigners were sent directly to combat assignments. When the Poles arrived in Africa they were distributed among the rifle companies with a limit of two in any one group, the equivalent of an American squad. In 1944, a Luxemburger, who was anti-Nazi, was reclassified from Class IV to III, inducted, given four days training, and sent to an artillery battalion in southern France.[19]

Foreigners also were used to man the large number of antiaircraft guns defending Germany from Allied air attacks. By 1944, over 1,000 antiaircraft battalions plus independent batteries with up to a million individuals defended Germany and the occupied countries. In January 1943, the air defense of Germany was augmented because of the increasingly heavy raids. As early as January 17, 1943, a night raid on Berlin killed 88, wounded 177, and left 11 missing.[20] Foreigners helped to man the guns. In January 1943 three heavy antiaircraft batteries were formed in Denmark with Danish Nazi sympathizers to guard the ports.[21] However, attempts failed to recruit French, Belgians, and Dutch into antiaircraft units.[22] In the January 1943 plan proposed to bring total war to Germany, 500,000 men in antiaircraft units in Germany were to be replaced with women, youngsters, and foreigners.[23]

The use of teenagers to perform military tasks in Germany had begun even earlier. On September 20, 1942, Hitler had ordered the formation of the Antiaircraft Militia to replace men in antiaircraft batteries. In January 1943, the age limit was dropped to include fifteen-year-old boys and girls who were to be excused from school to man the guns.[24]

All of the above extraordinary measures had the central objective of releasing combat-fit Germans to serve on the Eastern Front. However the most important source of new combat soldiers was the annual class of young recruits that passed through the replacement system. The ordinary eighteen-year-old entering the army passed through a system based on a prewar organization linking divisions, not only to military districts, but to geographical subdivisions within the district. For each regiment in the peacetime army, a replacement battalion was created at the beginning of the war, located in the home station of the regiment. The purpose of this battalion was to induct, train, and send new recruits to the parent division, thereby preserving the geographical identity of the division. The replacement battalion also held recuperating wounded until they were ready to rejoin the division. The demand for replacements varied greatly during the first three years of the war, and all of the available replacements were not needed. New divisions were formed using the surplus men that overloaded the system when casualties began to mount after June 1941. Late in the war, replacement battalions, rather than regiments, were required to serve entire divisions. During the last two years of the war, divisions were created that combined men from two or more military districts, and the division was arbitrarily assigned to one of the districts. Despite many alterations, the basic system continued of relating the home of the recruit to the division in which he would serve.

By 1942 the replacement and training battalion consisted of a cadre company that included the administrative and training personnel, one or more companies of recuperating wounded, and one or more companies of men in training. The replacement and advanced training companies were separated into replacement battalions and training battalions, the latter comprised of men who had completed the eight weeks of basic training and were receiving eight weeks of advanced training. In 1943, the training battalions were redesignated as reserve battalions and formed into reserve divisions. The reserve divisions, recruits completing their training, were used to maintain order in the occupied areas. In October 1942 five training divisions had been formed in Russia to provide advanced training and to combat the partisans. By February 1943 there were ten reserve divisions in the West, four in Russia, one in Croatia, and three in Poland.[25] The numerous German returning wounded served as the major source of replacements. From July 1, 1942, to June 30, 1943, the Germans lost 1,985,000 men in the East. During the same period 850,000 wounded returned, a little less than half.[26] The Germans estimated that 80% of wounded would return to combat. The report assumed that of those lost about 10 percent would be killed or missing; 10 percent would be permanently disabled; about 40 percent would return within thirty days from hospitals in Russia; and the remaining 40 percent would be sent to Germany for hospital care to return in sixty days. British intelligence made an estimate in September 1942 based on German State Insurance Company records. The records indicated that 61 percent of men wounded or sick were permanently disabled. The British estimated that 30 percent was more accurate because the insurance company records excluded those treated in forward hospitals.[27] A fair estimate of losses would be 10 percent killed and missing, 30 percent permanent disabled, 30 percent returned within thirty days, and 30 percent returned within sixty days. The Russians estimated that 27 percent of the hospitalized would not return to duty.

The newly trained recruits were sent to the front in march battalions, while the wounded returned in companies at more frequent intervals, another indication that the returning wounded exceeded the number of new recruits. The replacement companies were given three component numbers. On July 12, 1943, the German 255th Infantry Division received a company number IV/255/14 with 22 noncommissioned officers and 113 men. The first roman numeral referred to the military district, the second number the receiving division, and the final number indicated that it was the fourteenth company sent. On July 11, 1943, the VIII/57/20 company with one officer, seventeen NCOs, and ten men arrived at the headquarters of the 57th German Infantry Division.[28]

In 1943 the 7th Military District, providing replacements for six divisions, sent an average of one march battalion with new recruits every three months and two returning wounded companies each month (or twelve companies in three months), about three times as many returning wounded as new recruits.[29]

The manpower problem in 1943 extended to the SS. Unable to replace its losses with volunteers, the SS resorted to conscripted men. In 1943, the SS received only 10,000 volunteers, instead of the 27,000 needed, so an additional 20,000 men were selected from army inductees. To form two new divisions in the West, the SS took 27,000 men from the Labor Service (RAD) and 10,000 conscripted from industry. Another 5,000 men included Volksdeutsch, eighteen-year-old volunteers, and 800 former border security guards.[30]

Even with all these measures to provide manpower, the enormous losses of the winter of 1942–43 were only partially replaced. The heaviest losses occurred from November 1942 through March 1943. In the first quarter of 1943 the Eastern Front lost 689,260 men killed, wounded, and missing, and received only 370,700 replacements. However, beginning in March, major additions came from Germany including replacements and returning wounded. In March, April, and May, 441,000 new men arrived while only 124,000 were lost in March, and 78,000 in April and May. In the first half of 1943, 823,433 men were lost and 720,100 replacements arrived, a net loss on the Eastern Front of

103,333 men, despite determined German efforts to find manpower. While the Germans lost over 100,000 men, the Red Army field armies gained over a million men in the same period.

At the core of the German problem in the east was the need to match the growth of the number of Red Army divisions. In early 1941 a host of substandard divisions had been created in the west to replace the divisions transferred to the east. In 1942 the German occupation army in France, Belgium, the Netherlands, Denmark, and Norway had served as the strategic reserve for the army, gave advanced training for recruits emerging from the replacement battalions in Germany, provided recuperation for returning wounded, and posed as a deterrent force for any British or American invasion plans.

To form new divisions over a million men were diverted from the replacement stream in the period from June 1941 to July 1943.[31] New German divisions were formed in "waves." All of the divisions in a wave usually had similar characteristics. The Fifteenth Wave of nine divisions began forming in April 1941 and remained the core of the defensive force in France until June 1944. The divisions had only two infantry regiments, a single artillery battalion, very few machine guns, and limited service personnel.[32]

The German Thirteenth Wave with eight divisions and the Fourteenth Wave with six divisions, were created in November 1940 for occupation duties in anticipation of the transfer in 1941 of all combat-fit divisions to the east for the attack on the Soviet Union. The divisions had three infantry regiments, but only three battalions of Czech or obsolete German artillery. The infantry had captured Czech or French weapons and equipment. In 1942 these divisions were reequipped with modern German weapons and sent to the Eastern Front. As part of the preparation for combat duty in the east, the divisions received an antitank company and an infantry cannon platoon for each rifle regiment, and an additional field artillery battery in each of the artillery battalions.

Most of the divisions of the Thirteenth and Fourteenth Waves were sent to Russia between June 1942 and March 1943. In June 1942, four German divisions (305th, 323rd, 336th, and 340th Infantry Divisions) left the west to participate in the summer campaign. The 305th was subsequently lost at Stalingrad. The 323rd was badly mauled in the Soviet breakthrough in January 1943 that destroyed the Hungarian 2nd Army, and only a battle group of the 223rd Division survived. The division was rebuilt as part of the 2nd Army in the spring of 1943, but had not regained full strength by July 1943. The 336th Division was outside the Stalingrad pocket with the 3rd Rumanian Army and in January 1943 formed part of the Mieth Corps in the Hollidt Army Detachment that later was redesignated as a new 6th Army. The 340th Division was sent to the 2nd Army, but was not mauled as badly as the 323rd. It remained with the 2nd Army, along with the 323rd Division, through the Battle of Kursk.

In November 1942 more German divisions were sent from the west in response to the Soviet offensive that surrounded Stalingrad beginning with the 337th Infantry Division that bolstered the 9th Army in Army Group Center. In January 1943 the mass transfer of the Thirteenth and Fourteenth Wave divisions began with the 304th, 306th, and 321st. The 304th joined the 30th Corps in Army Detachment Fretter Pico in the Ukraine, and sustained heavy losses in the battle in the Don Bend. The 306th went to the 16th Corps in Army Detachment Hollidt, holding the southern flank of the line. The 321st Division was sent to the 4th Army in Army Group Center and saw little action in 1943.

In February, three more German divisions went to the east. The 302nd and the 335th joined the 304th in the 30th Corps of Army Detachment Fretter Pico in the Ukraine, and the 320th became part of Army Detachment Lanz near Belgorod. In March the last three of the fourteen divisions of the 13th and 14th waves left France for the east. The 327th went to the 13th Corps of the 2nd Army to shore up the gap left by the Soviet drive through Kursk. The 332nd also went to the 2nd Army initially, but then transferred to the 52nd Corps of Army Detachment Kempf in April, and played a major role in holding the west flank of the 4th Panzer Army during the Kursk battle. The 333rd formed part of the new 3rd Corps in the 1st Panzer Army in the Ukraine.

Four of the divisions of the Thirteenth and Fourteenth Wave reinforced the summer drive on Stalingrad, and the remaining ten formed the bulk of the divisions that stopped the Soviet offensives in the spring of 1943.

Twenty divisions had been withdrawn from Russia to France in 1942 for rehabilitation. Nine of these divisions were sent back to Russia between December 1942 and March 1943 and helped reverse the Russian advance in the spring of 1943, and seven more were sent to Russia between April and June 1943, as part of the buildup for Kursk. Of the remaining four divisions, the 10th Panzer was sent to Tunisia in December 1942; the 1st Panzer was sent to the Balkans in June 1943; and the last two, the 65th Infantry and 26th Panzer remained in France until August 1943 when they were sent to Italy.

Of the sixteen sent to Russia, the 23rd Infantry Division was sent to the 18th Army in the Northern Army Group, but all of the rest went to the south. The 6th Panzer went to the 4th Panzer Army to join the forces attempting to rescue the trapped 6th Army at Stalingrad. In January 1943, the 7th Panzer went to the 1st Panzer Army, followed in February by the Adolf Hitler and Das Reich SS Panzer Grenadier Divisions that went to the 4th Panzer Army after it had withdrawn from the Caucasus. In March the 15th Infantry and the Death Head SS Panzer Grenadier Divisions also went to the 4th Panzer Army, while the 106th Infantry and 167th Infantry reinforced Army Detachment Kempf blocking Soviet advances around Kharkov. The German counteroffensive in March 1943 was made possible by nine returning rehabilitated divisions and the ten new divisions from the Thirteenth and Fourteenth Waves, for a total of nineteen divisions from France, the bulk of Manstein's forces in March 1943.

In the second quarter of 1943, Hitler continued to draw on France for the buildup at Kursk. From April to June 1943 eight more divisions were withdrawn; the 1st Panzer went to the Balkans and the 17th, 38th, 39th, 161st, 257th, 282nd, and 328th Infantry to Russia. Two went to the 1st Panzer Army and one to the new 6th Army in the south, while the remaining four went to the Kempf Army Detachment that formed the right flank in the attack on Kursk. Of the thirty-four divisions taken from the forces defending Western Europe in mid-1942, thirty were sent to Russia and most to the crucial southern front where their presence made a major contribution.

The transfer of divisions from France to Russia between December 1942 and June 1943 was based on a decision by Hitler that there would be no second front in France in 1943. Whether this was a gamble on his part, or based on information gleaned from intelligence sources including transcripts of trans-Atlantic telephone calls between Roosevelt and Churchill, cannot be definitely established. However the decision of the leaders at Casablanca in January to forego an invasion of France in 1943 was made known to Hitler. In July 1943 the Germans had only a single combat ready division left in France, the 65th Infantry Division. All of the others were either static occupation divisions or new units in training.

The history of the German 65th Infantry Division provides an insight to the successes and failures of the rebuilding program, and, more significantly, the exhaustion of the strategic reserve previously held in the French occupation force. The 65th Infantry Division was formed in the summer of 1942 as a two-regiment division. The table of organization strength for officers was 202 and on February 4, 1943; the division had 209, seven over the authorized number.[33] The division in this period was well armed with 260 light machine guns, 66 heavy machine guns, 15 50mm antitank guns, 9 75mm antitank guns, 9 self-propelled 75mm guns, 22 105mm howitzers, and 8 150mm howitzers. In addition the division had numerous French and Polish machine guns and over fifty French artillery pieces of various calibers that formed the coastal defenses.[34] The 65th Division regiments had a full complement of German weapons in the two infantry regiments and three artillery battalions, but the service units were equipped with Polish light machine guns.[35]

A persistent activity during the next few months was exchanging combat-fit men in the German 65th Division for men with third-degree frostbite in divisions destined for transfer to the Eastern Front.[36] The 65th Division also received Volksdeutsch III men from divisions bound for Russia. A German who was the last son in a family or the father of five or more children was deferred from combat, and small groups of these men came to the 65th Division in February and March. A further upset was created by the exchange of older men in combat elements for younger men in the service units. In April alone 301 soldiers were exchanged.[37]

On February 19, 1943, over 100 cadre with a heavy proportion of officers and noncommissioned officers were sent to the 17th Luftwaffe Field Division in exchange for untrained privates, an attempt in part to alleviate the serious lack of experienced leadership at all levels in the Luftwaffe divisions. In late February the 65th Division was ordered to provide cadres equal to about three rifle companies and two artillery batteries to the 44th Division near Antwerp, one of the divisions being formed to replace those lost at Stalingrad. At the same time the 65th transferred over 600 combat-fit men to the 39th Division in exchange for men with frostbite. In March over 400 men were sent to the 39th Division, and in April, 220. Another 700 men went to the 44th Division in April as well.[38]

On May 31, 1943, the 65th Division had 158 unfit men, 907 men with third-degree frostbite, 375 men classified as Volksdeutsch III, 198 men missing, and 72 returning wounded, a total of 1,710 men of limited capacity of the approximately 10,000 in the division. In addition many of the other troops were over-aged. In June the 65th Division was ordered to prepare for combat, and the unqualified men were sloughed off to occupation divisions. During the month, the division received 2,101 men to replace the transfers.[39] In the summer of 1943 the 65th Division was in Vlissingen, Holland assigned to the 15th Army, the only mobile combat ready division in the west. In August 1943 the division was sent to Italy in anticipation of an Allied invasion.

To replace the divisions in France, the Germany created thirty-six new divisions in 1943. To address the problems caused by the heavy losses during the winter, on February 6, 1943, Hitler outlined a program to rebuild the Wermacht. Beginning in March 1943 the twenty divisions lost at Stalingrad were to be reconstituted, sixteen in France, and one each in Denmark, Germany, the Balkans, and Russia. Seven other divisions that had been lost were not reformed, and the 403rd Security Division was abolished.[40] The sixteen divisions formed in France were given the numbers of the divisions lost at Stalingrad. Some divisions were reformed with cadres from other divisions in France and from units that had not been captured with the original division, for example the bakery companies were often outside of the pocket. Replacements came from the returning wounded from the divisions, and the regular flow of recruits from the divisional replacement battalions assigned to these divisions. Other divisions absorbed existing training units, for example, the 3rd Panzer Grenadier Division incorporated the 386th Motorized Reserve Division in France, and the 29th Panzer Grenadier Division took the units of the 345th Motorized Reserve Division.[41] The 60th Panzer Grenadier Division used the 271st Infantry Regiment as cadre.

Seven other German divisions were rebuilt on the basis of especially created infantry regiments. In February 1943, each of fourteen military districts in Germany formed an infantry regiment by drawing men from the cadre and students in noncommissioned officer schools. Each regiment had twelve rifle companies, an infantry gun company, an antitank company, an artillery battalion, and a motorcycle squadron. The 44th Division absorbed the 887th and 888th Reserve Infantry Regiments; the 76th Division the 877th and 878th Regiments; the 94th Division the 875th and 876th Regiments; the 113th Division, the 881st and 882nd Regiments; the 71st Division, the 883rd and 885th Regiments; the 79th Division (in Russia), the 884th and 886th Regiments; and the 305th Division, the 879th and 880th Regiments. By mid-April each of the seven divisions that received the new regiments had approximately 15,000 men, very strong for a German division in 1943. The other five infantry divisions (297th, 371st, 376th, 384th, and 389th) were increased first to battle group size of about 3,000 men by March 1, 1943, and by mid-April averaged over 4,000 men. The 297th received returning wounded and recruits from the 156th Reserve Division. The three panzer divisions (14th, 16th and 24th) ranged in size from 7,000 to 15,000 by mid-April, but shared only eighty-two French tanks.[42] Two other divisions burned out in Russia were also refitted in France, the 25th Panzer and the 1st Parachute, as well as the 334th Division in Tunisia, for a total of nineteen refitted divisions.

The Germans formed four new mobile divisions, the 356th Infantry, the 2nd parachute, and the 9th and 10th SS Panzer Grenadier. The last two divisions, formed from seventeen-year-old members of the Hitler Youth, would not be fit for combat for over a year. The 13th SS Division was formed from Bosnian Muslim recruits. The resistance in Yugoslavia was primarily by Greek Orthodox Serbians, while the Catholic Croatians and Muslim Bosnians sided with the Germans. The Croatians formed a separate government and furnished an infantry regiment, which was lost at Stalingrad, and later two divisions used for fighting the partisans.

The Germans also formed twelve new occupation divisions that remained in France until driven out by the Allies in 1944. The Muslim division and the two young SS divisions also remained in France. However, the other twenty-one divisions were called away between June and November 1943. Twelve, including most of the Stalingrad divisions, went to Italy; one went to the Balkans; and eight returned to Russia, none of them in time to take part in the Battle of Kursk.

Two new German divisions (15th and 90th Panzer Grenadier) were created in Sicily from the few remnants that had escaped before the surrender. They were reinforced by units that had remained in Sicily and Italy, men

returning from leave, and replacement battalions of new recruits and returning wounded that were on the way to Tunisia before the surrender.[43]

The major impact of the creation of the thirty-six German divisions in
France was the drain on the replacement pool. The new recruits in the Class
of 1924 (nineteen-year-olds) that had been trained from October to December 1942 were used to fill out the Stalingrad divisions as well as divisions being
upgraded before going to Russia. By March 1943 all of the recruits in the Class
of 1924 had been absorbed by units, leaving none in the replacement pool.[44]
While the divisions in Russia desperately needed replacements in the rifle
companies, many of these troops were being sent to form new divisions that
would not see action until 1944.

The time to re-create the Stalingrad divisions and form new divisions
stretched to eight months because of shortages of equipment that delayed
training. There were shortages of tanks, vehicles, weapons, horses, and equipment of all kinds.[45] Although fifteen of the other new divisions were occupation divisions with limited service personnel or divisions with foreign troops or
youngsters, the remaining twenty-one absorbed up to 200,000 combat fit men,
and only eight returned to Russia too late for the crucial summer offensive.
The first to return was the 113th Infantry that went to the 4th Army in Army
Group Center in August.

How all of these German measures played out in the infantry divisions in
the East is of vital concern. The divisions already on the Eastern Front, but not
scheduled for the Kursk offensive, were not rebuilt; even the German 2nd
Army on the west face of the bulge was short of men. The nine infantry divisions lacked 54,200 men in April and on June 1, 1943, still lacked 48,350 German replacements. All of the divisions in the 2nd Army had been reduced from
nine battalions to eight or even four battalions. The weakest was the 323rd Division with only four battalions; the strongest was the 327th Division with eight.
The 26th Division had six strong battalions and a field training battalion of new
recruits. The divisions were rated according to combat capability. Only the
327th was rated as capable of attack; four others had limited attack capability;
one had full defense ability; and the remaining two had only limited defensive
ability. The 2nd Army even lacked artillery, with the batteries reduced from the
normal four guns to only three.[46]

The changes that were occurring in German infantry divisions on the Eastern Front in 1943 are illustrated by the 134th Infantry Division, part of the
52nd Corps of the 2nd Panzer Army. On January 1, 1943, the division was
ordered to comb the 134th Artillery Regiment and divisional service units for
combat-fit men and to replace them with hiwis. A school company was established to retrain the German service personnel as infantry.[47] By March 1943,
the division made further use of Russians, forming the 134th Ost Battalion that

carried weapons. The battalion was assigned to work details, and on March 28, two platoons from the battalion were transferred to the 134th Engineer Battalion of the division.[48]

The 134th Division was in good condition in April 1943, despite heavy Russian attacks in the previous three months. The division had 14,100 Germans, 2,300 Ost troops, 1,100 hiwis, and 5,600 prisoners of war on work details.[49] At the same time the obligations of the division increased. For example, on January 19, 1943, the 134th Division assumed the responsibility of additional frontage formerly held by the 211th Division so that the 4th Panzer Division from the 2nd Panzer Army could be withdrawn to stop the Soviet breakthrough at Kursk. In February the 134th Division provided two battalions to assist its neighbor, the 211th Division, in withstanding an attack. While the total number of men in the division was high, it held a long front line, and few reserves were available. While 9,000 Russians performed much of the noncombat work and fought the partisans, they required German surveillance. The 134th Division was called for heavy duty when the Soviet offensive aimed at Orel opened in July 1943.

While the mainstay of the defense rested on the infantry divisions, the panzer forces held the offensive power of the German Army. A major task for the High Command in the east was the refitting panzer and motorized divisions that were combat weary after turning back the Russians in February and March. In April, south of the Kursk bulge, the Germans had five panzer corps in need of rehabilitation. The 24th Panzer Corps pulled the 16th Motorized Division and the 23rd Panzer Division from the front, replacing them with infantry. Other panzer corps did the same, the 3rd Panzer Corps with the 3rd and 19th Panzer Divisions; the 40th Panzer Corps with the 7th and 17th, and the Viking SS Panzer Divisions; the 57th Panzer Corps with the 6th and 11th Panzer Divisions and the Gross Deutschland Motorized Division; and the SS Panzer Corps with the Adolf Hitler, the Reich, and the Death Head SS Panzer Divisions. Infantry divisions were needed to replace the panzer divisions in the front line, and in one case, the 6th Panzer Division had to remain in the line while the refitting took place.[50]

To refit all of these German divisions required not only manpower, but also vast quantities of weapons and equipment. Sufficient weapons were not available in January 1943, and many units were partially equipped with captured weapons, especially in the west. In January 1943, the two new SS divisions forming in France were equipped with captured arms and transport.[51] In January 5,000 French trucks were sent to the Eastern Front to fill deficiencies.[52] However, during 1943, Albert Speer was redirecting German industry to war production. The resulting flow of weapons beginning in early 1943 eventually provided the German divisions in the east with an adequate, though not plentiful supply. In 1943 the Germans manufactured 9,200 tanks and assault guns compared to only 4,300 in 1942. German arsenals produced 2,600 artillery pieces compared to only 1,200 in 1942. Rifle and machine pistol production increased from 137,000 per month to 209,000 per month, and the production of machine guns doubled. While these totals were less than Russian production, the German Army had sufficient high quality weapons to arm most of the troops on the Eastern Front by the middle of 1943. However, divisions not slated for a part in the Kursk battle continued to use substandard weapons. In July 1943 the 134th Division lost two Russian howitzers, four French 45mm antitank guns, and five obsolete 37mm antitank guns in combat, indicating the continued use of substandard weapons, even by combat divisions.[53]

New higher quality weapons introduced in 1943 increased the firepower of German units. The introduction of the MG42, an improved light machine gun, gave the German infantry the most versatile and dependable machine gun of the war, capable of a high rate of fire and convenient to carry. The comparable Russian weapon had a large pan magazine making the weapon and extra magazines difficult to carry. By 1943 the Germans had introduced new heavier antitank guns to replace the ineffective 37mm guns of 1941. The advanced tank types will be described below.

The rebuilding of the German Army was a stupendous undertaking. German losses in men from the time of the first offensive in 1941 until March 1943 had been staggering. To rectify the situation, Hitler announced a massive buildup that progressed rapidly during the muddy season in the spring of 1943. A change in Nazi strategy was necessary because of the alarming German losses and the fear of increasing Soviet power. Hitler decreed that the German nation would devote itself to total war, including a much greater effort by the civilian population from women to school children, who were released from classes to operate antiaircraft guns. All of the measures were designed to release men for the Eastern Front.

By May 1943, the Wermacht reached its highest point of 9.5 million men. Women and foreigners played a large role in both the armed forces and the economy. Men previously exempted from service because of suspected disloyalty were inducted into the army. Even the prisoner of war camps were tapped for volunteers who received better conditions in return for working for Germany. Nearly a million Russians fought for the Germans in Ost battalions that battled the Partisans in the east and reinforced the occupation divisions in the west.

The major source of new manpower was the annual class of youngsters reaching the age of eighteen. The replacement system was based on the prewar system that linked a division to a geographical area, and gave the new recruits a sense of identity. The recovering wounded returned to their original units after recuperating in the same replacement battalions that trained new recruits. Still the shortage of men was widespread, and even the SS had to resort to conscripts.

All of the measures to find 800,000 replacements resulted in many substandard additions to the army. While the German Army had a net loss of 100,000 men in the first six months of 1943, the Red Army had a net gain of one million. The constantly expanding Red Army could not be matched by the Germans, even though Hitler stripped the west of all except one combat ready division by August.

Hitler's next challenge, the threat of the Allied invasion of Sicily and Italy in the summer of 1943, did not divert divisions from the Battle of Kursk. No divisions were sent from the Eastern Front to defend the "soft underbelly" of Europe. Instead sorely needed replacements were used to re-create the Stalingrad divisions and to refit others that would make up the armies to defend Italy. The only troops from the Russian Front sent to Italy were a single SS division and the headquarters of the II SS Panzer Corps that was stationed in northern Italy in August after fighting at Kursk.

In July 1943 the Eastern Front required not only manpower in huge numbers, but also large quantities of weapons. Albert Speer reorganized the economies of Western Europe and sharply increased the production of weapons, although still less than Soviet production. Speer improved the quality as well as quantity of weapons, which offset the Russian superiority in numbers.

All of the measures taken in the first half of 1943 resulted in a very powerful German Army in Russia by July 1943. However, the expansion was not sufficient to match the Soviet rebuilding program. The Germans were able to obtain superiority in only two sectors north and south of Kursk on July 5 when the attack commenced.

CHAPTER 4

The German Order of Battle

On July 5, 1943, the Germans had assembled their most awesome armored force of the war concentrated for a single campaign. The invasion in June 1941 had been spread over the entire length of the front and included three separate operations. The Kursk forces exceeded the forces gathered for the offensive in the south in 1942. The Kursk battle had drawn the cream of the German army from all over Europe. Many of the divisions had been transferred from France or from the Rzhev salient in early 1943. All of the divisions had been reinforced during the preceding three months.

The German armies involved in the battle were the 9th Army on the north shoulder, the 2nd Army on the face of the bulge, and the 4th Panzer Army and Army Detachment Kempf on the south shoulder.

On the northern fringe of the north shoulder, the 299th Infantry Division of the 2nd Panzer Army faced the right flank division of the 48th Soviet Army. In May 1943, the 299th Division had been reduced from a nine-battalion to a six-battalion division by the abolition of a battalion from each of the infantry regiments because of the shortage of infantry replacements. The division had been in the Livny area since January 1942 and was well settled in its fortified line that stretched over 20 km, a considerable span for six infantry battalions.

Opposing the remainder of the Soviet 48th Army and the right flank of the 13th Army was the 23rd Corps of the 9th German Army. Here the division sectors were only 8 km wide. From left to right the corps had the 383rd Infantry Division, the 216th Infantry Division, and the 78th Sturm division on the line and the 87th Infantry Regiment of the 36th Infantry Division in reserve. The 383rd Division was a hybrid division formed in January 1942 with replacement elements from three military districts and included regiments from Koenigsberg, Stettin, and Berlin. After two months of training, the division was sent to the 2nd Army north of Voronezh where it remained until driven back in February 1943 to its location on the north shoulder, still retaining nine battalions.

The 216th Infantry Division had been reduced to six battalions by the elimination of one of its regiments in June 1942 to make troops available for the southern offensive. The remainder of 1942 the division served in the Orel area under the 2nd Panzer Army. In December 1942, the division relocated to the 4th Army and later to the 2nd Panzer Army in the Orel salient until June, when it was transferred to the 9th Army.

The 78th Sturm division was reorganized from the 78th Infantry Division in January 1943. The new table of organization included three storm regiments each with a single infantry battalion and an artillery battalion. In June the organization was changed again, giving each regiment two infantry battalions and reestablishing the artillery regiment. The division also had a powerful armored component with an antitank battalion that included two companies of self-propelled guns and an assault gun battalion. Additional support units included a mortar battalion and an antiaircraft battalion. With over fifty armored vehicles and six battalions of infantry, the division was nearly equal to a panzer division.

The 36th Infantry Division had been reorganized in March 1943 from a motorized division, with two regiments of three battalions each producing a six-battalion division. The reorganization was completed in May 1943, but the division remained in army group reserve with one of its regiments, the 87th, attached to the 23rd Corps as a reserve. The 23rd Corps also had two rifle battalions in reserve, the 8th and 13th Jager Battalions placed behind the 216th Division. The 23rd Corps had two assault gun battalions including the 189th assigned to the 78th Sturm division, three artillery regiments, and a mortar regiment, not an especially strong allotment of supporting troops.

The main thrust would be provided by the three panzer corps. To the west of the 23rd Corps, the 41st Panzer Corps was astride the Orel-Kursk railroad opposing the west half of the 13th Soviet Army. The corps included two infantry divisions, the 86th on the left and the 292nd on the right, and the 18th Panzer Division in reserve to the north near Orel. The 86th Infantry Division had been holding static positions with the 9th Army in the Rzhev area from January 1942 and was one of the divisions released when the Rzhev salient was abandoned. In March 1943 the division lost three infantry battalions because of the late of replacements, leaving only six battalions. The other division, the 292nd, was moved to the 2nd Panzer Army at Orel in April 1943, from the 4th Army near Viasma. The 292nd Division had only two regiments with a total of six battalions, reflecting the long-term shortage of replacements in Army Group Center. In June 1943, the division was moved to the 41st Panzer Corps.

The 18th Panzer Division consisted of two panzer grenadier regiments each with two battalions, the 18th Panzer Battalion, a reconnaissance battalion, and an artillery regiment. The division had given two tank battalions to the 3rd and 60th Panzer Grenadier Divisions in 1942. With only thirty modern Mk IV and Mk III tanks and thirty-three older tanks, plus eleven in repair and in transit, the 18th Panzer was not a strong division.

The 41st Panzer Corps had the equivalent of two artillery regiments, two assault gun battalions, a mortar regiment, and the 656th Panzer Jager Regiment in two battalions, each with forty-five Ferdinands, the 216th Sturm Panzer Battalion with forty-five self-propelled 150mm howitzers, two tank companies, and a heavy mortar battalion. The corps was unbalanced with two weak infantry divisions, a weak panzer division, and about 185 armored vehicles assigned directly to the corps, some of which would reinforce the 18th Panzer Division. Although the Ferdinands were concentrated administratively, they were employed as individual companies of fifteen vehicles. Capable of destroying T34s and 76mm antitank guns at long range, the 9th Army dispersed them by company among the attacking units in the other panzer corps and made maximum use of their power. Very few were lost in the battle, suggesting that they were kept well behind the front out of range of Soviet antitank guns yet were still able to employ their 88mm guns.

West of the 41st Panzer Corps was the far stronger 47th Panzer Corps, which included three panzer divisions and an infantry division facing the east flank of the 70th Soviet Army. The 6th Infantry Division that held most of the sector was a full strength nine-battalion division. The division had been with the 9th Army in the Rzhev salient from November 1941 until it withdrew in March, joining the 4th Army at Smolensk. In June the division was moved to the 47th Panzer Corps on the north shoulder. The division had not been heavily engaged for eighteen months and had suffered few casualties.

The remainder of the corps sector was held by elements of the 20th Panzer Division. The 20th Panzer had four battalions of panzer grenadiers and two tank battalions with fifty-seven modern Mk IIIs and Mk IVs and twenty-one older tanks, plus eight tanks in repair. The division had been with the 2nd Panzer Army in the Orel area since March 1943 and joined the 9th Army in June.

Two panzer divisions were deep in reserve around Kromy, halfway to Orel. The 9th Panzer Division had two tank battalions, an assault gun battalion, and four panzer grenadier battalions. The tank contingent included sixty-six modern Mk IIIs and IVs, six older tanks, fifteen in repair, and twenty-six more tanks in transit, making it about equal to the 20th Panzer Division. The large number of tanks in transit is evidence that the Germans were reinforcing their panzer divisions right up until the day of battle and beyond.

The 2nd Panzer Division was much stronger with two tank battalions, one with Panthers, the other with Mk IVs and IIIs, and four panzer grenadier battalions. The division had eighty-four modern tanks and twenty-nine older models, plus twenty-three in repair and in transit. The division was transferred to the 9th Army from the 2nd Panzer Army in June 1943. Attached directly to the corps were the equivalent of three artillery battalions, a heavy mortar regiment, two assault gun battalions, the 505th Tiger Battalion, and an antiaircraft tank company. The 47th Panzer Corps was the shock force of the 9th Army, but had a total in all of its units of only one Tiger battalion with 45 Tigers, a Panther battalion with about 40 Panthers, five other tank battalions with about 260 Mk IIIs and IVs, and four or five assault gun battalions with about 150 assault guns for a total of about 500 operational armored vehicles.

The left flank of the 70th Soviet Army was opposite the German 46th Panzer Corps consisting of four infantry divisions. The 31st Infantry Division on the east end of the corps sector had been reduced to only six battalions in 1942 with only two battalions in each of the three infantry regiments. The division had been assigned to the 4th Army in the Rzhev area from February and moved to the 9th Army in June. The division had occupied quiet sectors since 1941 but had few replacements. The 7th Division to the west also had been in the Orel area since February with the 4th Army and 2nd Panzer Army and moved to the 9th Army in June. With little combat for over a year and at full strength with nine battalions, the division was one of the stronger infantry divisions in the 9th Army and held a wide sector.

The 258th Infantry Division, reduced to seven battalions in February 1943, had joined the 2nd Panzer Army in the Orel area in March and in June moved to the 9th Army. With little active service in the past year, the division was probably in good condition. Next in the line was Group Manteuffel with three jager battalions (independent rifle battalions) holding a sector nearly 10 km wide opposite the 106th Soviet Division. At this point the Germans were providing a thin screen of units in defensive positions against a similar configuration on the Russian side. The most westerly division in the corps was the 102nd Infantry Division holding a 20 km-wide sector. The 102nd Division had been in the Rzhev area since December 1941. In July 1942 the number of battalions had been reduced to six in keeping with the program to send all of the reinforcements to the south in that year. The division was another of those released by the abandonment of the Rzhev salient, and it moved to its current defensive position in June. The 46th Panzer Corps was really a low-grade defensive unit holding a 60 km wide sector with four weak divisions and a regimental group. The corps troops included the equivalent of five artillery battalions, one assault gun battalion, and a heavy mortar battalion.

The next corps to the right was stretched even more. The 20th Corps had four divisions opposing over half of the Soviet 65th Army. The 72nd Infantry Division had lost three battalions in November 1942, one from each of the regiments. The division had taken part in the Crimean campaign in 1942 and then moved to the Rzhev salient in September 1942. In February 1943 it was withdrawn from the salient and moved to the 20th Corps in April 1943. The next division, the 45th, had been in the heavy fighting with the 2nd Army in January and February and joined the 20th Corps in April after some refitting in reserve. The 130th Infantry Regiment was abolished in June 1943, reducing the division to two regiments each with three battalions. Because of the losses suffered in the winter, the division was probably in poor condition.

The 137th Infantry Division also held a wide sector. It had come from the Rzhev salient to the Orel area in March and was added to the 20th Corps in April. In 1942 the division had been reduced to six battalions. The last division È the corps was the 251st Infantry Division also from the Rzhev salient, joining the 20th Corps in April. The division still had nine battalions and had suffered few losses in the previous year. As the strongest division in the corps, it held the widest front. The 20th Corps had very few corps troops, only one artillery battalion, in keeping with its mission to provide a screening force with four comparatively weak divisions against the Soviet 65th Army.

The 9th Army had a strong reserve including the bulk of the 36th Infantry Division and Group Esebeck with two panzer divisions and one panzer grenadier division. The 4th Panzer Division, west of Orel, had served with the 2nd Panzer Army since January 1942 and was placed in army group reserve in April. The division had two tank battalions and four panzer grenadier battalions. The tank component was strong with eighty-eight modern tanks and fifteen older models, plus seven in repair. It had not been heavily engaged for over a year.

The 12th Panzer Division, located south of the 4th Panzer Division behind the 46th Panzer Corps, had also been in Army Group Center since November 1942. It had moved to the Orel area in March 1943 and went into army group reserve in June. The division had four panzer grenadier battalions and two tank battalions with fifty-one modern tanks and twenty-eight older models, plus four in repair, a comparatively weak division.

The 10th Panzer Grenadier Division had been with Army Group Center since 1941 and in the Orel area since April, another of the divisions freed up by the withdrawal from Rzhev. In June the division was transferred from the 47th Panzer Corps to army group reserve as it reorganized from a motorized division to a panzer grenadier division, picking up a tank battalion, a reconnaissance battalion, and an antiaircraft battalion in the process, while retaining two regiments each with three battalions.

Also assigned directly to 9th Army was the 21st Tank Brigade, a powerful unit with forty-five Tigers, thirty-one other modern tanks, eight older models, and thirty-five tanks in repair or in transit. The brigade probably provided tank battalions to attacking infantry divisions, or supplemented the panzer divisions. No mention of the brigade fighting as a unit has been found.

The 9th Army had four weak corps, two on either side of the assault area, with a total of eleven infantry divisions, all but one of which had only six battalions. The strongest two divisions were positioned on both sides of the assault zone. The 41st and 46th Panzer Corps held the assault front with three infantry divisions and a panzer division and had three panzer divisions poised to attack. In addition there were two panzer divisions and a panzer grenadier division in army group reserve. This powerful force was to strike on a sector held by three Soviet divisions in the first echelon, two in the second, and three rifle divisions and two tank corps in the third echelon, all heavily reinforced with tank destroyer units and artillery.

None of the divisions in the 9th Army had been refitted in France since 1941. All had been more or less continuously engaged in quiet sectors for over a year and a half. Starved for replacements, the divisions had been subjected to slow attrition that led to the disbanding of three battalions in most of the infantry divisions and the temporary loss of one of the two tank battalions in the panzer divisions in 1942. Many of the divisions had participated in the abandonment of the territory around Rzhev that they had so zealously guarded for over a year. This debilitating experience was certain to have a negative impact on morale, and could hardly produce the kind of *esprit de corps* necessary to conduct a sustained drive through formidable Russian defenses.

Holding the face of the Kursk bulge was the 2nd German Army, which was in even worse condition than the 9th Army. The army had been decisively beaten and nearly encircled in the bitter fighting in February and March 1943. Although reinforcements had enabled the army to stop the Soviet attack in March, the divisions were badly worn. The army was relegated to providing a thin screen across most of the face of the bulge with seven divisions and the remnant of an eighth. The northern half of the army sector was held by the 13th Corps with two divisions and a regiment of a third. The corps left was held by the 82nd Division, a remnant that had broken out of the Kastornoie pocket in January and reconstructed during a brief period in army reserve. The rehabilitation was so extensive that the units in the division received new field post office numbers, an indication that for all intents and purposes this was a new unit with new men. There were few survivors from the original 82nd division whose families would be using the old post office number.

The center of the corps area was held by the 340th Infantry Division. This division had also taken part in the January battle, but had not suffered as much as the 82nd. The 340th Division had been reduced to six battalions in 1942 and had been with the 2nd Army since August 1942. Attached to the 340th Division since May was the 769th Infantry Regiment and a light field artillery battalion, which was all that remained of the 377th Infantry Division after the fighting in February. The southern third of the corps sector was held by a regiment of the 327th Infantry Division. The other two regiments of the division formed the 7th Corps reserve. The division had been transferred from France in February, and was at full strength, having been reformed as a field division in early 1943.

The 7th Corps held the southern part of the army sector. Adjoining the 13th Corps was the 88th Division with the remainder of the 327th Division in reserve. The 88th Division had been with the 2nd Army since August 1942 and had suffered heavy casualties as part of the 7th Crops in the January and February defeats. However the division still had nine battalions. To the south, the 26th Division held the next sector. The 26th Division had been in the reserve of the 8th Italian Army in January 1943 and suffered heavy losses as that army collapsed. In February the division was in the 2nd Army reserve, and returned to the front in March where it remained, retaining the nine-battalion.

To the right of the 26th Division, the 75th Division was assigned to the army reserve, but was holding a sector of the front. The 75th Division had been with the 2nd Army since September 1942. Any losses suffered by the division in the winter were apparently replaced by July 1943, as the division continued to maintain nine battalions. The 68th Division, next in line, had lost three battalions in May 1942, but these were replaced on April 1, 1943, by the inclusion of an "alarm" regiment in the division. The alarm regiment had been formed in January by any available units and manpower to plug the gaps in the line caused by the Soviet offensive. The division had been with the 2nd Army since August 1942 and had suffered heavy casualties in the recent battles.

The 2nd Army had the 202nd Assault Gun Battalion in reserve, but no other combat troops. The reserve consisted of two regiments of the 327th Division of the 7th Corps. With only seven weak infantry divisions, the army provided a very thin screen on a 170 km front covering the 60th and 38th Soviet Armies.

The strongest army in the Kursk area was the 4th Panzer Army. The army had been on the south flank of the 6th Army at Stalingrad and had commanded scratch units as Army Detachment Weichs in December. In January 1943, the army was known as Army Detachment Hoth, and it commanded the defense of the right flank of Army Group Don. In the spring the army took part in the Manstein counteroffensive with the SS Panzer Corps and the 6th, 11th, and 17th Panzer Divisions. In April the 4th Panzer Army was withdrawn from the front and had no units assigned until reintroduced on the south shoulder of the Kursk bulge in June.

On July 7, 1943, the 4th Panzer Army had three corps with six panzer and panzer grenadier divisions and four infantry divisions. The 52nd Corps held the left sector with three infantry divisions opposing the Soviet 40th Army. The 57th Division on the left held a 30 km sector with nine battalions that had been in the Voronezh-Kharkov area since October 1941. As part of the 2nd Army 7th Corps, the division had experienced heavy fighting in January and February, but had most likely been brought up to strength with replacements.

The center of the corps sector was held by the 255th Infantry Division, a six-battalion division. It had been with the 3rd Panzer Army in Army Group

Center from May 1942 and was brought down to bolster the 2nd Army in March in the fight to halt the Russian offensive at Kursk. In April it moved to the 52nd Corps at Kharkov. Although it had seen some combat, the division was probably in good condition.

The right hand division in the 52nd Corps, the 332nd Division was a recent transfer from France with nine battalions. The division had arrived in March and was assigned to the 52nd Corps. It had not been involved in heavy fighting and was at full strength with fresh troops, the strongest division in the corps. The corps had two artillery battalions and a werfer (multiple-barrelled rocket launcher) battery attached, very slender resources compared to the opposing 40th Soviet Army.

The 48th Panzer Corps held the center of the army sector and the left of the assault area. The corps included four divisions on the line all poised for the attack. On the left was the Gross Deutschland Panzer Grenadier Division, a unique division in the German Army. It was the outgrowth of a pre-war regiment composed of selected men from all around Germany, hence the name Greater Germany, whereas men in all the other infantry regiments in the peacetime army had been drawn from a single town or area. This elite regiment was used for ceremonial purposes. When the war began, the regiment was motorized and employed independently in the same fashion as the SS regiments; however it remained part of the army and had no connection with the SS. In March 1942 the regiment was enlarged to a division with six infantry battalions. A tank battalion, an assault gun battalion, and other supporting troops. In January 1943 the tank element was increased to a regiment with the addition of the 2nd Battalion of the 203rd Tank Regiment, which became the 2nd Battalion of the Gross Deutschland Panzer Regiment. In May the division was designated a panzer grenadier division and on July 1, 1943, the tank regiment received a third battalion equipped with Tigers. The division had been at Rzhev in December 1942, but in January was moved to Corps Kramer at Kharkov and took part in its recapture. Although the division had seen considerable action, it had first call on quality replacements and was in good condition in July, with forty-six Tigers, sixty-seven other modern tanks, eleven older tanks, thirty-four assault guns, and fifty-one other tanks in repair and in transit.

The next division to the right was the 11th Panzer Division which had been part of Manstein's force that threw back the Russians in February. Earlier the division had served as a "fare brigade" on the Don River driving back Soviet penetrations of the thinly held line north of Rostov. The division was badly worn and was withdrawn for refitting in May and June in Kharkov. By July it was back up to strength with seventy-four modern tanks and fifteen older models, plus twenty-nine tanks in repair and in transit. The division had two tank battalions, four infantry battalions, and supporting units. A third Panther battalion was redesignated as the 52nd Panther Battalion and was assigned directly to the corps.

In the right sector of the corps was the 167th Infantry Division with one regiment holding part of the 2nd SS Panzer Corps sector. The division with nine strong infantry battalions had transferred from Holland in February. Prior to transfer from the west, all divisions were brought to full strength with combat-fit men drawn from other divisions and the training establishment, while at the same time exchanging noncombat fit men, usually men with frostbite who were still considered fit for combat in the milder weather in France and Italy. Having arrived recently, the 167th Division was in excellent condition.

The 3rd Panzer Division was in reserve south of Kharkov. In March 1943 the division lost its third tank battalion and was reduced to two plus four infantry battalions and supporting units. The division had been part of the 4th Panzer Army in the February battles and in March went to the Mius River line until June when it moved north to Kharkov. The division had been refitted behind the Mius in April and May and was in good condition with fifty-six modern tanks and thirty-two older tanks, plus nine tanks in repair and in transit.

The 48th Corps troops were exceptionally abundant including the 10th Panzer Brigade with a battalion of 45 Tigers and 200 Panthers in the 51st and 52nd Panther Battalions, the 911th Assault Gun Battalion, artillery battalions, and an antiaircraft battalion. The 48th Panzer Corps was in excellent condition and formed one of the three assault corps on the south shoulder.

The 2nd SS Panzer Corps was the strongest corps in the battle with three SS panzer grenadier divisions. On the left was the Adolf Hitler Division with two tank battalions, six infantry battalions, an assault gun battalion, and supporting units. The division had refitted in France from November 1942 to January 1943 and then moved to the Kharkov area where it was one of the prime players in the Manstein counteroffensive. In May and June it refitted at Kharkov and was in prime condition in July with 100 modern tanks, 13 attached Tigers, 7 older tanks, and 34 assault guns, plus 25 tanks in repair and in transit.

The Das Reich Division had the same organization and had moved from France in January 1943 to take part in the counteroffensive. It also had refitted at Kharkov and was in prime condition with 113 modern tanks, 14 attached Tigers, and 34 assault guns, plus 16 tanks in repair and in transit. The Death Head Division, with a similar organization, had moved to Russia in February and had taken part in the counteroffensive. The division was in army reserve in May, and in June it was withdrawn to Kharkov for refitting. It was in prime condition in July with 104 modern tanks, 15 attached Tigers, 12 older tanks, and 27 assault guns, plus 38 tanks and assault guns in repair and 9 tanks in transit. The number of tanks in repair was exceptionally high, but many of these vehicles would have been repaired within a few days and provided the

Death Head Division with more operational tanks than any other division in the battle. The 2nd SS Corps troops included a Tiger battalion with forty-five Tigers that were divided among the three divisions, an artillery battalion, two werfer regiments, and some engineers and service units. All three divisions were organized under larger tables of organization than army divisions, for example, the tank battalions had four companies instead of three. Replacements were young volunteers who had passed through the SS schools and were highly motivated. These three divisions were the cream of the German Army in the summer of 1943.

To the east of the 4th Panzer Army was Army Detachment Kempf consisting of three corps. An army detachment (*armee abteilung*) was a temporary organization of two or more corps given the name of the commander. Army Detachment Lanz had been renamed for its new commander, General Werner Kempf, on February 21, 1943, and was finally given permanent status as the 8th Army in August 1943. The 3rd Panzer Corps was on the left with three panzer divisions and an infantry division, the striking force of the army. The 6th Panzer Division on the left had come from France in December and had been part of the 4th Panzer Army in the counteroffensive. In February the division had absorbed the remnants of the 22nd Panzer Division and included two tank battalions and four panzer grenadier battalions. In April it had transferred to the Kempf army and was refitted in May. It was in good condition in July with seventy-eight modern tanks, twenty-nine older tanks, and ten tanks in repair and in transit.

To the right of the 6th Panzer was the 168th Infantry Division with nine battalions. The division had been with the 2nd Hungarian Army in January and had probably suffered considerable losses. The division was assigned to Kemp in March and refitted in April. It was probably in good condition in July. The 19th Panzer was the next division in line. It had two tank battalions and four grenadier battalions. The division had supported the 8th Italian Army in January and suffered severe losses when the Italian army collapsed. In February it was part of the 1st Panzer Army in the counteroffensive. In April and May it refitted and joined Kempf in June. In July the 19th Panzer had sixty-two modern tanks, nineteen older tanks, and nine in repair and in transit, not a strong division.

The third panzer division, the 7th, also had two tank battalions and four grenadier battalions. The division had transferred from France in December and joined the 1st Panzer Army for the counteroffensive in February. It refitted in May and returned to the front in June in good condition. In July it had eighty-one modern tanks, twenty-two older tanks, and nine in repair and in transit.

The 3rd Panzer Corps had a werfer regiment, two antiaircraft regiments. the 228th Assault Gun Battalion, the 503th Tiger Battalion, and artillery. The

3rd Panzer Corps was a strong formation in good condition that would play a significant role in the battle.

South of the 3rd Panzer Corps was Corps Raus, a temporary corps named after its commander with the 106th and 320th Infantry Divisions. The 106th Division was a nine-battalion division that had come from France in March and joined Kempf in April. Having refitted before moving to the Eastern Front, the division was in excellent condition. The 320th Division that arrived from France in January had nine battalions and joined Corps Raus in March in excellent condition. The corps had a werfer regiment and another battalion, three antiaircraft regiments, the 905th Assault Gun Battalion, an assault gun company, and artillery. The corps was in excellent condition and protected the flank of the attack against the 7th Soviet Guards Army.

The third corps of the army, the 42nd, had three divisions thinly spread in front of the Soviet 57th Army of the Southwest Front. The 282nd Infantry Division had been formed in France in March 1943 from the 165th Reserve Division and sent to Kempf in April. Although the division had nine battalions, it lacked experience and cohesion and was suited for the passive assignment. The 39th Infantry Division was also a nine-battalion unit that arrived from France in March and joined Kempf in April. The division lacked experience, having served as an occupation division since its formation in July 1942. The third division in the corps, the 161st Infantry Division, was also a recent arrival from France. The division joined Kempf in May after refitting for six months in France. The division had nine battalions, and the combination of combat veterans from previous service with the 9th Army and the lengthy refit made it a first-class formation.

The 42nd Corps had only one antiaircraft regiment and two heavy panzer hunter battalions with Hornisse tank destroyers that were still organizing with service and headquarters troops. The 42nd Corps held a wide sector with each division holding more than 40 km sectors. However, it was not planned to use the corps in attack, and the holding assignment behind the Donets River was ideal for the inexperienced divisions.

Of the total of fifty German divisions that took part in the Battle of Kursk, at least nine had come from the Rzhev salient, thirteen had been transferred from France in the previous six months, and ten were panzer divisions that had been siphoned from the reserves of Army Groups South and Center, leaving those army groups exposed to Soviet attack. Of the other eighteen divisions, seven were weak, combat weary units that held the 2nd Army sector.

The impact of the Western threat in the Mediterranean was manifested in the shortage of replacements that were used to rebuild the twenty Stalingrad divisions in the summer of 1943. Most of those divisions would eventually be used to defend Italy, but the process of rebuilding drained a major portion of the available replacements. As a result, thirteen of the infantry divisions at Kursk had only six rifle battalions, and one had only three battalions. The missing forty-five battalions would have a serious impact on the battle.

The 4th Panzer Army was chronically short of infantry to secure its flanks, and panzer divisions were diverted from the spearheads to hold the east and west tanks. When Manstein asked the 2nd Army commander for more infantry, the commander pleaded that his weak divisions were already stretched too thin, and no divisions were sent. The eastward drive of the 3rd Panzer Corps, that could have created a crisis for the 7th Soviet Guards Army, was aborted and the panzer corps turned north to clean up the gap that had developed between the 4th Panzer Army and Army Detachment Kempf which should have been taken care of by infantry.

CHAPTER 5

The Soviet Order of Battle

Battle tactics and technology determined the composition of the field armies in World War II that changed to react to differing weapons and methods. For every defensive or offensive technique, a counterbalance soon appeared. In World War I, infantry in trenches and covered bunkers were difficult to dislodge, even with lengthy artillery bombardments. The infantry hid in the deep shelters during the artillery shelling and emerged to lay down curtains of machine gun fire to halt the attacking infantry. In 1916 the tank was introduced to destroy the machine guns, but by the end of World War I, antitank guns were holding back the tanks. The faster, more heavily armored tanks regained the ascendancy early in World War II, but by 1943 the tracked tank destroyer emerged as a potent enemy to the tank, along with improved antitank guns. These are a few examples of the constant ebb and flow as new weapons and new techniques continually changed the balance on the battlefield and the organization of the armies.

The Red Army was continuously under pressure to find answers to German military developments. By 1943 the Soviet field army was a flexible unit that could be tailored to an assignment by attaching tanks, self-propelled artillery (SUs), artillery, antitank guns, antiaircraft guns, and other supporting units. Unlike the other major powers that made most of their supporting units permanent parts of divisions, corps, and armies, the Russians had hundreds of regiments and battalions that were attached to armies when required for an operation, and then withdrawn to be used elsewhere. In the areas where the German attack was expected, the Soviets provided each army with a plentiful supply of artillery, antitank guns, antiaircraft guns, SUs, and tanks. In the quiet areas, the armies would be practically devoid of supporting weapons.

In examining the Soviet order of battle, one should remember Napoleon's often repeated statement that morale was three times as important as material. Morale is related to the condition, training, experience, and perspective of the troops. Material includes the number of men and weapons. Some of the Russian divisions were battle weary after two years of war, and the new riflemen replacements were not well trained. In 1942 Stalin had made a major point that replacements were not to be added to rifle companies while at the front, but rather held in the divisional training battalions until the replacements had more training and could be added to companies in more favorable circumstances. Many of the Soviet divisions at Kursk had received numerous replacements in April, May, and June. To compensate for the condition of the men, the Soviets had a substantial numerical superiority in divisions and weapons, in effect, substituting material for morale. The Germans divisions also received many replacements, but not as many and not as recently because many of the German divisions had been transferred from France, beginning in December 1942, or had served on comparatively quiet sectors at Demyansk or in the Rzhev salient.

During May and June, the Russian divisions in the Voronezh Front were brought up to a strength of 8,000 to 9,000 men, somewhat smaller that the German divisions. However the German division had more service troops because the division had to fetch its supplies from army depots, while the Soviet army depots delivered supplies to their divisions, reducing the number of service troops in the division. The Russian field armies used trucks to deliver supplies, while the German division supply columns used horse-drawn wagons. Both countries used a three-regiment, nine-battalion organization, and their fire power was nearly equal because many German divisions were under-strength and short of weapons.

From their intelligence sources, the Russians learned that the major blow from the north would fall on the 13th Army of the Central Front. The 13th Army had been involved in offensive fighting for only twelve days in late February, advancing northeast to protect the northern shoulder of the Kursk bulge created by the attacking armies farther south. On July 1, 1943, the 13th Army consisted of eleven rifle divisions, a tank brigade, five tank regiments, two anti-aircraft divisions, an artillery corps with three divisions, and miscellaneous other regiments that gave the army enormous fire power, especially the artillery divisions that played a dominant role during the battle.

Five of the rifle divisions had been part of the 13th Army for some time. The 8th Rifle Division was formed in December 1941, the third formation with that number, and it joined the 13th Army in July 1942. The 15th Rifle Division had joined the 13th Army in May 1942 from the south. The 74th Rifle Division was formed in October 1942 (the second formation) and joined the 13th Army in the same month, indicating that the units of the division came from preexisting formations, probably a rifle brigade. The 81st Rifle Division formed in October 1942 using the 135th Rifle Brigade as cadre. The 81st Division was part of the 48th Army until January 1943 when it was transferred to the 13th Army. The 148th Rifle Division was a prewar division that became part of the 13th Army in November 1941. All five of these divisions were up to strength and experienced after long service at the front.

Six divisions were added to the 13th Army in April and May, including three guards rifle divisions. The 6th Guards Division, formerly the 120th Rifle Division, had been part of the Bryansk Front from September 1941, mostly with the 48th Army. In March 1943 the division was withdrawn to front reserve, and in April 1943 it joined the 13th Army. The 70th Guards Rifle Division, formerly the 138th Division, transferred in March 1943 from the Stavka Reserve to the Central Front Reserve, and to the 13th Army in May 1943. The 75th Guards Rifle Division, formerly the 95th Rifle Division, moved to the Central Front reserve in March 1943, and to the 13th Army in May. The last two guards divisions had been recently rehabilitated behind the lines, and all three of the guards divisions were at full strength.

Three guards airborne divisions were added to the 13th Army in May. The airborne received the best recruits and were excellent soldiers, although they had little if any parachute training. The 2nd, 3rd, and 4th Guards Parachute Divisions had been formed in December 1942 from three airborne corps. In February they were sent to the 1st Shock Army of the Northwest Front at Demyansk and experienced strenuous combat. By the end of March the three divisions had returned to the Stavka Reserve for rebuilding with the 53rd Army that became part of the Steppe Military District in April. In May the three divisions were transferred to the 13th Army. Two divisions of the 13th Army were transferred away in June. The 132nd went to the 70th Army, east of the 13th Army, to provide the inexperienced 70th Army with a well-trained division. The 307th Division went to the 3rd Guards Army in the Southwest Front.

The 13th Army had a strong tank component including the 129th Tank Brigade that had been with the 13th Army since January 1942. The brigade probably had about fifty mixed Lend Lease and light tanks. All five tank regiments were assigned in May 1943. The 27th and 30th Guards Tank Regiments, equipped with heavy KV tanks, were formed in the Moscow District in January 1943. The 43rd Tank Regiment had been formed at Gorki in September 1942, probably with T70 tanks made at Gorki, and had been with the Bryansk Front since November. The 58th Tank Regiment, formed in November 1942, had been at Demyansk and in early 1943 was refitted in the Moscow District. The 237th Tank Regiment was formed at Kosterevo in February 1943. The six tank units gave the army a strong armored reserve of 223 tanks, equal to two German panzer divisions.[1]

The 13th Army had an extremely large artillery component designed to break up the German attack. An entire artillery corps, including the 5th and 12th Artillery Divisions (each with six brigades) and the 5th Guards Mortar Division (with three brigades of Katusha rocket launchers), was augmented by five additional independent guards mortar regiments, an artillery regiment, and three mortar regiments. An artillery division had 108 120mm mortars, 68

76mm guns, 69 122mm howitzers, 20 152mm guns, 55 152mm gun-howitzers and 24 203mm howitzers.

The antitank component was not particularly strong, considering the expected tank attack. There were two 76mm gun brigades in the artillery divisions and an independent tank destroyer regiment for a total of seven regiments with 140 antitank guns. The army had only one or two SU regiments including the 1442nd with forty-seven SUs, formed in Moscow in January with no combat experience. On the other hand, the antiaircraft component was extraordinary with two divisions and an independent regiment, nine regiments for a single army. Some of the 85mm antiaircraft guns may have been used as long-range antitank guns. Most of the artillery units were assigned in May, two months before the attack. The 13th Army opposed the main force of the 9th Army's panzer divisions.

To the right of the 13th Army was the 48th Army, also part of the Central Front. Like the 13th Army, the 48th had not been engaged in severe fighting, and its six rifle divisions were probably at full strength with experienced men. Five of the rifle divisions (16th, 73rd, 137th, 143rd, and 339th) were with the army in February. The 170th and 202nd Divisions, which were added in May and June, were with the 27th Army on the Northwest Front in February, then in the Stavka Reserve with the 53rd Army in March and finally in the Central Front Reserve in May. In March the 48th Army had lost the 6th Guards Rifle Division that went to the front reserve and then to the 13th Army.

There were four tank regiments with the army with 134 tanks.[2] The 193rd Tank Regiment had been with the 48th Army before February. The other three arrived in June 1943, shortly before the battle. The 45th and 229th Tank Regiments had been refitting in the Moscow District, and the 30th Tank Regiment was at Demyansk with the 1st Shock Army in May. These regiments replaced four regiments that had been transferred. In April the 48th Army sent the 28th Guards Tank Regiment and the 42nd Tank Regiment back to the Moscow District, presumably for refitting, and in May sent the 30th Guards Tank Regiment and the 43rd Tank Regiment to the 13th Army to reinforce the area where the attack was expected. The impact of the exchange of the four tank regiments was significant. Two experienced tank regiments went to the 13th Army and were replaced by two newly formed regiments from Moscow. Two combat-weary tank regiments returned to the Moscow Military District for rehabilitation and were replaced by one experienced tank regiment from Demyansk. Of the four regiments available on July 1, 1943, three were recent arrivals, and of these, two had just been refitted.

Three SU regiments, the 1540th, the 1454th, and the 1455th, were added to the 48th Army in June 1943, giving the army a strong mobile tank destroyer force of over forty-four SUs. Also adding to the antitank component was the addition of the 220th Guards Tank Destroyer Regiment and the 2nd Tank Destroyer Brigade, formed in the Moscow District in April from three existing regiments. The 48th Army also had the 479th Mortar Regiment, the 1168th Gun Artillery Regiment, and the 16th Antiaircraft Division, standard supporting units for an army. The 48th Army, with seven rifle divisions, was oriented toward tank defense with an added tank destroyer brigade, four tank regiments, and three SU regiments.

To the left of the 13th Army was the 70th Army, formed from border guards in early 1943, excellent soldiers but they lacked combat experience. In March 1943, the 70th Army had been added to the Central Front to protect the right flank of the 65th Army, which had been on the leading edge of the force that took Kursk and created the bulge in the spring. Four of its rifle divisions (102nd, 140th, 162nd, and 175th) and the 106th Rifle Brigade were from the original army, and three divisions were additions. The new divisions (132nd, 211th, and 280th) were transferred from the 13th Army to give the 70th Army combat experienced divisions. The three new divisions were placed in the first defense zone immediately to the left of the 13th Army. The border guard divisions may have had replacements for losses suffered in the spring, but the army had little combat experience other than the three divisions from the 13th army.

Three tank regiments had been with the army since February, and the 27th Tank Brigade arrived in June from the 1st Shock Army at Demyansk, providing the army with over 125 tanks, a reasonable number for immediate local counterattacks.[3] The army had the standard antiaircraft, tank destroyer, and mortar regiments, and three strong additions—the 1st Guards Artillery Division, the 12th Antiaircraft Division, and the 2nd Destroyer Division. The latter unit was one of the few remaining destroyer divisions that was being replaced by the new tank destroyers brigades. The destroyer division probably had about a hundred antitank guns as each brigade was used to form five new regiments each with twenty guns.

The 70th Army had an unusually large quota of artillery and antitank guns that shut down the west flank of the German 9th Army's attack and severely limited the penetration farther east. The 211th Division and the 106th Brigade gave no ground, though they were not seriously attacked. The 175th, 132nd, and 280th Divisions formed a tough shoulder against the German 46th Panzer Corps.

To the west, the 65th and 60th Armies played a small part in the battle and were faced by six weak divisions of the German 2nd Army. Four divisions and three brigades of the 60th Army had suffered heavy losses in the spring and were still with the army, probably absorbing large numbers of replacements in anticipation of the Soviet summer offensive. The army had only one tank brigade with sixty-seven tanks, and the only additions to the standard allotment of supporting units were three mortar regiments, sufficient to provide a minimum of support to hold the German divisions from being transferred elsewhere.[4] The only reinforcement was the 55th Rifle Division, one of the Soviet divisions released by the German withdrawal at Rzhev, which arrived in June from the 53rd Army in the Steppe Front.

The 65th Army had changed little from February 1943, when it had been involved in the offensive against the German 2nd Army. The nine rifle divisions and the rifle brigade had all been part of either the 65th or the 2nd Tank Army. The four tank regiments with 124 tanks had also been with the 65th Army since February.[5] In July 1943 the army had an extra tank destroyer regiment and two extra mortar regiments, but otherwise it had only standard supporting units. The 65th and 60th Armies had probably received many replacements since March. But that took time to absorb and train. Keeping these two worn armies in the quiet zone was a good decision. The combined strength of the two armies far exceeded the opposing German units and prevented the transfer of sorely needed German infantry to the active sectors.

While five armies of the Central Front manned the first two defensive lines, the Central Front had a powerful reserve of armored and rifle formations to mount counterattacks. The major reserve was the 2nd Tank Army that had been with the Central Front since February and had been engaged in heavy fighting in the February offensive that had carved out the Kursk salient. In March 1943, the tank army was reorganized, shedding the infantry divisions and acquiring more armor. The three rifle divisions and the rifle brigade in the tank army were sent to the 65th Army or to the Central Front reserve, along with a tank brigade and a regiment, two tank destroyer regiments, and a guards mortar regiment. The 28th Ski Brigade left in April along with the 11th Tank Corps that went to the Moscow District, presumably for a refit. The only remaining units in April 1943 were the 16th Tank Corps and the 51st Motorcycle Battalion. In April the army was rebuilt, receiving the 3rd Tank Corps, which had been rehabilitated after heavy losses with Group Popov in the Ukraine in February, and the 11th Guards Tank Brigade. In April both the 3rd and 16th Tank Corps were reinforced with tank destroyer regiments and mortar regiments. The 3rd Corps received the 121st Antiaircraft Regiment and the 74th Motorcycle Battalion, while the 16th Corps received the 1441st SU Regiment. Both corps received a newly formed antitank battalion of twelve 85mm guns in June. The 2nd Tank Army still had no mechanized corps, however, it had 452 tanks, 50 SUs, and 12 battalions of motorized infantry, comparable to three German panzer divisions.[6] The 16th Tank Corps was placed behind the second defense line on the boundary between the 70th and 13th Army north of Fatesh. The 3rd Tank Corps was in the center of the 13th Army area behind the third defense line.

The Central Front reserve also included two additional independent tank corps, the 9th and 19th, both of which included three tank brigades and a mechanized brigade. The 9th Corps received one of the new 85mm gun antitank battalions in June. The 9th Corps was in deep reserve south of Kursk, while the 19th Corps was astride the second defense line at the rear of the 70th Army. The Central Front reserve tank corps had 387 tanks, and the front had a total of 1,516 tanks and 91 SUs to oppose the six panzer divisions and other armored units of the 9th Army, that had about 600 operational tanks and 280 assault guns. The Russians had nearly twice as many tanks and SUs as did the Germans.[7]

The Central Front had a large reserve of antitank units, two destroyer brigades (each equal to five regiments), two tank destroyer brigades, and two independent tank destroyer regiments, the equivalent of 18 regiments and 360 guns. All of the units had been part of the Central Front since February 1943, except the tank destroyer brigades formed in April from existing regiments. The front reserve had a single SU regiment, the 1541st formed in the Moscow District in March. This unusually large antitank force was in addition to the guns assigned to the five front line armies and the tank corps. The tank destroyer regiments were extremely mobile with guns towed by American four-wheel drive trucks and could be dispatched to any sector of the front within a few hours. Each regiment could delay, if not disable, a full German panzer battalion. However, the mobile tank destroyer regiments, in their rudimentary gun positions, were especially vulnerable to long-range fire from the 88mm guns on the Tigers and Ferdinands once the Soviet antitank guns fired the first few rounds revealing their positions.

The Central Front commander retained the new 68th Artillery Brigade under his control. All other artillery had been distributed to the armies in the front. The front reserve included three guards mortar regiments (two of them newly formed), the new 21st Mortar Brigade, the 10th Antiaircraft Division, and two antiaircraft regiments. The numerous antiaircraft units assigned throughout the front provided the Russian troops with cover from low-flying Nazi aircraft, and, with the assistance of the Red Air Force, they gave the Soviet forces a much friendlier sky than in previous battles. The Central Front included three fortified regions directly under front control. These units usually had six battalions of elderly men heavily equipped with machine guns and artillery plus some artillery battalions. The units were normally assigned to hold quiet sectors, and were probably used to fill gaps in the wide sector held by the 60th and 65th Armies.

On the south shoulder of the bulge, the Voronezh Front had no army in prime condition to cover the area where the major attack was expected as the 13th Army did in the north. The threatened sector of the front was assigned to two very battle-worn armies, the 6th and 7th Guards that had been transferred from the Stalingrad pocket in March to ward off the German 4th Panzer Army advance north from Kharkov. The 6th Guards Army, formerly the 21st Army, had played a prominent role in the battle of Stalingrad. Six of the seven divisions (the 89th Guards, 67th Guards, 71st Guards, 90th Guards, 51st Guards, and the 52nd Guards Divisions) had been granted guards status in February, but these divisions had sustained many casualties at Stalingrad and were then moved without rest to the Kursk bulge to bolster the southern shoulder. The seventh division in the army was the 375th Rifle Division, which would play a major role in the battle, by holding the east flank of the 2nd SS Panzer Corps and tying up the Death Head SS Division for four crucial days. The 375th Division had joined the 21st Army (later the 6th Guards Army) in February 1943 from the Western Front reserve. The division had been in Rzhev area since December 1941 and was an experienced division with relatively few replacements.

In the course of the move of the 21st Army to the Kursk area, all of the supporting units were lost and the army troops had to be reconstituted. The rifle divisions were refilled with replacements, many of them hastily trained conscripts from the Kursk area and others from central Asia who had little command of the Russian language. The combination of the few experienced veterans who had seen too much combat, with many young men having no combat experience was not the optimum condition. Fortunately, Hitler,s decision to delay the offensive gave these divisions some time to assimilate the replacements, but some did not arrive until June, only days before the battle.

Anticipating a major German armored assault the 6th Guards Army received a major infusion of support units. The 96th Tank Brigade came from the front reserve and the 230th and 245th Tank Regiments from the Moscow District where they recently had been formed, for a total of 135 tanks.[8] Some of the tanks were Land Lease, as German photographs show burning Lees (the British version of the Grant medium tank) and Stuart light tanks.

The 6th Guards Army also had strong artillery support. The 27th Artillery Brigade came from the front reserve, and the 33rd Artillery Brigade came from the Northwest Front. The powerful artillery and 135 tanks reinforced the Soviet counterattacks in the first few days and delayed the Germans long enough for the reserves to be positioned in the second defense line.

The antitank defense was also potent, with seven independent tank destroyer regiments added to the 6th Guards Army in April and May, four from the front reserve, one from the Northwest Front, one from the Southwest Front, and one from the Bryansk Front. Two tank destroyer brigades also joined the army, the 28th Tank Destroyer Brigade and two new independent regiments were formed from the 6th Destroyer Brigade, and the 27th Tank Destroyer Brigade was formed from the 10th Destroyer Brigade. The army had a total of fifteen tank destroyer regiments with 300 antitank guns in July, an incredible number, considering that two regiments could stop a panzer division. The army received the new 1440th SU Regiment from the Stavka Reserve in May 1943, a highly mobile source of antitank fire.

The 6th Guards Army had four guards mortar regiments, two mortar regiments, an antiaircraft regiment, and the 26th Antiaircraft Division, drawn mostly from the Stavka Reserve. Most of these new units arrived in March and April, allowing ample time for them to be integrated into the army. The antiaircraft guns made it possible for the Russians to move units in daylight hours without undue loss to air attack.

The weakness of the army was in the inexperience and lack of training of the replacements. Faced by the awesome power of the 2nd SS Panzer Corps and the 48th Panzer Corps, the veterans could expect a difficult time keeping the rifle units together. That practically all of the 6th Guards Army divisions were still intact and fighting after ten days of intense pounding by the 4th Panzer Army was a great credit to the spirit of the Russian soldiers. Another weakness was the lack of an artillery division headquarters, with the result that twenty-three artillery units were directly subordinate to army headquarters.

The 7th Guards Army, slated to blunt the attack of Army Detachment Kempf, had fought at Stalingrad as the 64th Army. Six of the seven rifle divisions had received guards status (15th Guards, 36th Guards, 72nd Guards, 73rd Guards, 78th Guards, and 81st Guards), the latter four receiving the honor in March. However, the six guards divisions were well worn at Stalingrad and had moved to the Kursk area without a period of rehabilitation to absorb and train the numerous replacements. The 213th Rifle Division, the only new division, was added to the army in March from the Stavka Reserve, but was relegated to the second defense line in July, possibly because of lack of experience.

The 7th Guards Army with 224 tanks had a stronger armored component than the 6th Guards Army.[9] The 27th Guards Tank Brigade had been with the 64th Army at Stalingrad. The 201st Tank Brigade was added in May from the 69th Army, while the three tank regiments had come from the Volga District, the Stavka Reserve, and the 69th Army in March and April. Many of the tanks probably were Lend Lease and light tanks, as the German claims seldom mention T34s in the first few days of the offensive when these brigades and regiments supported the local counterattacks. The 1438th SU Regiment, a newly formed unit from the Moscow District, and the 1529th SU Regiment, formed in the Ural District, arrived in May.[10]

The 7th Guards Army had fewer tank destroyer units than the 6th Guards Army. There were four independent regiments, two regiments that were offspring of the 8th Destroyer Brigade and two regiments that had been with the 7th Guards Army since February. The 30th Tank Destroyer Brigade was also formed from the 8th Destroyer Brigade, giving the army a total of seven tank destroyer regiments with 140 guns, a far less powerful group than the 7th Guards Army, but they had only one German panzer corps to face, rather than the two over-strength panzer corps of the 4th Panzer Army.

The artillery segment was small, including the 1112th Gun Regiment from the 69th Army, the 161st Guards Gun Regiment, and the 290th Mortar Regiment. The antiaircraft force was strong, the 5th Antiaircraft Division from the front reserve and three independent regiments including the 82nd Regiment taken from the Moscow air defenses. The weakness of the army was in its limited artillery support and combat-weary rifle divisions, weaknesses that were not apparent in the opening phase of the battle as the army firmly held their positions near Belgorod, creating a gap between the 4th Panzer Army and Army Detachment Kempf.

Holding the southeast face of the bulge for the Voronezh Front were the 38th and 40th Armies. Both of these armies had been involved in severe fighting in the winter and spring and had been rebuilt with replacements. Four of the six divisions in the 38th Army had been with the army since February. The 180th Division had joined in March from the 69th Army, and the 204th Division was formed from the 37th Rifle Brigade that had been with the 38th Army since March. Therefore, the rifle units were essentially the same as they had been six months previously. Both the 180th and 192nd Tank Brigades had served in that period with the 38th Army and had a total of 150 tanks.[11] Given the weakness of the opposing German 7th Corps, the 38th Soviet Army was able to transfer many units to the active sector during the battle.

The 38th Army had a strong tank destroyer component; the 7th Destroyer Brigade formed the 29th Tank Destroyer Brigade and two independent regiments (1658th and 1660th) in June. In May both the 222nd Guards Tank Destroyer Regiment and the 438th Regiment came from the Moscow District giving the army a total of seven regiments with 140 guns, more than adequate for the assignment, considering that there were no panzer units in the 7th German Corps. Some of the tank destroyer regiments were moved east during the battle to oppose the 48th Panzer Corps.

The artillery component was weak with only the 111th Guards Howitzer Regiment, the 112th Guards Gun Regiment, an antiaircraft regiment, a guard mortar regiment, and two mortar regiments, all of which had long service with the 38th Army. In March and April the army had relinquished a tank brigade, two tank destroyer regiments, a guards mortar brigade, and an antiaircraft division to the 40th Army and the 6th Guards Army. In general, the 38th Army was a well-worn army holding a quiet sector opposite a sparsely held German line.

Closer to the expected attack zone, the 40th Army was a much stronger force. Three of the rifle divisions (100th, 206th, and 309th) had been with the

40th Army since the heavy fighting in February. The 161st and 237th joined in March from the 69th and 38th Armies, replacing the 107th and 183rd that were sent to the 69th Army. The 184th and 219th Divisions arrived in April from the Southwest Front and the Voronezh Front reserve, replacing the 340th Division that went to 69th Army. Presumably the three divisions sent to the 69th Army had been badly depleted and were therefore sent into reserve with the 69th, while strong divisions from the 69th were sent to the 40th Army. However, all of the rifle divisions in the 40th Army had experienced heavy fighting and therefore had a high proportion of inexperienced replacements.

The 40th Army had the 86th Tank Brigade, which was added in May from the Southwest Front reserve, and two new tank regiments that came from the Stavka reserve in March with a total of 237 tanks.[12] The antitank defense of the army was unusually strong, including one new regiment, five experienced regiments, and three regiments in the 32nd Tank Destroyer Brigade. The 32nd Brigade was formed from the 16th Destroyer Brigade that also produced the 1663rd and 1664th Regiments. The army had a total of nine tank destroyer regiments with 180 guns. A gun brigade and a howitzer brigade were added to the army in June. The army also had an additional artillery regiment, four mortar regiments, an antiaircraft division, and an additional antiaircraft regiment. The army had no guards mortar regiments. Although the Russians expected little activity in the 40th Army zone, the army had an unusually strong array of supporting arms. These units would play a vital role in the battle, providing strong support to the divisions that pressured the west flank of the German 4th Panzer Army.

In reserve behind the four front line armies of the Voronezh Front were the 69th Army, the 1st Tank Army, and independent corps plus other units. The 69th Army had been formed from the 18th Independent Rifle Corps, and in March 1943, included five divisions, all of which had been in heavy fighting in February. Three divisions had been sent to the 38th and 40th Armies in March, and these were replaced by two divisions from the 40th Army and one from the 3rd Tank Army. Although the casualties in the divisions had been replaced, the army was in reserve to give the new men a better environment for additional training. The 69th Army was called on in the later phase of the battle to secure the south flank of the 5th Guards Tank Army.

The 69th Army had few supporting units, an antiaircraft regiment, a tank destroyer regiment, and a mortar regiment. There were no tank, artillery, guards mortar, or SU regiments. Most of the supporting units had been transferred to other armies in the Voronezh and Southwest Fronts. The army was spread in a thin line at the rear of the 6th and 7th Guards Armies.

The other reserve army, the 1st Tank Army, was a much more powerful force designed to counterattack any penetration of the three army defense lines. The former 1st Tank Army had fought at Demyansk in February and transferred to the Stavka Reserve in March, leaving behind three ski brigades, the 11th Antiaircraft Division, and other units. The army was sent to the Voronezh Front in April. The army was comprised of the 6th and 31st Tank Corps and the 3rd Mechanized Corps plus supporting units.

The 6th Tank Corps had been part of the 1st Tank Army in the February fighting. The 112th Tank Brigade of the corps was replaced in March with a fresh tank brigade, the 100th. The corps also received a tank destroyer regiment, a mortar regiment, and a motorcycle battalion in March and a new SU regiment in June. However, the corps did not receive an 85mm antitank battalion nor an antiaircraft regiment.

The 3rd Mechanized Corps had also been part of the 1st Tank Army in the February battles. The corps had three mechanized brigades and two tank brigades and in March received a tank destroyer regiment, a mortar regiment, and a guards mortar battalion, but no antiaircraft regiment.

The 31st Tank Corps was a new unit formed at Noginsk in the Moscow District in April with two new tank brigades (237th and 242nd) and no supporting units, not even a mechanized brigade! The corps served as a school unit before being reformed for combat. The tank brigades were probably formed from existing tank regiments. The 237th Brigade was the former 7th Tank Regiment that had been with the 1st Tank Army at Demyansk. The 242nd Brigade, consisting of the 63rd and 64th Tank Regiments plus a motorized rifle battalion, was formed early in 1943 and given an abbreviated training period, but the allocation of equipment was unusually large with forty-four T34 tanks in the 63rd Tank Regiment.[13]

The tank army reserve included the 316th Guards Mortar Regiment and the new 8th Antiaircraft Division formed in February. The tank army had 542 tanks, mostly T34s and T60 or T70 light tanks, and about twenty motorized rifle battalions.[14]

The three corps were strung along a fourth defense line at the rear of the 40th and 6th Guards Army in preparation for the 4th Panzer Army strike toward Kursk. The two strongest corps, the 6th Tank and the 3rd Mechanized were placed on either side of Oboyan road. The presence of the 1st Tank Army on the Oboyan road constituted a major obstacle to the German attack.

The Voronezh Front reserve had 369 tanks and included the 2nd and 5th Independent Guards Tank Corps. Both corps had been reinforced with tank destroyer regiments, antiaircraft regiments, mortar regiments, and heavy tank regiments. Most of these units were new formations. The 2nd Guards Tank Corps was redesignated in December 1942 from the 24th Tank Corps and assigned to the Southwest Front reserve till March 1943. At that time the corps was moved to the Voronezh Front reserve. In addition to three tank brigades and a mechanized brigade, the corps had the 1500th SU Regiment, the 1695th Antiaircraft Regiment, the 273rd Mortar Regiment, and the 755th Antitank Battalion, one of the new 85mm antitank battalions.[15]

The 5th Guards Tank Corps had suffered heavy losses during the battle at Stalingrad and was refitted at Rossoch in February 1943 with two T34 tank companies in each battalion. In May 1943, the corps was built up to full strength by replacement tanks and crews from the tank factory and school at Nishnij Tagil in the Urals.[16] These two corps were stationed at the rear of the 69th Army, but they came forward early in the battle to harass the open east flank of the 2nd SS Panzer Corps, diverting the Death Head SS Division from the main thrust.

An additional tank corps joined the 6th Guards Army early in the battle. The 2nd Tank Corps was in the Southwest Front reserve in early July, but was moved to support the 6th Guards Army. The corps included the 26th, 99th, and 169th Tank Brigades and the 58th Mechanized Brigade. The 169th Tank Brigade had fought at Stalingrad as part of the 13th Tank Corps. In November 1942, the brigade was refitted in the Volga Military District as part of the 2nd Tank Corps and sent to the Southwest Front reserve in December 1942.

The 99th Tank Brigade received replacements for 85 percent of its strength, including men from exhausted units in the Kharkov-Belgorod area and returning wounded. Officer replacements came from schools in Vladivostok (on the Pacific Coast!) and Charabarovsk.[17] The only support units in the 2nd Tank Corps were the 1502nd Tank Destroyer Regiment and the 83rd Motorcycle Battalion.

The Voronezh Front had a total of 1,657 tanks and 42 SUs to oppose the nine panzer divisions of the 4th Panzer Army and Army Detachment Kempf. The 2nd Tank Corps added an additional 150 tanks, bringing the total to over 1,800, far more than the opposing German forces.[18]

The tank destroyer forces in the Voronezh Front reserve included two brigades and two regiments, for a total of eight regiments with 160 guns. These mobile regiments with 45mm and 76mm guns towed by American trucks gave the front commander a potent blocking force. For example, the 538th Tank Destroyer, formed near Moscow in October 1942 and assigned to the 6th Soviet Tank Corps had five batteries with four 45mm guns towed by light American four-wheel drive trucks. On July 10, two batteries were attached to the 155th Guards Rifle Regiment of the 52nd Guards Rifle Division.[19]

The Voronezh Front also had five guards mortar regiments, a mortar brigade and a regiment, and two artillery regiments. The reserve also included three guards rifle divisions that had been formed in April from rifle brigades, which were still in the process of assimilating the new men. The Voronezh reserves were concentrated in the area behind the 6th Guards Army where the main assault was expected. By holding a substantial number of supporting units under front control, rather than dividing them among the five front line armies, the front commander was able to concentrate the maximum force in the endangered area.

While the Germans put most of their goods in the shop window and had few reserves, the Red Army had an entire front in reserve with four field armies, a tank army, three Guards cavalry corps, and four armored corps. The Steppe Front was established to serve as a reserve in the event of a German breakthrough and also to provide fresh forces for a counteroffensive to begin as soon as the German attack was halted.

The 27th Army was stationed behind the 48th Army on the north shoulder of bulge in July. In April the headquarters of the 27th Army had been transferred from the Northwest Front to the Stavka Reserve after the Germans withdrew from the Demyansk pocket. Most of its divisions and supporting units were reassigned to other armies in the Northwest Front in March. The 27th Army acquired six new divisions in April, two from the Volkhov Front, three from the Northwest Front, and one from the Kalinin Front. The 93rd Tank Brigade and 39th Tank Regiment were new units from the Moscow District with about ninety tanks. The 680th Tank Destroyer Regiment came from the Western Front, and the 1070th Tank Destroyer Regiment had been in the Moscow Military Zone. The guards mortar regiment and the 23rd Antiaircraft Division had been on the Northwest Front, while the 480th Mortar Regiment had been part of the 27th Army. At the beginning of the battle on July 5, the army had been together only two months and probably lacked cohesion. The divisions had, however, been restored to strength, and there was an adequate number of supporting units. The Russian defense on the north shoulder held so well that the 27th Army was not needed and did not play any role in the battle.

The 53rd Army east of the bulge, slightly to the north of Kursk, like the 27th Army, had been withdrawn from the Northwest Front when the Germans abandoned Demyansk. The army headquarters left its divisions and supporting units behind and was transferred to the Stavka reserve. In April, the army was assigned to the Steppe Military District and received seven rifle divisions— six from the Stalingrad area and one from the 27th Army. The six Stalingrad divisions were from the 24th and 66th Armies that fought on the north side of the pocket against fierce German resistance. The divisions probably were built up with replacements beginning in April 1943. The other division, the 28th Guards Rifle Division, joined the 53rd Army in March and was probably in good condition.

Like the 27th Army, the 53rd had a minimum of supporting units: two tank regiments (with about 80 tanks) that had refitted in the Moscow District in May; one experienced and one new tank destroyer regiment that also arrived in May. The guards mortar regiment, an army mortar regiment, and an antiaircraft division were all new units from military districts. The 53rd Army had been assembled for two months on July 1 and needed time to reach peak performance. The army was not needed in the battle and remained in reserve.

The 5th Guards Army, the former 66th Army, lay immediately south of the 53rd. Like the 53rd, of the seven rifle divisions, four of the divisions had been with the 66th Army at Stalingrad, but these divisions had been awarded guards status. Although the four Stalingrad divisions were probably heavy on replacements, the remaining three divisions should have been in excellent condition. The 6th and 9th Guards Parachute Divisions had been at Demyansk and joined the 5th Guards Army in May. The 9th Guards Parachute Division was at Staryi Oskol from April until July 9, when it moved to Prokorovka. The division had no jump training nor parachute equipment.[20] The 42nd Guards Rifle Division came from the 31st Army in the Western Front also in May. The 42nd Guards Rifle Division had received 3,000 replacements beginning in May 1943 from the 15th, 19th, and 23rd Replacement Regiments in Chelyabinsk. The replacements had arrived in groups of thirty to fifty men.[21]

Attached to the 5th Guards Army was the 10th Tank Corps (with about 170 tanks) which had been refitted after heavy losses as part of Group Popov in the abortive attempt to cut off the Germans with a drive south from the Dnieper during the winter. In addition to rebuilding its mechanized brigade and three tank brigades, the Corps was reinforced in April with a tank destroyer regiment, an SU regiment, and antiaircraft regiment, a mortar regiment, and a motorcycle battalion, mostly newly formed units. The 5th Guards Army also had a standard allotment of an artillery regiment, a tank destroyer regiment, a guards mortar regiment, and an antiaircraft division. The 5th Guards Army played an essential role in the battle, blocking the advance of the Death Head SS Division as it attempted to outflank the Prokorovka defenders.

Far to the south behind the Southwest Front was the 47th Army that had come from the North Caucasus in April, bringing along the 337th Rifle Division and six or more rifle brigades that were reorganized into five rifle divisions in May and June. The army also had a minimum of supporting units, a new mortar regiment, a new tank destroyer regiment, a tank destroyer regiment from Kalinin Front, and an antiaircraft division and a guards mortar regiment from the Northwest Front. The 47th Army was in the difficult process of organizing divisions from brigade cadres that entailed splitting the rifle battalions in half and filling the two halves with replacements to form two new battalions. Although two months had elapsed, the army was not up to the standard of the other units. Like the 27th and 53rd Armies, the 47th Army was not needed as the Voronezh Front infantry reserves were sufficient to halt the eastward drive of Army Detachment Kempf.

By the end of June the Steppe Front had one first-class army, two average armies, and one substandard. In addition the Front had powerful mechanized forces including the 5th Guards Tank Army, two Guards cavalry corps, and four independent armored corps. The 5th Guards Tank Army had been in the Southwest Front during the February battles and had moved into the Stavka Reserve in March. As part of the reorganization of the tank armies, four rifle divisions were sent to other armies in the Southwest Front along with two tank destroyer regiments. In April the army lost its last rifle division and other supporting units to the Southwest Front. In April the army was made part of the Steppe Military District that became the Steppe Front in May.

The 5th Guards Tank Army with about 395 tanks contained the 29th Tank Corps and the 5th Guards Mechanized Corps. Both corps joined the 5th Tank Army in March; the 29th Tank came from the Moscow District where it had been formed. The manpower of the 29th Tank Corps was far superior to the rifle units. The new recruits were eighteen and nineteen years old, and returning wounded provided experienced leadership. The ethnic composition was 90 percent Russian and Ukrainian and 10 percent central Asian. Most of the recruits came from the industrialized areas around Gorki and Ivanov.[22]

The 29th Tank Corps had a full complement of men and equipment, beginning with three tank brigades and a mechanized brigade. The 1446th SU Regiment and the 271st Mortar Regiment were added in February; the 108th Tank Destroyer Regiment and the 75th Motorcycle Battalion in March; the 38th Mechanized Battalion in May; and the 747th 85mm Antitank Battalion in June. Most of the supporting units were newly formed and lacked experience.

The 5th Guards Mechanized Corps, which came from the Southwest Front reserve, had three mechanized brigades and a tank brigade plus two SU regiments, a guards mortar battalion, a motorcycle battalion, a mortar regiment, a mechanized battalion, and an 85mm antitank battalion. The 24th Guards Tank Brigade of the 5th Guards Mechanized Corps had been battered at Stalingrad and sent to Rossoch for refitting. Replacements for the tank battalions that arrived in February included two companies of T34 tanks. In May 1943, the brigade was at full strength with replacements from the tank factory and school at Nishnij Tagil.[23] Most units were experienced with the exception of the antitank battalion, which had been formed in May. The tank army reserve included a heavy tank regiment, an SU regiment, the 6th Antiaircraft Division, a tank destroyer regiment, a motorcycle regiment, and a guards mortar regiment. The 1549th SU Regiment had been formed in the Ural District in March and joined the 5th Guards Tank Army in June. The other supporting units came from the Moscow District in March, except the 53rd Guards Tank Regiment that came from the 5th Guards Mechanized Corps.

The 5th Guards Tank Army was dispersed in a wide band behind the 47th Army on the east side of the Don River. The 7th Guards Cavalry Corps and the 3rd Guards Mechanized Corps, together nearly equivalent to another tank army, were stationed behind the 5th Guards Tank Army astride the Don River. The 7th Guards Cavalry Corps had joined the Steppe Front in May from the Southwest Front. It contained three cavalry divisions, an antiaircraft regiment, a tank destroyer regiment, an antitank battalion, and a mortar battalion, and each cavalry division included a tank regiment.

The 3rd Guards Mechanized Corps, placed behind the south flank of the 5th Guards Tank Army, had the usual complement of units including a tank destroyer regiment, an antiaircraft regiment, a mortar regiment, and an 85mm antitank battalion, all added in June. The late arrival of the supporting units would have created some dislocation during the time that the regiments were assimilated and worked into the plans and tactics of the corps.

North of the 5th Guards Tank Army and directly east of Voronezh was another group of three armored corps equal to a tank army. The 10th Tank Corps was assigned to the 5th Guards Army, which was described above. The 1st Mechanized Corps was located in the 53rd Army area and included three mechanized brigades, a tank brigade, and some of the usual supporting units— a tank destroyer regiment, a mortar regiment, and a motorcycle battalion. The corps had been with the 1st Shock Army on the Kalinin Front in March and had not recently been in combat. The corps went to the Stavka reserve in April and to the Steppe Front in May. The supporting units had been with the corps for some time, but the guards mortar battalion, the antiaircraft regiment, and the 85mm antitank battalion were missing.

The 4th Guards Tank Corps was placed between Voronezh and the 1st Mechanized Corps, both near the Voronezh-Kursk railroad. The tank corps had three tank brigades and a mechanized brigade, all of which had been with corps during the disastrous drive south with the Popov Group in February. The corps had gone into the Stavka reserve in March and presumably was rebuilt with replacement tanks and crews, and in April it was assigned to the Steppe reserve. In March and April the corps received an influx of supporting units— the 756th Tank Destroyer Regiment, the 120th Guards Antiaircraft Regiment, the 264th Mortar Regiment, and the 76th Motorcycle Battalion. In May the 1451st SU Regiment arrived and in June the 752nd 85mm Antitank Battalion. The corps had a full complement of supporting units, most newly formed, and was the most powerful of the three corps.

The Steppe reserve contained three additional mobile corps, the 3rd and 5th Guards Cavalry Corps and the 2nd Mechanized Corps with over 800 tanks, nearly equal to a tank army with cavalry instead of motorized infantry. The 2nd Mechanized Corps had a full complement of supporting units including one of the new 85mm antitank battalions. The two cavalry corps both had the full complement of supporting units, most of which had been added in March and fully assimilated.

The Steppe Front had a total of 1,700 tanks in four tank corps, four mechanized corps, and three cavalry corps, including those assigned to armies. The table of organization strength of these eleven units included 1,575 medium tanks, 147 light tanks, and 320 SUs. Given the fact that the Red Army was receiving 2,000 tanks per month and had no significant losses in the previous four months, it is safe to assume that all of the units were at strength with modern tanks. The Voronezh, Central, and Steppe Fronts had nearly 4,900 tanks and 400 SUs.

However, this was not the sum total of reserves of the Red Army. The Stavka reserve units, few of which were needed in the defeat of the Germans at Kursk, included a tank army, four field armies, two tank corps, a mechanized corps, twenty parachute brigades, and two cavalry corps.

The four field armies included the 3rd Reserve, 11th, 52nd, and 68th Armies. The 11th Army consisted of eight rifle divisions and the standard allotment of supporting artillery and tanks. The divisions were reconstituted units from Stalingrad, as well as three from other fronts. The 3rd Reserve Army had eight divisions and the standard supporting units. Most of the divisions had been formed from rifle brigades in March and lacked experience. The 52nd Army had seven divisions from the Volkhov, Northwest, and Kalinin Fronts, presumably withdrawn for refitting, and lacked supporting units. The 68th Army had eight new divisions formed in May and some supporting units. The four armies had a total of thirty-one rifle divisions but comparatively few supporting units. All of the armies would have been available if needed.

The armored forces in the Stavka Reserve were especially strong. The 3rd Guards Tank Army had the 12th and 15th Tank Corps and had been in heavy fighting in Kharkov in February. The units, in reserve for four months, were probably refitted and ready. The independent 18th Tank Corps had been part of the Popov Group and with that group suffered heavy losses in February. The 18th Tank Corps had been refitted at Rossoch and was ready for action in July. The corps was equipped with T34s, T70s, and Churchills, and had a mortar regiment, antiaircraft regiment, tank destroyer regiment, and an 85mm antitank gun battalion, along with the usual three tank brigades and motorized rifle brigades. On July 9, 1943, the corps was taken from the Stavka Reserve and added to the 5th Guards Tank Army at Andreivka. On July 12, the corps took part in the attack at Vassilievka.[24]

The 25th Tank Corps was in the Southwest Front in February and saw heavy action, but had been refitting since March. The 2nd Guards Cavalry Corps had been in the Central Front in February and had not seen any heavy fighting. The 6th Guards Cavalry Corps, in the Voronezh Front until April, had seen action in February and had gone into reserve in May presumably for refitting. The 5th Mechanized Corps had formed in the Volga Military District in February and March and was ready for combat with all the supporting units. The Stavka Reserve had a total of four tank corps, one mechanized corps, and two cavalry corps with over a thousand tanks. By August all of the forces in the Stavka Reserve would have been able to fight if the Germans had broken through the Steppe Front.

Although the Russians had concentrated their tank resources for the Kursk battle and the subsequent counteroffensive, there were substantial tank forces available elsewhere if needed. The closest were the two tank corps and cavalry corps in the Southwest Front reserve poised for the offensive that would begin as soon as the Germans had been exhausted at Kursk.

The Southwest Front reserve included the 1st Guards Cavalry Corps, the 1st Guards Mechanized Corps, the 23th Tank Corps, and the 2nd Tank Corps. The 2nd Tank Corps was committed to the Battle at Kursk almost immediately. The 2nd Tank Corps included the 15th Guards Heavy Tank Regiment, the 58th Mechanized Brigade, and the 26th, 99th, and 169th Tank Brigades plus a tank destroyer regiment, an antiaircraft regiment, a rocket launcher battalion, a mortar regiment, and a motorcycle regiment.

The 2nd Tank Corps had suffered heavy losses in the February and March battles and was refitted in the spring of 1943. One of the tank brigades of the corps, the 169th, received some Churchill tanks on June 21, 1943, just weeks before the battle. The rifle battalion in the 99th Tank Brigade consisted of 85 percent survivors of units worn down at Kharkov and Belgorod in March and the remainder were returning wounded. Officer replacements came from schools at Vladivostok and Charabarovsk.[25]

In the Southern Front reserve were two mechanized corps that would support the attack to draw off German reserves in mid-July. The Western Front had two tank corps and the Bryansk had one tank corps. The four fronts had a total of five tanks corps, two mechanized corps, and a cavalry corps, all in reserve. In addition three tank corps and three mechanized corps were in the Moscow and Volga Military Districts. The 7th, 8th, and 9th Mechanized Corps had been formed in January 1943 and were not ready for combat. The 11th and 20th Tank Corps had been in combat in February and were refitting. The 30th Tank Corps was a new unit formed in the Ural Military District in February and in June was ready for combat, complete with all supporting units. Any suggestion that the Russians had exhausted their tank reserves by the end of the Battle at Kursk is not supported by the facts. Less than 5,000 Soviet tanks were involved in the battle of the 20,000 tanks on hand in mid-1943.

A few major points emerge from this exhaustive examination of the Soviet order of battle at Kursk on the eve of the battle. First, the Red Army had ample reserves of all types of units and weapons. Previously published totals of tanks at Kursk referred to the organization strength of the units in the immediate area and ignored the thousands available in reserve units and replacement depots, luxuries that the Germans did not enjoy. In addition to the tanks and SUs in the organized units, the Russian tank depots had large stocks of replacements and hundreds of new tanks were coming off the assembly lines each week. Within a week or so the tank was prepared for combat, and then shipped to a depot awaiting a request for a replacement. The tank training schools provided crews stat were assigned to new tanks.

Second, the Russians, fearing the impact of the new German tank designs, had taken steps to cope. New antitank battalions with 85mm antiaircraft guns were assigned to the armored corps. The number of antitank regiments assigned to the assault areas increased dramatically. The plentiful supply of medium artillery allowed the diversion of the divisional 76mm guns to the antitank role. There were more antitank guns awaiting than there were German tanks. The guns at Kursk destroyed more that half the total German tanks lost. Although the Russians believed that the antitank gun was the best defense, they also created five new heavy tank regiments in June 1943, equipped with the old KV1 and KV2 tanks that had heavier armor than the current KV1S model. The move was probably based on the assumption that the older models would be better at combating the new German tanks.

The third factor that emerges is the significance of the supporting units and the time needed to assimilate them. Some armies, such as the 13th, had nearly as many men in the supporting units as in the rifle divisions, while other armies on quiet sectors were devoid of the additional artillery and tanks. The presence of antitank guns, artillery, mortars, rocket launchers, and armored vehicles was essential to withstand the concentrated German attack.

A fourth factor, poor morale of the Soviet troops, could have reversed the balance. Without the steadfast infantry to defend the strong points, the guns could have been overrun and the tanks left isolated on the battlefield. The difference between the German success in the south and failure in the north could have been the difference between the rested divisions in the 13th Army and the battle weary divisions in the 6th and 7th Guards Armies. However, contrary to Manstein's opinion, neither in the north nor in the south did the Germans exhaust Soviet resources.

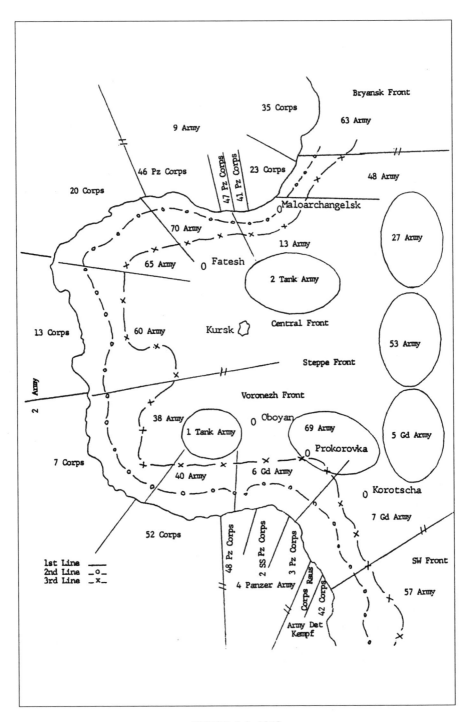

KURSK, July 1943

CHAPTER 6

Soviet and German Armor

Both the Germans and the Russians rebuilt their tank forces during the spring of 1943. The Germans introduced the Tiger and Panther tanks, the former in special heavy tank battalions to spearhead attacks and counter the Soviet tanks, and the latter to replace the Mark IV as the mainstay of the panzer divisions. In July 1943 the bulk of the German panzer force was concentrated around Kursk at the expense of the other areas of the Eastern Front and Western Europe.

Tanks were the key to unlocking the elaborate Russian defenses designed to dissipate the impact of artillery barrages and to withstand the effect of infiltrating infantry. The primary purpose of the tank was to enable the infantry to break through a defensive line and either to envelope the enemy, or to range deep into the enemy rear, disrupting communications and creating havoc. To perform these tasks a tank required a turret-mounted gun capable of firing a high explosive round to destroy bunkers and other defenses and a turret-mounted coaxial machine gun to drive the enemy infantry from their trenches. By 1943 the tank had acquired the other role of destroying opposing tanks that required a high-velocity gun capable of penetrating armor.

As soon as the first British tank appeared in battle, the Germans began to develop ways to destroy tanks. In World War I the tanks were slow and prone to mechanical failure, and once stopped they became easy targets for field artillery. The thin armor of the early tanks was vulnerable to the 12.6mm or .50 caliber round used in World War I antitank rifles by both the Allies and the Germans. As late as 1940 the American Army still considered the .50 caliber machine gun an antitank weapon.

Better automotive quality and thicker armor on World War II tanks dictated more effective counterweapons. The British theory that the best way to stop a tank was with another tank promoted the tank's function as an antitank weapon. Therefore they placed the extremely effective two-pounder (about 40mm antitank gun on all of their tanks early in the war. The two-pounder was effective against existing tanks, and superior to the 37mm gun mounted on the German Pz III. The ability of an antitank gun to penetrate the armor of an opposing tank resulted from the energy per square inch when the projectile contacted the surface of the opposing tank, not from the total weight or diameter of the round. A larger projectile, such as that fired from the low-velocity 75mm howitzers on the early German Pz IV, was useless against armor because the little energy the projectile had was dispersed by the larger area. Later in the war, shaped charge projectiles were developed that gave low-velocity weapons effective antitank capabilities, but the guns usually lacked the range and accuracy of the special purpose antitank gun. Once the armor was penetrated, the crew was disabled by the ricocheting projectile and pieces of metal flying about the interior of the tank. Larger guns, for example, the Soviet 122mm howitzer used on one of their SUs, would simply blow off the turret of a German tank, even if it could not penetrate the armor, because of the tremendous energy of the round.

When the British adopted the two-pounder as their tank gun, they sacrificed the benefits of the ability of the tank to fire an effective high explosive round against fortifications and limited the tank's infantry support arsenal to the coaxial machine gun.

The Germans realized the dichotomy of the two roles of the tank before 1939 and placed the 37mm antitank gun on the Pz III to fight other tanks and the low-velocity 75mm howitzer on the Pz IV to assist the infantry. As early as 1940 the Germans were developing self-propelled guns, vehicles on tracks but without turrets, that would function either to support the infantry or fight tanks.

In July 1943 the Germans were using four types of tanks—the Pz III, the Pz IV, the Tiger, and the Panther. The latest model Pz III had a good 50mm antitank gun and was still considered modern. The Pz IV had a high-velocity dual purpose 75mm gun, and the Panther had an even better 75mm gun that had excellent tank destroyer capability. The Tiger was the king of the battlefield with heavy armor and an 88mm gun. In addition, the Germans were using assault guns with 75mm guns, 105mm howitzers, 150mm howitzers, and 88mm guns to support the infantry and as tank destroyers. The Germans also had over a thousand self-propelled 75mm and 88mm guns with minimal armor to provide close artillery support for the infantry.

The production of tanks to reequip the panzer divisions with new advanced types was the most crucial segment of the armaments program set forth by Speer on November 22, 1942. An example of the significance of the tank production schedule is the fact that Hitler delayed the attack at Kursk in order to obtain delivery of more Tigers and Panthers. Although German industry produced 2,816 tanks and self-propelled guns in April, May, and June, 484 were Panthers, most of which were not ready on July 5, 1943, and 156 Tigers, bringing the total to 240, but only 178 were used at Kursk.[1] Delaying the attack worked against Hitler because the Germans were losing the tank and guns production battle, and the Red Army received over 6,000 tanks and assault guns in the three months before Kursk.[2] Of 6,291 modern German tanks, assault guns, and self-propelled guns available on July 1, 1943, nearly 3,000 were at Kursk. The German forces employed at Kursk had 1,865 modern tanks, 384 obsolete tanks, 533 assault guns, and about 200 self-propelled guns, vastly outnumbered not only by the 5,300 Soviet tanks and SUs in units in the Voronezh, Central, and Steppe Fronts, but also by thousands in units in the Stavka reserve and the Moscow Military District, and more in tank depots, complete with crews, waiting to replace losses as they occurred. The Germans also had additional tanks, but nearly half were siphoned off to other fronts in Russia, to France, and to other occupied countries.

The Germans had used the first Tigers near Leningrad and in Tunisia in late 1942. By February 1943 the mechanical problems of the early machines made by Henschel had been solved, and mass production began in March. From April 1943 to June, 156 Tigers were manufactured, and a total of 240 were available on July 1, 1943. The Tigers were organized in heavy tank battalions spearhead the attacks in July.[3] In terms of quality the Tiger still had mechanical defects and was prone to breakdown, but it had a superior gun (88mm high-velocity) to the Soviet KVIS then being produced with a 76mm gun. The KV85, with a comparable 85mm gun, was not produced until October 1943. The Tiger was a superb tank destroyer although the 88mm gun found few suitable targets other than antitank gun emplacements in the infantry support role. The Tiger in use in July 1943 had up to 100mm of armor in the front and mounted an 88mm L56 gun. The heavy weight of the Tiger required special bridges, and its slow speed resulted in failure to keep up with the infantry. In the crucial days before July 12, 1943, on the approach to Prokorovka, when the Reich SS and Adolf Hitler SS Divisions south of the Psel River were being harassed by artillery fire from the north bank, the Death Head SS Division was given the task of clearing the north bank of the Psel River. However, the Death Head Division Tigers could not cross the river until a 60-ton capacity bridge was built, and without the Tigers the Death Head Division could not keep pace with the two other SS divisions.

A competing version of the Tiger that was made by Porsche was not accepted for production, but was converted into an assault gun without a turret, dubbed the Ferdinand or Elephant. By May 12, 1943, ninety of these heavily armored monsters with long L71 88mm guns, compared to the less powerful L56 88mm on the Tiger tank, were ready and organized in two heavy tank hunter battalions. The two battalions (653rd and 654th) were assigned to the 9th Army. Designed to destroy tanks from positions behind the leading edge, the Ferdinand had only one ineffective machine gun for use against the infantry. The lack of a turret-mounted machine gun for all around defense made them vulnerable to infantrymen carrying explosives and short-range antitank rocket Launchers. Of the eighty-nine available on July 1, 1943, thirty-nine were lost during the month of July, but most losses came after July 12 when the Kursk offensive had been terminated in the north because of the Soviet offensives against Orel.[4]

The Ferdinand was a defensive weapon that was of limited use in an attack. In attacks, the Ferdinands remained at the rear of the panzer wedge and used their long-range 88mm gun to dispatch Soviet antitank guns before they could fire effectively on the Tigers and Mark IVs. Any Soviet tanks that appeared could be destroyed by the Ferdinands before the guns on the Russian tanks were able to fire on the other German tanks.

The Panther, which suffered woefully from mechanical problems in July 1943, was a German attempt to copy the qualities of the Soviet T34. The Panther was a new design that incorporated many of the good points of the Soviet T34 and had, in addition, more sophisticated optical equipment and a better gun. The Panther had 80mm of frontal armor and 100mm on the turret. The gun was the high velocity 75mm KwK42 (L70), compared to the L48 on the Pz IV. However the Panther was a complex machine and because the design was original and untested, it lead to many mechanical problems.

From April to June 1943, 484 Panthers were completed, but not all were ready for combat. By July there were 428 Panthers available and even these were prone to mechanical failure. General Heinz Guderian, then inspector of panzer troops and responsible for refitting the panzer divisions, reported to Hitler on June 16, 1943, that although 200 Panthers were available at Kursk on June 15, 1943, sixty-five had problems.[5] The 200 Panthers were operational by July 5, 1943, but forty were put out of action on the first day and only thirty-eight were operational on July 13. During July 1943, eighty-three were total losses, indicating that they were either heavily engaged or suffered from mechanical problems.[6] The shortage of Panthers available for the Kursk operation resulted in none of the three SS panzer grenadier divisions having any Panthers on July 4, 1943, nor did any arrive later in the battle.

The Pz IV was the workhorse of the panzer divisions. Two versions were used at Kursk, an earlier model referred to as a Pz IV (k) indicating that it was one of the earlier models of the Pz IV with the L24 gun, an older shorter gun with less velocity. Two modern versions were designated as the Pz IV (1) or long. The latest version, the Pz IV (H) mounted a 75mm KwK40 (L48) gun with higher velocity than the L43 gun on the earlier version. The Pz IV (H) had 80mm of armor on the front and turret and was mechanically reliable. The Pz IV was an excellent all around tank for work against both infantry and other tanks. The Germans manufactured 738 Pz IVs in the three months preceding Kursk, bringing the total to 1,305.[7]

The Germans placed little faith in the Mark III as a battle tank. Two models of the Pz III were employed at Kursk, the Pz III (1) with an L60 50mm gun and the Pz III (k) with the 37mm gun. The 50mm gun was still effective against the Russian light tanks and the Lend Lease tanks, but was no match for the T34 and the KV. However, 1,400 of the Pz IIIs were in use in July, and the model with the 50mm gun was still considered a modern tank. On July 4, 1943, the 2nd SS Panzer Corps, which was given priority in the distribution of weapons, had 117 Pz III (1)s compared to 151 Pz IVs and 35 Tigers. The Pz III was still a major factor in the inventory of the German panzer force.[8]

A few Pz IIs continued in use as a reconnaissance tank. Mounting a 20mm gun and with only 35mm of frontal armor, the Pz II could not be considered a battle tank, and few were used at Kursk. The 2nd SS Panzer Corps had only four.[9]

To supplement their limited numbers of tanks, the Germans manufactured or converted a sizable number of assault guns. The origin of the assault gun was the horse-drawn regimental 75mm howitzer used in World War I to provide close support for the infantry. The most successful German designs were based on the Czech T38 chassis, but others used the Pz III or Pz IV chassis. The turret was eliminated, which reduced the weight, as well as the center of gravity and the silhouette. The result was a mobile gun, that in the words of an American paratrooper, could hide behind a bush.[10] The increased space in the firing compartment enabled the assault gunners to fire more rapidly and bracket their targets, rather than fire a single round directly at the target.[11]

The best assault guns were the Hetzer, using the Czech chassis; and the SG III, using the Pz III chassis, both of which carried an L48 75mm gun, the same gun as the Pz IV but on the smaller chassis. The Germans were able to use the production facilities available at the Skoda Works in Czechoslovakia and the German Pz III production lines to build an armored vehicle with an excellent gun. The SG III was truly an armored vehicle, with 50mm of frontal armor and, unlike its Soviet equivalent, an armored top.[12]

The 2nd SS Panzer Corps had 137 assault guns and self-propelled antitank guns on July 4, 1943, one-third of the total armored strength of the corps. The assault guns were in greater numbers in the 9th Army to support the weaker panzer divisions. The Germans produced over a thousand assault guns in the three months prior to Kursk and had 1,737 on hand on July 1, 1943, including 1,452.[13]

In addition the Germans had a wide variety of fully tracked and half tracked self-propelled guns with a minimum of armor. Of the 1,102 on hand on July 1, 1943, 971 were 75mm and 76mm guns and 131 were lightly armored Hornets (Hornisse) mounting the same L71 88mm guns on a Mark IV chassis. Only ninety took part in the Kursk battle. On the north shoulder, forty-five Hornets were assigned to the 655th Battalion of the 9th Army, and on the south shoulder, forty-five more were assigned to the 560th Battalion with Army Detachment Kempf. Only four were lost in July 1943, indicating that they were properly employed, being held back for artillery support missions.[14]

Even though the offensive was postponed by Hitler to give German tank manufacturers more time to deliver Tigers, Panthers, and Mk IVs, the full impact of the reforms in German industry introduced by Albert Speer were still in the future. The German Army fought the Battle of Kursk with a limited number of quality tanks, plus a number of obsolescent varieties including the Mk III and the Mk IV with the short gun. One SS division had a company of captured T34s.

Although the Soviets had a preponderance of numbers, about 50 percent of their tanks at Kursk were light, and many of these were obsolete. The Russians began the year with a stock of 20,600 tanks on January 1, 1943, 11,000 light, 7,600 medium, and 2,000 heavy tanks, including Lend Lease tanks. The Germans started the year with only 7,927 tanks. In 1943 the Red Army received per quarter an average of 225 heavy tanks (compared to the Germans 156); 4,100 medium tanks (compared to the German 1,315); 1,400 light tanks (compared to the German 100); and 1,100 self-propelled guns (compared to the German 1,325) for a total per quarter of 6,825 Soviet tanks and SUs versus 2,804 German tanks and self-propelled guns in the second quarter of 1943.[15]

The mainstays of the Russian tank park were the T34 medium and the KV heavy tanks. The Soviet production of numerous light tanks were of marginal value on the battlefield. Of the 3,600 tanks in the Central and Voronezh Fronts in July 1943, 1,061 were light.[16] With thin armor and being outgunned by the German tanks, the light tanks were of most value in reconnaissance, but were pressed into other roles, most notably infantry support. The light tanks included the BT models, the T60, and the T70, all rather small vehicles with three-man crews. The best of the light tanks was the T70 that was driven by two GAZ202 truck engines in tandem. The GAZ engines were derived from the Ford Model A engines that were very reliable, but not very powerful. The tank weighed 9.8 tons, and was about 4.5 m long (slightly over half the length of an American automobile), and less than 2 m high (only slightly taller than a man). The major weakness was the one-man turret, giving the tank commander the tasks of loading and firing the 45mm gun and the coaxial machine gun. The tank was made at the GAZ Factory No. 37 near Moscow, where the GAZ trucks had been made before the war based on Ford Model A designs, and at Factory No. 38 in Kirov. The T70 went into production in March 1942 using many available T60 parts to reduce the design time and the time needed to create production tools. During 1942, 4,883 T70s were made and 3,343 in 1943, an average of about 400 tanks per month for twenty months, until production was discontinued in October 1943. The T70 was probably the most numerous light tank in the Soviet arsenal in July 1943.[17]

In September 1942 the T70 replaced the T60 that had gone into production on July 1941 at the GAZ Factory No. 37 near Moscow. The factory was evacuated as the Germans advanced, and most production then took place at the GAZ factory in Gorki and Factory No. 38 in Kirov. An improved model of the T60 was made in 1942 with a more powerful engine. The T60 mounted a 20mm gun and, with a one man turret, had the same problem of an overworked tank commander as the T70. A total of 6,022 were made, 1,818 in 1941 and 4,474 in 1942. Many of the T60s remained in July 1943, even after the immense losses of light tanks by the Russians in 1942. The Soviets began 1942 with 6,300 light tanks, received 11,900 (including 4,883 T70s, 4,472 T60s, and possibly 2,500 Lend Lease light tanks), and lost 7,200, leaving 11,000 light tanks on January 1, 1943, probably including over 2,000 Lend Lease light tanks.[18]

In July 1943 the only Soviet medium tank was the superb T34 mounting a 76mm gun and 52mm of frontal armor with excellent mechanical reliability.[19] The T34 was still a superior battle tank, though lacking the sophisticated features of the Panther that made the German tank more comfortable for the crew. The T34 was equal to the German Pz IVs, but was outgunned by the Panther and the Tigers. Fortunately for the Russians, there were very few Panthers or Tigers at Kursk, and many of the adversaries of the T34 were Pz IIIs and Pz IVs. From limited evidence available in German photographs and reports of destroyed Soviet tanks, the T34s were apparently concentrated in the tank armies and independent tank corps, while the independent tank regiments, which took the brunt of the 2nd SS Panzer Corps attack in the first two days of the battle, were equipped with light tanks and Lend Lease tanks. When the T34s were encountered later in the battle, the German claims of tanks destroyed decreased.

The Soviets had 7,600 medium tanks in January 1943, received 16,300 during the year, lost 14,700 during 1943, and ended the year with 9,200. In an average month during 1943, the Soviets lost 1,200 medium tanks, including T34s and Lend Lease tanks, but more than replaced them with new tanks.[20]

Once the Germans revealed the Tiger in later 1942, the Soviets were galvanized to find a means to counter this potent force on the battlefield. The current Russian heavy tank, the KV1 was heavily armored with 100mm of frontal armor, but carried the same 76mm gun as the T34, unequal to the 88mm gun on the Tiger. In a tank versus tank encounter, the KV I would have been destroyed before the Tiger came in range of the Russian gun. An improved model of the KV 1, the KV 1 S, was in production in July with a better engine and other improvements, but the same 76mm gun. Unlike the Tiger, the KV1S had been redesigned to improve the weight versus horsepower ratio and had gained in mechanical reliability. Some of the KV2s were still available armed with the 152mm howitzer that had the power to knock the turret from a Tiger if it came in range. The Soviets had 2,000 heavy tanks in January 1942, received 900 in the year, lost 1,300, and ended the year with only 1,600 heavy tanks, one of the few categories of weapons in which 1942 receipts did not exceed losses.[21]

Given the threat of the Tiger, the Russians formed heavy tank regiments. In the urgency to have as many heavy tank units as possible ready for July 1943, the Russians probably scraped the barrel for KVs and formed them into regiments equipped with KV1s and KV2s. The emptying of the arsenals would have turned up a few KV2s left over when the type was abandoned in early 1942. There were no KV85s at Kursk; production had begun after August 1943, and only 130 were made by the end of 1943. Five new heavy tank regiments were formed during July 1943, including the 202nd and 203rd in the Moscow Military District. The 203rd was assigned immediately to the 39th. Army (Kalinin Front), and the 202nd went to the 40th Army (Voronezh Front) by the end of July. The 204th and 205th Regiments were formed in Leningrad, home of the KV production before the war, and the last regiment was formed in the Volga Military District. Possibly these five regiments pulled together independent tank companies or provisional detachments because there was no training time involved. None of the new tank regiments took part in the Battle of Kursk, but their availability was an indication of the concern to bolster the defense against the Tigers.

Another alternative to combating the Tigers was the self-propelled gun.[22] By eliminating the turret, a heavier gun could be played on a chassis. The Soviets developed three SUs (mechanized artillery) in 1942, the SU76 with 76mm gun on a light tank chassis, the SU122 with a 122mm howitzer on the chassis of a captured German Pz III, and the AA SU37 with a 37mm antiaircraft gun on a T60 chassis. By the end of 1942, SU regiments had been formed with SU76s and SU122s, but the mixture of two types of vehicles was not effective because of the differences in speed and the ability to move over difficult terrain.

During 1943 the Russians produced 1,300 heavy SUs, 800 medium SUs, and 2,300 light SUs.[23] The 122mm howitzer on the medium SU and the 152mm howitzer on the heavy SU had the power to destroy the Tiger at short range, but were not equal to the 88mm gun on the Tiger at long range. Design of the SU152 began in January 1943, and the first models were produced in February. In May 1943 the first regiments were organized with only twelve SU152s and sent to Kursk.[24] Of the 2,100 heavy and medium SUs made in 1943, 600 were lost during the year, nearly 30 percent compared to only 20 percent losses of the SU76, indicating that taking on the Tigers was hazardous.

In April 1943 light regiments with twenty-one SU76s and medium regiments with sixteen SU122s were formed. The regiments were often based on cadres of tank regiments and were organized in a few weeks. The process of forming the SUs into regiments was still in its infancy on July 1, 1943. Of the total fifty-seven SU regiments identified, twenty were still organizing in the Moscow Military District, four were in the Stavka reserve, six were assigned to the Steppe District, six to the Central Front, four to the Voronezh Front, five to the Western Front, six to the Bryansk Front, and the remaining six scattered in the other fronts. Of the thirty-seven trained regiments, sixteen were with the three fronts engaged at Kursk and twelve with the two fronts to the north, where major operations were planned. This distribution does not reflect a total priority for Kursk. The Russians did not station a major portion of their SU resources in the Kursk area and had considerable reserves if faced with an adverse turn.

British and American tanks played a significant role in the Battle of Kursk.[25] About 6,000 Lend Lease tanks had been delivered to the Russians by July 1943 (4,500 in 1942 and 3,650 in all of 1943), and a total of 14,430 during the entire war. In June 1943 German intelligence estimated that of the 256 Soviet tank brigades identified, sixty-one were either fully or partially equipped with British and American tanks.

The British sent surplus Grants and Stuarts by way of the Persian Gulf from their tank maintenance shops in Alexandria, and additional American tanks came directly from the United States. From both sources the Russians received 1,386 Grants during the war. The Grant medium tank carried both a medium velocity 75mm gun and a 37mm gun, which was obsolete by 1943. The maximum armor was only 37mm, and the high silhouette (ten feet, three inches high, lowered to nine feet, four inches in a special version called a Lee for British use) made it a good target for the German gunners, which earned it the reputation among Russian tank men as a coffin for seven comrades. The 75mm gun was mounted in a half turret on the starboard side with a very limited traverse, reducing its effectiveness in a tank-versus-tank encounter. The Grant was usually given to Soviet independent tank regiments assigned to field armies for infantry support. Sherman tanks were sent to Russia beginning in June 1943, but none saw action at Kursk.

The Stuart light tank weighed only thirteen tons but had a two-man turret and a high speed of nearly 60 km per hour. The Russians received 1,676 Stuarts during the war, most before July 1943. The 37mm gun was comparable to the 37mm gun on the early versions of the Pz III. The Stuart was an excellent light tank with a very reliable engine, and the ready availability of these tanks, along with British light tanks, may have led to the Soviet decision to halt the production of light tanks and to use the manufacturing resources for the SU76 that had the T70 chassis. German photographs of the Kursk battlefields show destroyed Lees and Stuarts together, leading to the assumption that the tank regiments were equipped with both types.

The British provided the Russians with Matildas, Valentines, and Churchills. The British sent 1,084 Matildas to Russia. The Matilda infantry tank was a pre-war design with up to 78mm of armor and the two-pounder gun. Its narrow tracks and low speed had relegated it to a training tank in Britain by the end of 1942. The surplus stock was given to the Russians in 1941 and 1942, and some were still left in 1943.

The Valentine was also an infantry tank with heavy armor and low speed. In March 1942 the Valentine gun was upgraded to a 57mm six-pounder, one of the best antitank guns of the war. In March 1943 the British fitted a medium velocity 75mm gun in the turret. The Russians also converted some of the earlier model Valentines to a 76mm Soviet gun. The Valentine was the British tank preferred by the Russians, and production continued in Britain and Canada for Russian export after use had ended by the British armored forces. A total of 5,282 were sent. The heavy armor and the 75mm gun capable of firing a good high explosive shell made the Valentine an excellent infantry support tank.

The Churchill, also an infantry tank, was in use by the Russians at Kursk. It had 102mm of armor and a speed of only 15 mph, the two marks of British infantry tanks. The medium velocity 75mm made it an excellent infantry support tank and the Russians assigned it to independent tank regiments for that purpose. The Soviet 169th Tank Brigade, assigned to the 2nd Tank Corps that moved against the 2nd SS Corps early in the battle, was given some Churchills on June 21, 1943.[26]

The British and American tanks filled the role of infantry support tanks in the Red Army and were assigned to independent tank brigades and regiments. The Soviet T34s were assigned to the tank corps and tank armies where their superior tank fighting qualities were required. The Russians had ample supplies of tanks in July 1943 to carry out their plans and far more than the Germans were able to build.

The German shortage of tanks was the major reason for Hitler's delay of the Kursk offensive, and this shortage would plague the German Army for the rest of the war. Hitler believed that significant numbers of higher quality Tigers and Panthers and additional Pz IVs would alter the balance on the Eastern Front. Despite the opposition of the generals, Hitler delayed the offensive to give the German tank factories time to produce more tanks. There was solid reasoning behind the delay. The Germans produced 2,804 tanks and self-propelled guns in the three months preceding July 1943, about equal to the total number of German tanks involved in the battle.

The German panzer divisions were not in good condition in April when Manstein urged Hitler to launch an immediate attack on Kursk. In April 1943 the 18th Panzer Division had only thirty-one tanks including twenty Pz III and Pz IVs, eight Pz IIs, and three command tanks. An additional eight tanks were being repaired. The division had only twenty-nine antitank guns including ten 37mm guns and ten captured Soviet 76mm guns.[27] In May 1943 the 18th Panzer Division received 89 officers and 2,700 men as replacements. Half of the officer replacements were cadets, and the others were elderly men without combat experience.[28] This division would have been a very weak opponent to a Soviet tank brigade, let alone a Soviet tank corps.

The deliveries of tanks and assault guns to the Eastern Front during April, May, and June 1943 were essential for rebuilding panzer divisions like the 18th Panzer. Between April 25 and July 18, 308 tanks and 140 self-propelled guns and specialized tanks were delivered to the 9th Army on the north shoulder.[29] The total deliveries to the Eastern Front from March 1 to June 22, 1943, were 699 tanks, 318 assault guns, 90 Hornets, 45 Ferdinands, 45 150mm howitzer sturm panzers, 637 75mm antitank guns, and 162 88mm antitank guns.[30] Without these weapons the Germans would have been unable to launch a major offensive. Even in April 1943, the Russians had worked on their defenses for a month after the spring offensives ended in March. To break through would have required considerable strength, unlike catching the Soviet units in the open as occurred in February.

The balance of tank numbers shifted decisively against the Germans during 1943 even though total losses of German tanks and SUs in 1943 was 8,992, compared to the much higher Soviet losses of 22,400. Soviet production of 27,300 tanks exceeded losses by nearly 5,000 and made up the losses, while the Germans produced only 10,747 tanks in 1943, for a net gain of less than 2,000 tanks. While the German tanks were better in some respects than their Soviet counterparts, and Soviet tank losses were more than double those sustained by the Germans, these factors were not enough to sway the balance at Kursk.

German troops marching to the front. The vast majority of German infantry traveled by train and then on foot during the war on the Eastern Front. SCOTT PICK/SUMMIT PHOTOGRAPHICS

A German soldier sits watching the skies over the Russian steppe on a camouflaged 2cm flak gun. SCOTT PICK/SUMMIT PHOTOGRAPHICS

A German 10.5cm artillery crew stand watch in a wheat field. The low elevation of the barrel suggests they are shooting at targets close by, by direct fire. SCOTT PICK/SUMMIT PHOTOGRAPHICS

A German towed 7.5cm anti-tank gun is brought forward. The soldier on the far left carries a captured Russian submachine gun which German soldiers found to be a superior weapon to their own.

A German 10.5cm artillery position. The lack of empty shell casings would suggest the crew is waiting for their first fire mission at this location. SCOTT PICK/SUMMIT PHOTOGRAPHICS

The German Stuka served as a close support aircraft on the battlefield attacking bunkers, troop positions, bridges, artillery, and especially Russian tanks. SCOTT PICK/SUMMIT PHOTOGRAPHICS

A destroyed Russian 152mm heavy artillery piece and S-65 tractor. SCOTT PICK/SUMMIT PHOTOGRAPHICS

A Russian Maxim heavy machine gun lies abandoned in a field. SCOTT PICK/SUMMIT PHOTOGRAPHICS

An abandoned Russian 152mm artillery gun after having fallen partway through a wooden bridge.

CHAPTER 7

The Soviet Defense System

The Soviet defenses at the battle of Kursk were based on the concept of elastic defense developed by the Germans in the later part of World War I. Prior to 1917, defenses had tended to be linear, shallow, and brittle, thin lines that would break under a severe blow. Defensive techniques evolved over the centuries to counter advances in offensive technology, a continuous interplay between the invention of new offensive weapons and the development of ways to withstand them.

In the eighteenth century, battles were fought by armies in parallel lines beyond the limited range of the smooth bore musket, about 100 meters. The attacking army would advance at the speed of a walking man until within range of the opposing force. At that time both armies might exchange volleys, or, as Americans did at Bunker Hill, wait until they could see the whites of the eyes of the charging British. Both sides would attempt to reload, and the advantage lay with the defender who stood his ground and was able to reload with greater ease. The attacker tried to cover the 100-meters before the defender could reload. (Perhaps this requirement is relative to the continued emphasis on the 100-meter dash in track and field sports, rather than a 125- or 150-meter dash.)

In the Napoleonic Wars the French infantry advanced in a column, striking a small sector of the defending army. The theory was that only the defending infantry immediately in front of the column could fire at the attacking column when it came in range, and only the leading men in the column were threatened by musket fire as they advanced. The men behind were able to break through the line with bayonets and attack the remaining enemy forces from the flank and rear before they could rearrange their lines to bring musket fire on the attacker. In this way the poorly trained French were able to overcome the professional armies of England, Prussia, and Austria.

To counter the massed column, the British army replaced the continuous line with a series of squares with muskets facing in all four directions and capable of dealing with any force attempting to exploit a breakthrough, the forerunner of the strong points of World War I. The men on the flanks of the square could provide supporting fire to adjacent squares during a frontal attack. If the enemy chose to attack in line, the British units were trained to execute a drill that converted the squares into a continuous line.

The invention of the machine gun in the late nineteenth century forced the infantry to take cover. Defensive machine gun fire was most effective when the path of the bullets was parallel to the front being defended. If fired directly at the oncoming infantry, the stream of bullets might hit one man, but the rest of the burst of fire would continue on the same path with no likely target. If the machine gun fired parallel to the front, the attacking infantry would be forced to move through a curtain of fire that could be created at the precise moment that the infantry reached a point predetermined by the defender. The stream of bullets might find many targets, as attacking infantry approached the defenses in a line roughly parallel to the line of resistance. To take advantage of the curtain of fire provided by the machine gun, the armies on the Western Front in World War I constructed elaborate zigzag trench systems with machine guns at the rear angles firing parallel to the sides of the protruding points.

However, the concentration of men and weapons in the lines of trenches was an ideal target for the artillery. The elastic defense developed by the Germans was planned to counteract the heavy artillery barrages that preceded British and French attacks on the Western Front. For days the enemy artillery would pound the Germans, destroying the trenches, driving those defenders who were not killed nearly mad, and opening the way for the attacker. The elastic defense philosophy was first to scatter the defensive positions in the main line of resistance in a series of strong points in place of the continuous trench line that was so vulnerable to artillery fire. By spreading the troops the artillery effectiveness was reduced, as most of the shells fell on unoccupied ground.

The main line of resistance of strong points was up to 3 km deep requiring the artillery barrage to be dispersed over a much greater area than a single trench line. Immediately behind the main line would be another series of strong points held by the reserve battalions of the rifle regiments, and 3 km behind that line would be a third line held by the reserve regiment of the rifle division. The total depth of the main line of resistance was from 6 to 8 km.[1]

The intervening spaces between the strong points was covered with interlocking fire from machine guns, mortars, and light infantry cannon, as well as minefields, barbed wire, and other obstacles. A strong point could rely on fire from neighboring strong points for protection, as well as the strong point's own weapons.[2]

When the main line of resistance was breached at one or more points, and the strong points could no longer benefit from supporting fire from adjoining strong points, the defending troops would withdraw to a second line, usually at least 5 km to the rear, reinforcing the troops already there. The result was a maximum loss to the attackers from the heavy fire in the initial stage of the attack, and a minimum loss to the defenders who left before the attackers could move close enough to more than a few strong points to inflict heavy casualties on the defenders. The attacker would have to reorganize, move up his artillery, the another barrage on the second line, and launch a new attack. Generally it took at least a day to break through one line and prepare to attack the second line on the following day. The distance between the first and second lines, from 5 to 7 km, was far enough that the attacker would have to move some of his artillery causing a critical delay.

Unless the attacker was able to break through the successive lines promptly, the defender would have the opportunity to gather reserves and concentrate them in the most strategic areas and often launch counterattacks. Once a defensive line had been broken, the attacker needed reserve power to roll up the adjoining sectors from the weakened flank (deprived of supporting fire) as quickly as possible to prevent the defenders from withdrawing and reinforcing the next line, making the task of cracking that line more difficult. The inability of the 4th Panzer Army to roll up the second line on the south shoulder of the Kursk bulge on the second day of the battle gave the Russians the opportunity to pull in tank and infantry reserves and launch counterattacks from the east, north, and west, further slowing the process of breaking through. By the time the Germans closed to the third line, the defending Russians far outnumbered the attackers.

A major factor in the Soviet success was the depth of the defensive system that was constructed in the months prior to the battle. The defenses were more elaborate than any constructed before or after in World War II by the Red Army.[3] In late March 1943 the Central Front, the former Don Front headquarters with new armies, ceased offensive actions and moved to defense. The front was expanded to include the 48th Army and the 13th Army of the Bryansk Front and the 60th Army of the Voronezh Front and covered the northern half of the Kursk bulge. The southern portion of the bulge was held by the Voronezh Front.

Construction of fortifications began in late March. By early April Stalin had agreed with his advisers not to launch a preemptive strike, as had been attempted in the spring of 1942 at Izium. The strategy adopted was to meet the German attack with deeply echeloned defenses supplemented by counterattacks with reserves at every level.

On April 15, the work to improve the defenses was intensified, based on intelligence reports that the Germans would strike at the base of the Kursk salient in the 13th Army zone, in the north of the salient, and the sector held by the 6th and 7th Guards Armies in the south. Attacks at any other point in the Kursk bulge would be relatively harmless, at worst driving some of the Soviet forces out of the tip of the salient.

On May 22, 1943, Marshal Zhukov reported that the 13th and 70th Army defenses were in good order, but that the 48th Army still lacked sufficient artillery. The reserves for the 48th Army were concentrated behind the 13th and 70th Armies too far away to launch immediate counterattacks. Zhukov recommended that the 48th Army receive two rifle divisions, three tank regiments, two tank destroyer regiments, and two mortar or artillery regiments. These reinforcements would enable the 48th Army to flesh out its defense and be ready to participate in the offensive.[4]

Zhukov also pointed out the weakness of the antitank defenses of the Central Front. In May the front had only four tank destroyer regiments, and the two regiments in reserve had no trucks to tow their guns, an essential element, as the guns would have to move quickly to threatened areas. There was a shortage of 45mm guns in the battalion and regimental antitank units in the front lines. Zhukov insisted that four more tank destroyer regiments be sent to the Central Front, along with three regiments of 152mm SUs. These recommendations were carried out, and the Central Front was reinforced. Four additional regiments were sent from the Moscow District to the Central Front in June, two to the 48th Army, one to the 9th Tank Corps in the 48th Army, and one to the Central Front reserve, giving the front a total of six SU regiments. Reinforced to twenty-one SUs during the battle, the SU 152 regiments proved effective in coping with the Tigers and Panthers.

With the memories of German ability to penetrate Soviet defensive lines at will in 1941 and 1942, the Red Army indulged in what could be considered overkill. To an extent never seen before on the Eastern Front, the Red Army built multiple defensive lines around the Kursk salient. On much of the front there existed three "army" level defense lines, manned by units of a given army. Three "front" lines, manned by front reserves, and two reserve lines manned by the Steppe Front, a total of eight lines.

The first lines of fortification were built by the troops in the front lines, but the second and third lines of the army level defenses were built with the assistance of the local people. In the Central Front sector the works included 5,000 km of trenches and 400,000 mines. In the threatened sector of the 13th and 48th Armies, 112 km of barbed wire was installed with 10.7 km electrified.

A typical defensive position for a rifle corps at Kursk in 1943 had a depth of 20 km and a width of 15 to 30 km. The main line of resistance was protected in the front by a series of minefields and lines of barbed wire. In a divisional sector of the main line of defense, the Soviets usually placed two rifle battalions of two rifle regiments in front, the third battalion of the front line regiments about 2 km to the rear, and the three battalions of the third regiment in a third line about 5 km from the front. All of these battalions were in prepared defensive positions that were tied together, often forming switch lines, diagonal defenses that would be used to protect the flanks of the regiment in the event of a breakthrough in a neighboring sector.

In advance of the main line, each regiment had an outpost line with three positions. Each position was protected by a minefield and was linked to the other positions and the rear by a communications trench. The outposts had antitank rifles and were mutually supporting but were not intended to fend off any serious attack. The purpose was to prevent small reconnaissance detachments from closing in to the main line.

Behind the outpost line was a dense series of minefields, both antitank and antipersonnel, and an elaborate barbed wire entanglement. The strong points behind were staggered and covered both the minefields and barbed wire with machine gun fire to make it more difficult for German engineers to clear a path.

The battalion defense area was the basic element of the main line of resistance. A battalion area varied from 2 to 2.5 km in width and 1.5 to 2 km in depth. The battalion area included a multitude of strong points with automatic weapons. The volume of small arms fire at Kursk averaged thirteen to fourteen rounds per meter. As advancing infantry usually spread out with several meters between each man, the Russians allocated about fifty rounds of small arms fire for each attacking German. The automatic weapons were organized to create a fire zone up to 400 meters in front of the main line. Therefore, on the final approach the German infantry would have to move through a hail of small arms fire for at least ten minutes, the time needed to walk the 400 meters. No advance was possible until the machine guns had been silenced.[5]

About 15 to 20 km from the front, the third division in the rifle corps manned a second line of resistance organized the same way with two battalions in the leading edge and a third battalion in reserve. In some sectors an entire rifle division was placed in the second position behind each front line rifle division.

Of the three armies in sectors attacked by the Germans, the 6th Guards Army had four divisions in the first line and three in the second line; in the 7th Guards Army there were three divisions in the first line and three in the second line; and in the 13th Army there were four divisions in the first line and two in the second.

About 15 km behind the second line of resistance was a third line of prepared field fortifications. This third line was not always manned by troops at the beginning of the battle, on the assumption that by the time the Germans had penetrated the first two lines, the units surviving from the first two lines would retreat into the third line to be joined by reserve divisions moved in from other sectors.

An example of the complexity of the mutually supporting strong points was the 151st Rifle Regiment of the 8th Rifle Division holding the eastern most sector of the 13th Army on the boundary with the 48th Army on the north face of the bulge. The 151st Rifle Regiment had two battalions forward, the 2nd Battalion on the right, and the 3rd Battalion on the left. The 1st Battalion was in reserve. Each battalion had an outpost line armed with machine guns and antitank rifles and was protected by antitank minefields. The outposts were linked to their parent battalion with a communications trench that would enable the troops to withdraw under cover in the event of a major attack.

The main line of resistance was protected by both antitank and antipersonnel minefields backed by a barbed wire entanglement. Each of the two forward battalions had two companies in line and the third in reserve. The 2nd Company of the 3rd Battalion held a continuous line of trenches immediately behind the barbed wire with four machine gun nests. About 500 meters behind this line was a broken series of trenches containing four more machine gun nests, two artillery positions, two observation posts, and three bunkers. The 1st Company on the left was positioned in a similar manner. The 3rd Company, in reserve about 500 meters behind the rear of the forward company areas, had a forward continuous trench and three noncontiguous trenches in a second line behind the first trench. The 3rd Company had only two machine gun nests, an antitank gun position, an artillery position, four observation posts, and four bunkers.

The other two battalions were positioned much like the 3rd Battalion with two companies forward and one in reserve. The regiment was supported by the 2nd and 3rd Batteries of the divisional artillery regiment located immediately behind the reserve battalion. The total depth of the position was about 4 km and a duplicate system of the strong points manned by the reserve regiment was located about 1 km behind the rear of the front line regiments. The total depth of the main line of resistance was about 6 km. Penetrating this dense array of strong points presented the Germans with a formidable task.

Another example of the way in which the Russians employed the technique of elastic defense was provided by the 13th Soviet Army on the north shoulder of the Kursk bulge. The 17th Guards Rifle Corps of the 13th Army manned the west end of the third line, but the German 47th Panzer Corps never penetrated that far. The 17th Guards Rifle Corps moved forward to the second line positions to hold the German panzer divisions while the 280th Rifle Division and the 132nd Rifle Division withdrew from the first line to the second line, joining the 140th and 175th Rifle Divisions there, and held the west shoulder of the German salient preventing the German 46th Panzer Corps from widening the bulge. In the center of the army sector, the 75th and 81st Rifle Divisions withdrew from the first line to the second line and joined the 307th Rifle Division that had been in reserve at Ponyri.

The story was repeated on the east end of the 13th Army sector. The third line was held by the 18th Guards Rifle Corps made up of parachute divisions When the Germans broke through the first line, the 8th and 148th Rifle Divisions joined the 74th Rifle Division in the second line and held the east shoulder of the bulge, while the 18th Guards Rifle Corps moved forward from the third line. The entire action unfolded like a textbook example of elastic defense.

Breaking through a complex defense system such as the Russians had constructed required a massive application of artillery and infantry supported by tanks in a limited area to overwhelm the defenders. The artillery barrage could destroy the first line of strong points in advance of the attacking infantry, but once the infantry had fought their way through the devastated front line, they would be faced with relatively intact reserve positions.

The tank was the obvious weapon to silence the machine guns and the key to providing the needed support to exploit the breakthrough. During World War I the British introduced the tank, which provided the necessary artillery and machine gun support to the infantry as it advanced through the strong points, eliminating the critical delay in bringing forward the artillery as well as providing machine gun fire to reinforce the light machine guns carried by the infantry. The guns on the tanks could destroy the bunkers, and the machine guns could dispose of the unprotected infantry driven out of their trenches.

To counter the tank, antitank rifles and antitank guns were added to the strong points in 1918, but not in numbers great enough to reduce substantially the effectiveness of the tanks. Mechanical unreliability was the most serious enemy of the French and British tanks. Once the tanks stopped, the defender's artillery could more easily destroy the stationary targets.

By 1943 the tank had been improved significantly compared to the 1918 models. German Mk III and Mk IV tanks were very reliable mechanically, although the Tiger and Panther were still experiencing problems in 1943. The German assault guns based on the Mk III and Mk IV chassis were work horses for the Germans providing support for the infantry in the counterattack and mobile antitank fire in defense. The armor on the German tanks had been thickened to the point that antitank rifles were useless, except when fired at the side of a tank at close range. Antitank rifleman was not the safest military occupation specialty. The Russian 45mm antitank gun was effective only at close range, usually fewer than 600 yards and again against the side, not the front of the tank, making it necessary to wait until the tanks were in the defensive line positions. If the elastic defense were to work in 1943, the number and power of antitank weapons would have to be increased greatly, which did occur at Kursk.

By the beginning of July the Russians created an incredibly powerful line of antitank weapons beginning with the antitank minefields that prevented the tanks from closing to the main line. The antitank gun line was based on a

series of strong points with heavier concentrations in the areas most likely to
be used by the German panzers. The individual strong points were combined
into antitank areas. In the battalion antitank area there were at least three
company strong points each with four to six antitank guns, fifteen to twenty
antitank rifles, a platoon of engineers trained to attack tanks with mines and
grenades, and several tanks and self-propelled guns.[6]

All types of artillery were called on to take part in the antitank defense,
including the antiaircraft guns. The 6th Guards Army used 152mm howitzers
and 85mm antiaircraft guns in its antitank strong points.[7] The antitank
defenses were from 30 to 35 km deep. In the 13th Army main line, there were
thirteen antitank areas including forty-four strong points, thirty-four strong
points in the second line, and fifteen areas with sixty strong points in the third
line.[8] The field of fire of each strong point was coordinated with others in a
system that enabled the Russians to concentrate fire on any threatened location. Overall the Central Front had 3,110 antitank guns, 10 per km, and 25
other guns and mortars per km, but most of the guns were concentrated in
the 13th Army area where the density of artillery was much higher.[9]

In the south, the 375th Rifle Division had seven battalion antitank areas
and three regimental antitank areas. The total number of guns in the ten
areas was 68 76mm divisional guns, 12 76mm antitank guns, 41 45mm antitank
guns, 134 antitank rifles, and 61 tanks of the 96th Tank Brigade in the tank
reserve. The 375th Division held up the right flank of the 2nd SS Panzer Corps
and required the full attention of the Death Head SS Panzer Division for over
two days, and also its replacement, the 167th Infantry Division, for two more.

The 1247th Regiment of the 375th Division defended the road leading from
Iachnev Kolodez to a bridge over the North Donets River to Petropavlovka The
regiment was supported by the 5th battalion antitank area (eight divisional
76mm guns, two 76mm antitank guns, eight 45mm antitank guns, and twenty-
seven antitank rifles), the 6th battalion antitank area (two 76mm antitank guns,
four 45mm antitank guns, and nine antitank rifles), and the 1st Regimental antitank area (twenty 76mm divisional guns and twenty-three antitank rifles). The
263rd Tank Regiment was placed just behind the 3rd Rifle Battalion area. The
96th Tank Brigade was deep in reserve on the east side of the North Donets at
Koklova, and the 3rd regimental antitank area (eight 76mm divisional guns) was
also in deep reserve at Dalniaia Igumenka. Six of the seven rifle battalions on the
front had an antitank area. There was more than one antitank gun for every
tank in the Death Head Division. With this incredible concentration of strength,
there is little wonder that the 375th Rifle Division was able to delay the German
effort, separating the 4th Panzer Army and Army Detachment Kempf, until the
375th Division finally withdrew on July 12 when threatened in the rear from
both the east and west.

At the beginning of the battle the Central and Voronezh Fronts had ten tank destroyer brigades (each sixty to seventy-two guns), forty tank destroyer regiments (each twenty to twenty-four guns), and three destroyer brigades (up to ninety-six guns) with a total of about 2,000 antitank guns. In other units in the two fronts were another 2,700 antitank guns.[10] The 13th Army in the north had 30 antitank guns per km while in the south the 6th Guards and 7th Guards Armies had an average of 15.6 guns in the first echelon and over 14 in the second echelon. Additional guns were held in mobile reserves along with engineers prepared to create antitank minefields and other obstacles.[11]

Artillery was to play a major role in the defense beginning with a maximum effort barrage from all guns and mortars preceding the German attack to throw the assembling Germans into confusion and to reduce the effectiveness of the German artillery. The large number of Russian artillery units has been described above.

The generous antiaircraft support for the Central Front included five divisions and many regiments and battalions. The Voronezh Front had four antiaircraft divisions, twenty-five antiaircraft regiments, and three independent battalions. The front commanders could provide a two- to five-tier defense, that is an attacking German aircraft would be within range of as many as five antiaircraft batteries rather than only one. Combined with the efforts of the Russian fighters, the German ground attack aircraft were far less effective than in previous battles. Soviet units and tanks could move in the daylight hours without suffering heavy losses to air attacks. The relative safety from air attack was a marked change from the devastation experienced by Soviet armies in the summer of 1942 whenever they attempted to move by day. This freedom to move greatly enhanced Soviet mobility and access to reserves at crucial timer.[12]

Elastic defense worked at Kursk as the Soviets gave ground but delayed the German attackers. During the battle, the inability of the 4th Panzer Army on the south side of the bulge to penetrate the second line quickly gave the Russians the opportunity to pull in tank reserves from the Steppe Front and adjoining armies and launch counterattacks from the east, north, and west, further slowing the process of breaking through. By the time the Germans approached the third line, the defending Russians outnumbered the attackers. The Germans breached the third line at Prokorovka, but there were still five more lines with ample reserves to man them. In the north, the 9th Army was stopped at the second line. The Soviets held the Germans at the second line with available "front" reserves and did not need additional reserves in the Steppe Front.

At Kursk the Russians applied the lessons of World War I and improved the technique of elastic defense. When the Germans went on the defensive after Kursk, they became the grand masters of defense as illustrated in Italy and Normandy, as well as on the Eastern Front.

CHAPTER 8

Breaking Through in the South

The offensive began on July 5, 1943 with a series of attacks and counterattacks by relatively small units, usually a regiment or a battalion of infantry with tank support. The average Soviet counterattack was made by a battalion of infantry with the support of up to sixty tanks (a tank regiment or a reduced tank brigade). The use of the terms army, corps, division, brigade, and battalion can be quite confusing. The Soviet tank army was stronger than a German panzer corps, with twenty-two infantry battalions and thirty-one tank battalions (twenty-one tanks each for a total of about 600 tanks, equal to about ten German tank battalions. A German panzer corps of three panzer divisions had six tank battalions (about 300 tanks) and twelve infantry battalions. The German SS panzer grenadier divisions were stronger, with three tank battalions and six infantry battalions plus an assault gun battalion. The 2nd SS Panzer Corps had eighteen battalions of infantry and nine tank battalions with 474 tanks and assault guns on July 5.

The Soviet tank corps was stronger than a German panzer division with six infantry battalions, eleven tank battalions (equal to nearly four German tank battalions), and often a self-propelled artillery regiment (equal to the German assault gun battalion). The German panzer divisions had two tank battalions and four infantry battalions. However, given the German advantages in training and experience, one can equate a Soviet tank army with a panzer corps and a Soviet tank corps with a panzer division. The Soviet tank brigades and regiments were similar to a German tank battalion. Therefore, the collision of the 2nd SS Panzer Corps and the 5th Soviet Guards Tank Army was between two comparable units.

The Kursk offensive took place in a relatively small area; the entire Kursk salient was about the size of four midwestern U.S. counties, less than 200 km from the base to the tip, about 125 miles, a two-hour drive on a good road. On the south shoulder of the Kursk bulge, the countryside of ripening grain was interspersed with small villages and woods. The base of the southern bulge created by the 4th Panzer Army was only 30 km, a distance equal to that covered by a horse-drawn wagon in a single day, and less than a day and half's march. The depth of the salient was also about 30 km. The German panzers in the south advanced at an average of less than 3 km per day compared to gains of over ten times that average in previous offensives. In comparison the width of the Kiev salient in September 1941 was nearly 300 km and pocket was closed in about five days with the north and south prongs advancing about 150 km each. If the Kursk offensive had similar success, the pocket would have been closed in three or four days, trapping two tank armies and seven infantry armies inside the pocket and denying the Russians the time to bring up more than one additional tank army that would have been brushed aside by the combined forces of the 9th Army, the 4th Panzer Army, and Army Detachment Kempf.

The offensive did not come as a surprise to the Soviets. As the time grew nearer, the information concerning the time and place became more detailed. On July 2, 1943, the Stavka warned the front commanders that the German offensive would begin between July 3 and 6. On the evening of July 4, Zhukov and General Alexandr M. Vasilevsky, chief of the General Staff, discussed a report from a soldier who had been captured by the Russians from the German 168th Infantry Division and had informed his captors that the attack would begin at dawn on July 5. At 2 A.M. on July 5 an engineer from the German 6th Infantry Division was captured, and he informed the Russians that the attack would begin about 3 A.M. on that date.

Zhukov ordered General Konstantin Rokossovsky, commander of the Central Front, to begin the counter-preparation artillery barrage immediately and that Zhukov would inform Stalin. The previously planned barrage began at 2:20 A.M. with all guns of the front directed at German artillery batteries and the infantry and tank assembly areas. The barrage inflicted many German casualties, destroyed some artillery positions, and cut telephone lines.

The impact of a barrage on the Eastern Front is difficult to imagine. The testimony of Guy Sajer, a member of the Gross Deutschland Division, was striking, but the real terror of seemingly endless crashing explosions, even on those in comparatively safe shelter, cannot be expressed. Daylight turned to darkness and was interrupted by brilliant flashes of nearby explosions. The earth trembled and bushes and trees exploded into flame by spontaneous combustion from the intense heat. The German troops were frozen with fear, unable to move or even scream at times and at other times driven to howling like animals while desperately trying to bury themselves deeper to escape the terror, while clutching one another like children. Those who peered out were thrown back into the shelter in pieces. A close hit would flood the darkness with blinding light for a brief second followed by even blacker closeness as dust and dirt poured into the shelter through every crevice. The barrage would go on for seemingly an eternity until all hope for survival had vanished and then would suddenly stop. The eerie silence that followed was soon interrupted by individual sounds of motors and automatic weapons signaling that the even more dangerous war in the open was to resume.[1]

However, in Zhukov's opinion the Russian barrage began too soon while the Germans were still in their dugouts and their tanks were in concealed waiting areas, rather than in the open, assembling for the attack. The Soviets had not located all of the concentration areas for German tanks and troops, and even if some of the German were gathering there, these troops survived unscathed. Although the Russians had located some artillery positions, they were firing at broad areas rather than specific targets. Had the artillery barrage been delayed until a half hour before the time of the attack, the German casualties would have been greater, according to Zhukov, and the Germans would have been less successful on the first day.[2] However, the information from the prisoner was the attack would be launched at 3 A.M., and the Russian artillery barrage began at 2:20 A.M. Ten minutes would not have made a difference. A second barrage at 5 A.M., a half hour before the time of the delayed attack, would have accomplished much, but the Russians had no way of knowing when the actual attack would take place once it had been delayed.

The 4th Panzer Army had well-equipped panzer divisions and used its tanks in the initial assault, rather than holding them for the exploitation phase on the second day, as did the 9th Army in the north. German tanks usually attacked in battalion force of about fifty tanks spread over a frontage of about 1,200 m, with the two lead companies forming the first wave, another company in the second wave, and the remaining company in the third wave. Each forward company placed two platoons of five tanks in a 500-meter line with ten tanks spaced about 50 m apart. The two remaining platoons and the headquarters troop followed in file. The tanks of each of the platoons were arranged in a wedge shape. The lead companies were dispersed in depth about 500 m and the total depth of the battalion was nearly 1,500 m. This formation has many advantages, including giving the battalion commander the ability to see all of his tanks and to provide supporting fire from the reserve companies in the battalion.

The first wave of tanks would attack the enemy antitank defense and artillery. The German Tigers were probably very effective at this point in the battle. Standing off at 1,000 meters, beyond the effective range of the Soviet 76mm antitank guns, the tank gunners could locate an antitank gun as soon as it fired. With an 88mm gun and excellent fire direction equipment, the Tigers wrecked havoc with the Russian tanks and antitank guns. A platoon commander of the 6th Company of the Reich SS Tank Regiment in his Tiger tank claimed eight Soviet tanks on July 7, ten on July 8, and six more on July 10.[3] Russian anecdotes relate the heroism of the antitank gunners winning posthumous Hero of the Soviet Union medals while their regiments were eliminated, gun by gun, as they fired on the German tanks. Once the Soviet antitank guns were silenced, the

German first wave would crash through the defense main line, attack the Russian artillery positions, and disrupt the rear echelon of the enemy.

The German second wave would provide covering fire for the first wave as it advanced and would then attack the enemy infantry with the help of one or two companies of the division's panzer grenadiers, who moved forward in half-track personnel carriers, supported by the assault guns, and then dismounted to clear the enemy infantry. The third wave with the bulk of the panzer grenadiers would eliminate any remaining resistance. The flanks were protected by antitank guns.[4]

The tanks provided mutual support in the attack. The medium and heavy tanks would provide covering fire while the light tanks moved quickly to the next enemy defensive position. Once that position was taken, the light tanks in turn provided covering fire while the medium and heavy tanks moved forward.

The infantry accompanied the tanks in the attack. To attack and break through heavily defended positions required a great deal of skill, luck, and guts. In the words of a former World War II paratrooper, who on more than one occasion led a platoon in breaking through similar German defenses in the West in 1944 and 1945.[5] The German technique, as described by Sajer, was to send engineers and discipline battalions (made up of convicted men sentenced to the battalions for a crime) to clear the minefields during the night preceding the attack. One of the German engineers clearing the mines on July 4 deserted and told the Russians the time of the attack.

Once the mines were cleared, a few infantry groups (equal to an American squad or British section) were sent forward to make paths through the barbed wire by cutting gaps and to silence the outpost line, preferably without shooting The duties of the advance patrols were probably the most dangerous of all and required the greatest skill. Typically the group would begin crawling forward before dawn keeping close together and as close to the ground as possible, hoping to advance unnoticed. The group was in as much danger from their own troops as from the Russians because one could not determine the nationality of a few muffled sounds fifty meters away in the darkness, and the safest course was to shoot first and ask questions later. According to an American paratrooper, an extremely valuable skill in this work was the ability to detect the nationality of a nearby position from its odor. The Germans smelled of horse blankets, an odor familiar to a man raised on a farm. On patrol one paratrooper would be continually questioned by the new replacements, "Can you smell them yet?"[6] The Russians also had a distinct odor of cabbage soup that could be detected fifty meters away by a skilled infantryman.

However as in all armies, the most dangerous assignments often went not to those who were the most skilled, but to the newcomers. Sajer's experience as a member of one of these advance groups was typical. He joined the Gross Deutschland Division as a member of a group made up entirely of replacements. Before the new group even met anyone in their new rifle company, they were assigned to move out in advance of the assault to neutralize the Russian outpost line. Sajer's patrol was unsuccessful, as the man assigned to kill a Russian in the outpost line with a knife lacked experience and was shot by the Russian, which alerted the entire sector that erupted with flares, automatic weapons, artillery, and grenades that rained on Sajer's group and the approaching main assault force.

The theory was that once the outpost line was eliminated, the main assault force would crawl in the darkness to within a few hundred meters of the main line of resistance. In Sajer's sector the Russians did not perceive the true meaning of the attack on the outpost line and assumed this was merely routine patrol activity. After the fire stopped for lack of visible targets, the Russians did not give the general alarm, but simply sent a patrol out to see if anything was happening. The patrol found nothing after a cursory look and returned to the main line.

Meanwhile the assault troops continued to crawl forward. When the mass of the assault troops was finally discovered, German fire teams of a machine gunner, his assistant, a team leader, and one or two riflemen and grenadiers would rush the final hundred yards or more to the first foxhole. At this point success depended on the ability of the second fire team in the section to cover the first team to prevent the Russians from firing at the running men. The company mortars and attached tanks were also effective in this protective role, although the tanks were reluctant to advance without infantry to ward off close range fire from Russian antitank weapons and Russian engineers who would leap on a German tank, place a mine on the deck, and blow off the turret.

Once the Germans entered the Soviet front line company strong points and began to eliminate the Russian positions one by one, an essential link in the chain of interlocking fire was broken. Each Soviet company depended on its neighboring companies to lay down a curtain of fire parallel to the front, while the company itself provided the same service to its neighbors. Once the chain was broken, the neighboring company would be open for assault not only from the flank, but also from the front as its protective curtain was weakened by the loss of its neighbor. Although the company strong points were laid out with all around defense in mind, the protection of the flank was never as strong as the front. Once the Germans penetrated the first company line, they could begin to roll up the companies on either flank.

The task of the 4th Panzer Army was made easier by the character of the three divisions of the 6th Guards Army that defended the sector. The 71st Guards Rifle Division, the 67th Guards Rifle Division, and the 52nd Guards Rifle Division, each with from 8,000 to 9,000 men, took the full brunt of the 4th Panzer Army attack. These divisions had fought at Stalingrad and suffered heavy casualties. They were among the divisions hurriedly moved by rail to the Kursk area, leaving army supporting combat units and service units behind, to prevent any expansion of the German offensive that took Kharkov and Belgorod in the spring of 1943. Through prisoner interrogation, the Germans learned that the weakened divisions had been filled in May and June with new recruits with brief training from the recently liberated area around Kursk, and by Central Asians, who had passed through the normal training cycle in the replacement system, but probably lacked the language skills that would have enabled them to fit into the rifle companies in a short period.[7] As combat veterans testified, recent replacements in a company that had gone through many battles and lost many men were a liability to the company and were at high risk to themselves. Having lost many friends, veterans were reluctant to make new friends among the replacements who soon would become casualties because they lacked the skills needed to stay alive. Shunning the newcomers meant few opportunities for the replacements to learn from the veterans. Adding language barriers in the case of the trained replacements on one hand, and the complete lack of skill of the hastily drafted farm boys from the Kursk area on the other, produced a very unstable element in the rifle companies defending the first line against the 4th Panzer Army.

On the first day, the SS Corps captured a number of prisoners from the 155th Rifle Regiment of the 51st Guards Division that had moved from reserve 20 km to the rear at Teterevino in the second line of resistance to a position between the 52nd Guards Rifle Division and the 375th Rifle Division. The prisoners informed the Germans that the rifle company strength was 120 to 130 men. The officers were all Russians, but the replacements were 60 percent recent draftees from the Kursk area and 40 percent from Central Asia.[8] The 155th Rifle Regiment had received 1,000 replacements (over one-third of the total strength) at the end of May. The men were from eighteen to fifty-three years of age. The prisoners said that they had American rations and the morale was very good.[9] The 3rd Battalion of the 155th Rifle Regiment had received eighty replacements from the 508th Horse Hospital in March and forty men from replacement depots in May.[10] The 1st Battalion of the 155th Rifle Regiment prisoners informed the Germans that there were 180 to 190 men in the rifle companies, and that they were well armed with machine guns and mortars. The supply of ammunition was good except for the machine pistols. The daily ration was 700 grams of bread, vegetables, and barley soup.[11] These first hand accounts bear out the problems and strengths of the three guards divisions facing the 4th German Panzer Army.

The attack on the southern shoulder began at 4 A.M. on July 4. The 6th Guards Army was subjected to a heavy air attack by bombers and Stukas, and over 2,500 bombs were dropped on the 67th Guards Rifle Division in ten minutes. The German 4th Panzer Army tanks and infantry attacked at 5 A.M. On the 71st Guards Rifle Division front, on the east of the 48th Panzer Corps, a ten-minute barrage was followed by a German attack with five battalions of infantry and thirty tanks of the 52nd German Corps at Gertsovka. The 332nd German Infantry Division launched an attack with two regiments of infantry supported by thirty tanks west of Butovo, near the boundary between the 67th and 71st Guards Rifle Division. The Germans took the village of Bereso about 3 km north of the start line and drove the 71st Division nearly 8 km north toward Krasnia Pochinka. By evening the 71st Division was defending Krasnia Pochinka against elements of the German 332nd Infantry Division.[12] However, the left flank of the German division experienced some pressure from Russian counterattacks from the west. The classic method to defeat a breakthrough was to attack the salient at the base, which the Soviets started to do on the first day.[13] To shore up the western flank of the offensive in the south, the 52nd German Corps had attacked east and north of Bubny on July 5, supported by a heavy artillery barrage. Bubny became the anchor for the west shoulder of the salient held by the 255th German Infantry Division.[14]

To the east, an infantry regiment of the 332nd Infantry Division supported by seventy tanks of the 3rd Panzer Division attacked the 67th Guards Rifle Division at Butovo on the west flank of the Soviet division.[15] Later 200 tanks of the 3rd Panzer Division attacked Butovo against elements of the 67th and 71st Guards Rifle Divisions supported by the 27th Tank Destroyer Brigade and four independent tank destroyer regiments. [16] By 7:10 A.M. the 3rd Panzer Division and Gross Deutschland had broken through the first line of defense and had driven the 67th Guards Division back 5 km toward Cherkasskoe. According to the Russians, the German 48th Panzer Corps suffered heavy losses moving through the first defense line. By the evening of July 5, of the 200 Panthers assigned to the 48th Panzer Corps, forty were out of action from Soviet fire.[17]

The Russians counterattacked at Cherkasskoe at 8:10 A.M. with fifteen to twenty tanks and the 196th Guards Rifle Regiment, hitting twenty-five German tanks and 300 men.[18] However, by evening the tank regiment of the Gross Deutschland with eighty tanks took Cherkasskoe, about 5 km from the start line. The 3rd Panzer Division and the Gross Deutschland had advanced a little more than an hour's march from the start, far short of expectations.[19] They were only half way to the second line and were not able to position themselves to launch an attack on the second line by the next morning.

In the sector east of the 67th Guards Rifle Division, the Gross Deutschland hit the 52nd Guards Rifle Division, first with a thirty-minute artillery barrage then followed by an attack at Iakontov near the center of the 52nd Guards Division sector. The 11th Panzer Division and 167th Infantry Division attacked the east flank of the 52nd Guards Division at Berezov at 11 A.M. with 200 tanks and air support. The 52nd Division had the support of the 1008th and 538th Tank Destroyer Regiments and claimed 18 German tanks, including 10 Tigers, 4 assault guns, and 200 infantry.[20] By 4 P.M. the division had been driven out of its first line positions and was withdrawing with the support of the 28th Tank Destroyer Brigade, destroying twenty-five German tanks. The 52nd Soviet Guards Division retreated 6 km to Bukovka on the Vorskla River, where it was joined by the 96th Tank Brigade with thirty to forty tanks and elements of the 51st Guards Rifle Division, and held the town overnight.

The 2nd SS Panzer Corps to the east had more success. East of the 52nd Guards Rifle Division sector, the 375th Rifle Division held a 15-km-wide sector leading southwest from the area of Gremuchii and Berezov to a point on the Belgorod-Prokorovka-Kursk railroad just south of Belomestniai. Opposite this single rifle division was the 2nd SS Panzer Corps with three SS panzer grenadier divisions and a regiment of the 167th Infantry Division.[21]

The entire corps of three SS divisions struck the 375th Rifle Division. The center point of the German attack at Ternovka was in the middle of the division sector. The Soviet division gave way and moved northwest to the west bank of the Novi Donets River pursued by the Death Head Division, while the Adolf Hitler and Reich Divisions bypassed the resistance and pushed north against light opposition. Beginning at 2:30 P.M., despite a Soviet artillery barrage, the Adolf Hitler Division advanced and at 4:30 P.M. was attacking Bukovka on the Vorskla River about 8 km north of the start line with the east flank units of the 48th Panzer Corps. At 2:15 P.M. the Reich Division was also through the main line of resistance and moving through the open country.[22]

By 6:40 P.M. the Adolf Hitler Division had moved another 5 km north and was only 500 m south of the second line, reaching positions near the second line in the sector from Iakovlevo on the west to the Donets on the right about 15 km from the start line. The Soviets brought up elements of the 51st Guards Division from the second line and the 230th Tank Regiment to delay the Adolf Hitler SS, but to no avail.

The tanks of the Reich Division were stopped farther south, and its attack on the second line was delayed until 3 A.M. as the infantry came up during the night. The Death Head Division was still on the Belgorod Oboyan Road behind the other two divisions slowly driving the 375th Soviet Rifle Division eastward toward the Donets. Remarkably, the 375th Rifle Division retained its integrity, despite the fearsome assault of the 2nd SS Corps and held a front line divisional sector for the next week.[23]

The SS Panzer Corps had done well on the first day. The report of the 2nd SS Panzer Corps on the damage done to their opponents on July 5 is revealing. The corps claimed seventeen aircraft destroyed, an indication that the Red Air Force was very active in attacking the ground troops. Only seven tanks were destroyed or captured by the entire corps, positive evidence that the Soviets did not have time to bring up major tank units, and the tank regiments with the 6th Guards Army managed to withdraw with few losses. The Germans destroyed or captured twenty-seven antitank guns, a comparatively small number considering that they broke through over 20 km of front with an average of nine antitank guns and over twenty-six guns and mortars per km.[24] The Germans destroyed only one gun, two mortars, and thirteen rocket launchers. The corps captured 552 prisoners the first day but made no estimate of Russians killed and wounded. Only 300 rifles, 68 machine pistols, and 73 machine guns were captured or destroyed, indicating the toll of killed and wounded could not have been high. The Reich Division reported the highest total in most of the categories, indicating more combat.[25]

A note of caution is necessary regarding claims of tanks destroyed. Both Russians and Germans made extravagant claims of enemy tanks destroyed during the battle. At the same time German records indicate that few German tanks were total losses. Gunners and tank commanders on both sides claimed a tank if they fired and it stopped, effectively putting it out of action. However, both Germans and Russians had extremely efficient salvage and repair organizations for damaged tanks. For every tank written off as a total loss, three were repaired and returned to battle in a few days. On July 13, the number of operational Panthers had dropped to 38 of the original 200, while 31 had been declared total losses and 131 were still being repaired.[26] None of the Panthers had been involved in the clash southwest of Prokorovka, so these losses were the result of the slow grinding attrition that took place as the 48th Panzer Corps fought its way north on the Oboyan road.

The Germans did a study of tank and assault gun repairs in October and November 1943. In October 973 tanks were repaired and 450 written off as lost, 652 assault guns were repaired and 208 written off, and 200 self-propelled guns were repaired and only 62 were written off, for a total of 1,825 armored vehicles repaired and only 720 lost. In November the numbers were very similar: 911 tanks repaired and 524 lost, 698 assault guns repaired and 243 lost, and 195 self-propelled guns repaired and 20 lost, for a total of 1,804 repaired compared to 787 lost. Most of the repaired tanks would have been claimed as destroyed by the Soviet gunners that inflicted the damage. However, most of the vehicles were back in action within a few days, and very few were sent back to Germany for complete rebuilding.[27]

Unless the ammunition or fuel exploded and burned the tank or the turret was blown off the turret ring, the field repair crews could often return a tank to action in a matter of days. The easiest way to stop a tank was to damage the track. The track presented a large target and could be broken even with an antitank rifle. However, many tanks carried extra links, and the crew had jacks and tools to repair track damage themselves. A gunner could claim a hit on a tank and report it destroyed, but that same tank could reappear within a few hours.

Some German records included tanks that were both operable and in repair without distinction. Other records did indicate a total number and a second number reflecting those that were operable. Before the Kursk battle, over one-tenth of the German tanks were listed as inoperable. In the course of the battle, many German tanks damaged by the Russians would have become inoperable, but, since the Germans controlled the battlefields at nightfall throughout the first week, after dark their salvage crews would tow damaged tanks to the repair shop. The damaged tanks continued on the roll of the unit, even though days might be needed for repairs. A turning point in the battle occurred later when the 4th Panzer Army commander issued a special order requiring all disabled tanks on the battlefield that could not be towed immediately to the rear to be destroyed with explosives to prevent capture by the Russians. This order was a tacit admission that the battle was lost and that the Russians would control the battlefields in the future.

The Russian divisions had fought well, and their training and morale were good according to a German report on the evening of July 5. The Soviet artillery and antitank gunnery had improved, and very few Russian tanks were destroyed. The report noted that major elements, including the artillery of the front line divisions, had withdrawn to the second line without heavy losses and had heavily reinforced the second line.[28] The Red Air Force was very active during the attack, strafing and bombing the advancing Germans.[29]

Better progress was needed if the trap was to be sprung in four or five days before the Soviets had time to react. The Germans had to break through a defense line each morning and close up to the next line by that evening to give the infantry and artillery time to advance overnight.

Army Detachment Kempf at Belgorod on the right of the 4th Panzer Army made even less progress on the first day. At 10:30 on the night before the attack, the Russians unleashed a five-minute barrage, followed three hours later by a second five-minute barrage, and additional short barrages designed to disrupt the German troop assembly.[30] The final barrage came at 2 A.M. concentrated on the bridgehead over the North Donets at Belgorod.[31]

At 2:25 A.M., the Kempf Detachment attacked with the 3rd Panzer Corps on the north and Corps Raus on the south preceded by a thirty-minute bombardment on a 25 km front from Belgorod to Maslova Pristani along the North Donets River. At 3:30 A.M. the Soviet 7th Guards Army countered with artillery and air attacks on German artillery positions and tank concentrations. The Germans crossed the North Donets at eight points. In the 3rd Panzer Corps sector at Belgorod the 6th Panzer Division, with the support of infantry elements and the artillery of the 168th Infantry Division, attacked north of

Belgorod toward Staryi Gorod, a few km east, forcing the south flank of the
81st Guards Rifle Division to retreat to the east. Another battle group of the
6th Panzer Division took Chernaia Poliana 5 km northwest of Belgorod forcing back the north flank of the 81st Guards Rifle Division. However, by
evening the Russians had reinforced the line at Staryi Gorod and had held the
6th Panzer Division advance to less than 3 km.[32]

The 19th Panzer Division attacked with thirty tanks, including some Tigers,
from the bridgehead southeast of Belgorod at Michailovka encountering stiff
Soviet resistance. By 11 A.M. the 19th Panzer had suffered heavy losses, but was
firmly established on the east ride of the Donets River. At 1 P.M. the 19th Panzer
attacked with 100 tanks and lost nineteen to Soviet tank destroyer guns. However elements of the 81st Guards Rifle Division were still delaying the 19th
Panzer at Michailovka on the North Donets.[33] During the night, the German
engineers completed a bridge at Pushkarnoie, southwest of Belgorod, that
enabled the 19th Panzer Division to bring its tanks across the river during the
night of July 5–6.[34]

The 7th Panzer Division crossed the river and built a bridge west of
Dorobushino, 12 km south of Belgorod. The 7th Panzer encountered stiff resistance and was stalled by the 78th Guards Rifle Division at the rail line that passed
through Dorobushino. The 78th Guards Rifle Division was reinforced by the
73rd Guards Rifle Division, but by evening both divisions were driven back several km to Razumnoe on the rail line from the south, located on the east bank of
the North Donets. The Germans occupied the town after heavy street fighting
and breaking up a Soviet tank supported counterattack. By nightfall the 7th
Panzer had a tank group on a hill near Krutoi Log, 5 km farther east.[35]

By evening the 3rd Panzer Corps had its left flank with the 6th Panzer Division at Staryi Oskol, but was under heavy Soviet fire from the north that halted
progress and had not cleared the first line of defense. The 19th Panzer Division had encountered strong opposition and was held up in the first line of
defense at Michailovka. The 7th Panzer Division had broken through the first
line and was halfway to the second line at Krutoi Log.[36] The events of the day
had not been favorable, as the 3rd Panzer Corps had even failed to pierce the
first line of defense, except at Dorobushino, in the 7th Panzer Division sector.

During the night, elements of the 6th Panzer Division withdrew from the
north flank and crossed the Donets about 12 km south on the 7th Panzer Division bridge and became the corps reserve in the area west of Krutoi Log.[37]
Although this move was in the classic tradition of support success (the break
through of the 7th Panzer) and starve failure (the inability to break through
the 81st Guards Division at Staryi Gorod), the failure to keep the 6th Panzer
on the north flank to clear the Soviet 81st Guards and 375th Rifle Divisions
from the east bank of the Novi Donets branch would haunt the overall offen-

sive. The Soviets quickly fed reinforcements into the salient that divided the 2nd SS Panzer Corps and the 3rd Panzer Corps, forcing the 2nd SS Panzer Corps to hold back the Death Head SS Panzer Grenadier Division to serve as a flank guard for several days, depriving the 2nd SS Panzer Corps spearhead of the much needed punch of a third division. Even when replaced by the 167th Infantry Division, the Death Head Division had to leave behind significant elements to bolster the 167th Division against continuous Soviet counterattacks. The decision to move the 6th Panzer Division may have been based on an optimistic evaluation of the situation with the expectation that by passing the 6th Panzer to the east of the heavy Soviet concentration at Staryi Gorod, the Germans would trap additional Soviet units, rather than drive them north and east out of the intended pocket.

South of the 3rd Panzer Corps, in the center of Army Detachment Kempf, Corps Raus with the 106th and 320th Infantry Divisions made little progress. The 106th Division with the support of the 905th Assault Gun Battalion crossed the Donets after a brief exchange of fire, and the engineers built an eight-ton bridge, not strong enough to carry the assault guns. The division advanced to the railway at Toblinka a few miles east of the river, but was stopped by a tank supported attack by the 72nd Guards Rifle Division reinforced by elements of the 213th Rifle Division. The 320th Division crossed the Donets after heavy fighting and by noon had reached the railroad connecting Belgorod to the south at Masslova Priston, a few km east of the river. Corps Raus failed to penetrate the first line of defense and failed to reach its July 5 objectives.[38]

The southernmost corps of Army Detachment Kempf, the 42nd Corps. crossed the Donets but was halted immediately by a minefield. The two southern corps of Army Detachment Kempf had managed to cross the Donets but had failed to advance more than a few km and were bogged down in the Soviet first line of defense.[39]

The entire effort of Army Detachment Kempf had been hampered by heavy Soviet artillery fire that delayed the building of bridges, and consequently the assault guns and the heavy antitank guns could not cross the river. Faced with very strong defensive positions without the help of assault guns or antitank guns to ward off Soviet tank supported counterattacks, the two infantry corps were unable to drive the Russians from their positions. The Red Air Force was very active on the first day of the battle on the south shoulder. The 2nd Air Army flew 1,322 missions and the 17th Air Army flew 569 missions, a total of 1,891 missions in support of the 6th Guards Army. The advancing German tanks had to be wary of air attack the entire day, a disadvantage that the Luftwaffe had usually placed on its opponents. At the same time, Soviet fighters protected the withdrawing tanks and infantry from German attack, a luxury not enjoyed to any great measure in any previous battle.

The day was one of victory for the Germans, but they had not gained enough to ensure the goal of encircling large Soviet forces. There were six defense lines between the start line and Kursk in the south and four lines in the north. If the trap were to close before the Russians made countermoves and brought up reserves, it was imperative that at least one line be broken each day, and the German forces had to close up to the next line by evening to allow the artillery and infantry to reposition during the night. This goal was achieved by only two of the SS panzer grenadier divisions.

The remainder of the German units failed to close up to the second line. On the left, the 332nd Infantry Division did pivot the 71st Guards Division to the west, but was experiencing counterattacks by evening. The remainder of the 48th Panzer Corps was able to advance only halfway to the second defense line after breaking through the first line in the morning. The Gross Deutschland was stopped at Bukovka by late afternoon. Although the Adolf Hitler and Reich Divisions did reach the second line by evening, the Death Head Division merely shunted the 375th Rifle Division to the east and was experiencing counterattacks during the afternoon. Several days would pass before the Death Head Division would be able to extricate itself and join the spearhead to the north. Army Detachment Kempf had a poor day, even though it was able to cross the Donets at many points. Once across the Donets, the attack was stalled while the German engineers built bridges to bring the panzers across the river. By the end of the day, most of the Army Detachment was still embroiled in the first line of defense. On the left flank of the Army Detachment, the 6th Panzer Division was withdrawn in the evening to reinforce the attack of the right flank of the 3rd Panzer Corps. Rather than resuming the attack on the following day and rolling up the 81st Guards Division and the 375th Rifle Division and clearing the Russian units on the west bank of the Novi Donets, the 6th Panzer Division withdrew and left the Russians in a position to pressure the Death Head Division on the right flank of the 2nd Panzer Corps.

The next day would be critical to the success of the German operation. The plan called for closing the pocket in four days, requiring the Germans to advance about 30 km per day. In the south, the 48th Panzer Corps was delayed at the second line and then stopped by the dug-in 1st Tank Army before it even approached the third line at Oboyan. The SS Panzer Crops overran two lines of defense and penetrated the third line at Prokorovka, but they were continually harassed by the counterattacks of Soviet tank units that slowed their advance.

While the strength of the German panzer divisions eroded gradually with few replacements coming from Germany, the Soviets were apparently able to replace many of their tank losses, either through repairing damaged tanks, receiving new ones from the several huge tank depots in the area, or absorbing the surviving tanks from battered independent regiments and brigades.

Even after ten days of battle, the Russian 1st Tank Army, the 5th Guards Tank Army, and many independent tank and mechanized corps were still launching multiple attacks supported by sixty or more tanks all along the line of the southern bulge.

The offensive developed into a costly battle of attrition, not in the midst of complex defensive positions as stated in the Soviet version, but in relatively open country between the second and third defense lines as Russian infantry if supported by tanks continuously counterattacked the advancing Germans.

CHAPTER 9

Cracking the Second Defense Line

Although the 4th Panzer Army had broken through the first defense line at two points on July 5, the Soviet divisions withdrew as functional units according to the philosophy of elastic defense, rather than fighting in untenable positions to the last man. Possibly the Soviet divisions may have left hastily in the 2nd SS Corps sector, but very few prisoners were taken. In keeping with the concept of an elastic defense, the Soviet High Command and the commanders of the Voronezh and Central Fronts began moving reserves into the areas threatened by the three German armies. General Nikolai F. Vatutin, commander of the Voronezh Front, ordered his operational reserves to move on the afternoon of July 5. The 1st Tank Army, with the 6th Tank Corps, the 31st Tank Corps, and the 3rd Mechanized Corps, was ordered at 4 P.M. move into the second defense line behind the 6th Guards Army, and to arrive by midnight with orders to counterattack the following day and stop the 48th Panzer Corps' breakthrough on the road to Oboyan. The 6th Tank Corps moved to the rear of the 90th Guards Rifle Division on the east, the 3rd Mechanized Corps behind the 67th Guards Rifle Division in the center, and the 31st Tank Corps in reserve on the Oboyan road behind the boundary between the 67th and 52nd Guards Rifle Divisions on the west end of the 6th Guards Army.[1]

To hold back the 48th Panzer Corps, the 6th Guards Army received additional reinforcements in the west from the 40th Army, including the 29th Tank Destroyer Brigade and the 1244th and 869th Tank Destroyer Regiments, a total of over 100 antitank guns. The 309th Rifle Division also moved from the 40th Army to a reserve position on the Oboyan road. One regiment of the 309th Division was supported by the 59th Tank Regiment, the 86th Tank Brigade, the 1461st SU Regiment, and the 12th and 1689th Tank Destroyer Regiments, a total of more than 120 armored vehicles and 40 antitank guns. The 192nd Tank Brigade was moved from the 40th Army to the 38th Army on the west flank of the 4th Panzer Army. The 180th Tank Brigade came from the 38th Army to a reserve position near Semenovka on the west flank of the 6th Guards Army. These two tank brigades with over 100 tanks would continue to harass the west flank of the 48th Panzer Corps. The 161st Rifle Division was also inserted on the west flank of the bulge, but the Germans made little effort to expand the bulge westward, being content to contain the Soviet counterattacks.[2]

To counter the advance of the 2nd SS Panzer Corps, the Stavka ordered the 2nd and 10th Tank Corps to move up to Prokorovka behind the Voronezh Front. In the late evening of July 5, the 5th Guards Tank Army was placed on alert for possible movement to the front. The tank army was moved to the area of Staryl Oskol on the evening of July 6.[3]

The condition of the units arriving to counter the SS Corps was excellent. The Soviet 2nd Guards Tank Corps at Korotscha, nearly 60 km northeast of Belgorod on the morning of July 5, was ordered to move to an area south of Prokorovka to strike the east flank of the advancing 4th Panzer Army. The 2nd Guards Tank Corps was in excellent condition and would give the Reich Division considerable trouble for the next few days. One of the components of the corps, the 1st Motor Rifle Battalion of the 26th Guards Tank Brigade, was comprised of half Russians and half Uzbeks at an average age of thirty years. Replacements had arrived as late as the first week of June when forty men and five women came to the battalion from the 230th Replacement Regiment located at Budyenny, southeast of Novi Oskol in the rear of the Southwest Front.

At 3 P.M. of July 5, the 1st Motor Battalion was alerted to move in its three-ton trucks to Petropavlovka by midnight and then proceed on foot for four hours to Redin to rest and reorganize. The tank battalions of the brigade also left for the front on the evening of July 5. On the morning of July 6, the sudden German advance caught the 1st Motor Rifle Battalion of the brigade unawares and broke it up, capturing many prisoners.

Other units of the 2nd Guards Tank Corps at Korotscha were the 25th Guards Tank Brigade and the 6th Guards Motorized Brigade. The 25th Guards Tank Brigade was organized in six tank companies with infantry mounted on the tanks. The 6th Guards Motor Brigade had been in Kursk for refit, but did not receive the authorized motor vehicles. According to a prisoner, the morale of the brigade was very poor and the political commissars were unpopular. All of the units of the 2nd Guards Tank Corps left Korotscha on July 5 and arrived at Gostishevo on the morning of July 6 to assist the 375th Rifle Division versus the Death Head SS Division.[4]

The 5th Guards Tank Corps moved to the Lutschki area by midnight of July 5–6, to support the 52nd Guards Rifle Division, which was being driven back by the Adolf Hitler and Reich SS Divisions. The 5th Guards Tank Corps included the 20th, 21st, and 22nd Guards Tank Brigades, the 48th Guards Tank Regiment, and the 6th Guards Motor Brigade. The corps was equipped with over 200 T34s, KVs, and Churchill tanks and six battalions of infantry, stronger than a German panzer division.[5]

With the 1st Tank Army and the other reinforcements in place in the 6th Guards Army sector, Vatutin ordered attacks against the northern face of the 4th Panzer Army on the morning of July 6. The Germans reported heavy Soviet air and artillery activity in the morning. The 2nd Guards Tank Corps and the 5th Guards Tank Corps attacked in the early hours of July 6.[6] Manstein had given orders to the 4th Panzer Army to break through the second line on the morning of July 6. On the extreme west flank of the 4th Panzer Army, the 52nd German Corps with the 255th and 57th Divisions experienced minor attacks by Soviet reconnaissance units and some artillery fire. In the afternoon, the 255th Division attacked southwest of Bubny, which formed the anchor to the west side of the salient. The 57th Division observed Soviet units moving east from the 40th Army area.[7]

The 48th Panzer Corps attacked at 8:30 A.M. on July 6, and drove back the 71st, 67th, and 52nd Guards Divisions with heavy losses, closing up to the second line despite wet weather. At 11:30 the German 48th Panzer Corps attacked again, and at 2 P.M. the 71st Guards Division was hit by two regiments of the 332nd German Infantry Division at Krasnia Pochinok, about 8 km north of the start line at the west edge of the 48th Panzer Corps sector. The southern regiments of the 332nd Division drove elements of the 71st Soviet Division out of Korovino and the rest of the division back about 5 km to the second defense line at Rakovo on the Pena River. As the 71st Guards Rifle Division began to pivot to the west to maintain contact with the 38th Army, the 90th Guards Rifle Division filled the gap between the 71st and 67th Divisions with the support of the 6th Tank Corps and 3rd Mechanized Corps and momentarily halted the Gross Deutschland, which attacked eight times with 250 tanks and infantry. Both Russians and Germans suffered heavy losses.[8]

The Gross Deutschland met the Russian tanks south of Luchanino, but kept moving in a northeast direction on the road to Dubrova. Late in the afternoon of July 6, the Gross Deutschland Panther Battalion encountered a unit of the 6th Soviet Tank Corps south of the Pena River. A Gross Deutschland panzer grenadier regiment and the reconnaissance battalion attacked north between Luchanino and Alexeievka to the east and created a small bridgehead over the Pena. Farther west, the 3rd Panzer Division had encountered heavy fire and had withdrawn to Tscherkasskoie and secured the left flank of the Gross Deutschland between Tscherkasskoie and Iaoki. Later the 3rd Panzer also crossed the Pena River and established a small bridgehead against heavy opposition.[9]

To the right of the Gross Deutschland, 200 tanks and motorized infantry of the 11th Panzer Division struck the 67th Guards Division at 11:30 A.M. on July 6, and by 3 P.M. drove the division back through Trirechnoe and Dmitrievka to Olikova, over 10 km from the start line, but still several km south of the second defense line. The 11th Panzer Division also drove elements of the 52nd Guards

Division back with heavy losses to the second line east of Dubrova. In the after-noon, the 11th Panzer hit the Soviet position at Dubrova on the second defense line and heavy fighting took place in the main line of resistance. The 11th Panzer Division attacked the 1st Soviet Mechanized Brigade supporting the 67th Guards Division eight times with 100 tanks, and by evening the 67th Guards Division had been forced back to the second line. By the evening of July 6, the 48th Panzer Corps broke through the second line at Dubrova on a road leading to the Oboyan road in the 67th Rifle Division sector.[10]

The most dramatic German gains took place in the 2nd SS Panzer Corps sector. On the previous morning, July 5, elements of the 51st Soviet Guards Rifle Division had moved forward from the second line to slow the advance of the 2nd SS Panzer Corps with little success and suffered serious losses. On July 6, the Reich Division attacked at 9:30 A.M. and by 10:30 reported weak resist-ance. At 11:30 the Reich and Adolf Hitler Divisions overran the 51st Guards Division after the Germans broke through the second line at Iakovlevo on the Oboyan road in the 52nd Guards Rifle Division sector. Prisoners from the 52nd Division informed the Germans that many of the replacements in the 52nd Division were untrustworthy, newly mobilized men from the Kursk region and that many had deserted. The gap left between the 52nd and 51st Guards Divi-sions was closed by the 31st Tank Corps and the 1st Guards Tank Brigade of the 3rd Mechanized Corps north of Iakovlevo. At 1 P.M. of July 6, the Germans at Iakovlevo beat off an attack by thirty-eight Soviet tanks of the 230th Soviet Tank Regiment and elements of the 31st Tank Corps and the 3rd Mechanized Corps. The 100th Tank Brigade of the 31st Tank Corps moved up to Bol Maiachki behind the 52nd Rifle Division at 5 P.M.[11] At the same time thirty-three Soviet tanks with air support attacked the Adolf Hitler Division near Iakovlevo. The German destroyed six T34s and seven heavy antitank guns.[12]

In the Reich Division sector at 2 P.M. of July 6, the division was still fighting in Lutschki, but it pressed the attack home late in the day with up to ninety-five tanks and assault guns, encountering among other units, the 48th Heavy Guards Tank Regiment of the 5th Guards Tank Corps equipped with British Churchill tanks.[13] East of Lutschki, the 2nd Guards Tank Corps counterat-tacked in the afternoon of July 6, hitting the Reich Division and the north flank of the Death Head Division, halting the German advance on the west bank of the Novi Donets River with the help of two divisions from the 69th Army.[14] In the evening, the Reich Division moved several km north of Iakovlevo, encoun-tering the 5th Guards Tank Corps, which was supported by the 122nd Guards Artillery Regiment, that claimed nine of the Reich Division tanks. The Reich Division was in a defensive position northwest of Iakovlevo at midnight.[15]

On the east flank of the Reich Division, the 155th Rifle Regiment of the 52nd Guards Division and the 2nd Guards Tank Corps were holding a defensive position on the Novi Donets, the east branch of the Donets River. To the south along the Novi Donets, the 375th Rifle Division, the 496th Tank Destroyer Regiment, and the 96th Tank Brigade were defending Schopino and Ternovka against the south flank of the Death Head Division, straddling the Belgorod-Kursk road. Strong Soviet counterattacks with infantry riding on tanks came in the evening and were repulsed with heavy losses. The Death Head Division reported the destruction of fifteen Soviet tanks (including twelve American tanks) in an attack at 7 P.M. evening of July 6. The continued pressure prevented the Death Head Division from moving north to reinforce the spearhead.[16]

Although the 2nd SS Panzer Corps had moved about 5 km north during the day and had pierced the second line at Iakovlevo and at Lutschki, the fighting was intense, with heavy casualties on both sides. By midnight of July 6, the Germans were in the second defense line positions. The Germans reported that the Russians fought well in the fortified areas, but were weaker in the open country. The 2nd SS Corps reported that on July 6 they had captured 1,609 prisoners and destroyed or captured ninety Soviet tanks and eighty-three antitank guns, indicating a heavy commitment by the Soviets of their tank destroyer regiments and consequent losses, probably to the Tiger's 88mm guns, which outranged the Russian 76mm guns, while the Tiger armor withstood the 76mm fire except at a short range of 300 meters or so. The Soviets were fighting the German panzers with antitank guns as well as tanks. The Russian antitank guns were exacting a toll on the Pz IIIs, Pz IVs, and Panthers, sapping the strength of the panzer divisions.[17]

To the west, the 48th German Panzer corps failed to move very far up the road toward Oboyan in the face of the reinforced 1st Tank Army. The Red Air Force made a major contribution on the second day, flying 1,632 sorties compared to the German 899. German air support declined from the first day total of 1,958, while the Red Air Force was getting stronger.[18]

To the south of the Death Head Division, Army Detachment Kempf had been ordered on the evening of July 5 to drive through the first defense line of the 7th Guards Army position between the Donets River and the railroad leading south from Belgorod on the following day. The 6th Panzer Division had been stopped on July 5 by strong Soviet opposition, and therefore, was withdrawn and ordered to cross the Donets farther south.[19]

To bolster the 7th Soviet Guards Army, the 35th Guards Rifle Corps, including the 92nd, 93rd, and 94th Guards Rifle Divisions, was ordered to move forward to arrive at 3 A.M. of July 6. The 111th, 183rd, and 270th Rifle Divisions of the 69th Army moved into reserve positions north of Prokorovka.[20] To the south flank opposing Army Detachment Kempf, Vatutin sent the 25th Guards Rifle Corps supported by the 31st Tank Destroyer Brigade, the 167th Tank Regiment, the 1438th SU Regiment, an artillery regiment, and two rocket launcher regiments to reinforce the second defense line east of Belgorod. This powerful force gathered in the region of Batratskaia Dacha 15 km east of the Donets River just to the rear of the second defense line and directly in the path of the advancing 19th Panzer Division. A second group, including the 201st Tank Brigade, the 1529th SU Regiment, and the 1669th Tank Destroyer Regiment assembled at Gremiachii between the first and second defense lines in front of the German 7th Panzer Division.[21]

To the south, in the path of the 320th German Infantry Division, another shock group gathered around Pristani, including the 24th Guards Rifle Corps, the 213th Rifle Division, and the 27th Tank Brigade. A fourth group, consisting of the 15th Guards Rifle Division and the 111th Rifle Division, moved into Nekludovo on the Koren River about 10 km behind the second defense line. All of these reserves, totaling nine rifle divisions, with more than 160 tanks, 40 self-propelled guns, and 80 antitank guns launched an attack at 3:30 A.M. of July 6 on the two panzer divisions and three infantry divisions that has crossed the Donets on July 5.[22]

The Soviet attacks ran head on to advancing German units. At 5 A.M. on July 6, the 7th and 19th Panzer Divisions of the 3rd Panzer Corps attacked eastward. In the south the 7th Panzer Division advanced about 5 km to Krutoi Log. The German 168th Infantry Division all had some success, reaching Staryi Gorod 5 km northeast of Belgorod, and finally broke through the first Soviet defense line southeast of Michailovka (about 5 km southeast of Belgorod). The 19th Panzer Division in the center drove the Soviet 78th Guards Rifle Division back to Blisnaiaia Igumenka, over 10 km northeast of Belgorod and attacked the flank of the Russians holding up the 168th Division. Despite heavy air attacks during the night of July 5–6, the 6th Panzer Division began crossing the Donets using the bridges built by the 7th Panzer Division, but it did not complete the crossing until 7 A.M. on July 6, and did not take part in the attack. Later in the day, the 6th Panzer Division was inserted between the 7th and 19th Panzer Divisions south of Belgorod. The 6th Panzer crossed the Rasumnoie River at Miassoiedovo 18 km east of Belgorod behind the 7th Panzer Division and then turned north in the direction of Melekovo just south of the Belgorod-Korotscha road about 22 km northeast of Belgorod. During July 6. The three panzer divisions of the 3rd Panzer Corps attacked with 300 tanks and despite heavy losses drove the Soviet defenders back.[23]

To the south, Corps Raus and the 42nd German Corps broke into the Soviet defense line in the morning of July 6. Later Corps Raus was counterattacked by a battalion-sized force with tank support aimed at the bridgehead. The Germans encountered stiff resistance between the Donets and Koren Rivers. The 78th Soviet Rifle Division fought very hard at the railroad line southeast of Belgorod.[24] Later in the day, the 106th Infantry Division was attached to the 7th

Panzer Division at Krutoi Log 15 km southeast of Belgorod and advanced due east driving back the Soviet 73rd Guards Rifle Division. The German right flank regiment made good progress, as the Russians fell back to the second defense line running north-south about 18 km east of the Donets River. By noon the 106th Division approached the second defense line at Poliana, 8 km southwest of Krutoi Log. The 320th German Infantry Division, the other division in Corps Raus, maintained liaison with the 106th Division, but neither division could make much headway against the well-developed complex defense line that was being reinforced by the 24th Soviet Guards Rifle Corps.[25]

By late afternoon of July 6, Vatutin was alarmed at the German progress against the 6th and 7th Guards Armies and asked the Stavka for an additional four tank corps and two air corps. At 6:30 P.M. Vassilevsky, the Stavka representative with Vatutin, received a telegram informing him that a tank corps would be sent to Prokorovki 30 km southeast of Oboyan, and another to Korotscha 60 km northeast of Belgorod. The 10th Tank Corps (5th Guards Army) was ordered to Iadova northeast of Prokorovka, and the 2nd Tank Corps from the Southwest Front was sent to the Oskol River, east of Prokorovka at Kamishevka.[26] The four tank corps, each larger than a German panzer division, arrived July 7.

Despite the advances of the 4th Panzer Army and Army Detachment Kempf, the Germans had moved only 10 to 15 km in two days from the start line of July 5, and the distance to Kursk was still over 110 km. German success depended on closing the gap between the 4th Panzer Army and the 9th Army at Kursk before the Soviet reserves arrived. The delays encountered by the fierce Russian resistance on the first day had already jeopardized the German chances for success, and the rapid movement of reserves on the night of July 5–6 reduced the German chances enormously. The delays encountered on July 6 as the Soviet reinforcements attacked the advancing Germans in the zone between the first and second defense further reduced the German chances. Unless events took a radical turn to German favor, there would be no hope of surrounding a large body of Soviet troops.

The weather on July 7 was warm and sunny and the roads were in excellent condition, a factor of major significance in the events of the day. The attacks of Army Detachment Kempf were confined to the northern sector held by the 3rd Panzer Corps. In the south, Corps Raus was on the defensive with most of the corps antiaircraft guns employed in the antitank role, as the Russians put pressure on the 320th Infantry Division defending the bridgehead at Besliudovka. The Russians attacked repeatedly with infantry supported by tanks. South of Volkovo the German defense line was still west of the Donets River, the 42nd German Corps confining itself to providing supporting artillery fire.[27]

The Soviet 7th Guards Army was reinforced during July 7 on the east flank of the 3rd Panzer Corps breakthrough by units of the 35th Guards Rifle Corps, the 92nd Guards Rifle Division, and the 31st Tank Brigade. The German 3rd Panzer Corps turned to strike almost due north on July 7, exposing its east flank. To reinforce the spearhead, the 168th Infantry Division replaced the 19th Panzer Division, taking over the defensive positions on its left, east of the Donets River at Michailovka, a heavily fortified region southeast of Belgorod, which was held by the 81st Soviet Guards Rifle Division. The 235th Soviet Rifle Regiment was subjected to heavy German attacks, and though the regiment destroyed five German tanks, the division was forced back from 3 to 5 km.[28]

The 19th Panzer Division concentrated its efforts on the 92nd and 94th Guards Rifle Divisions of the 35th Guards Corps around Blishniaia Igumenka, 10 km northeast of Michailovka. The 6th Panzer, 5 km to the east of the 19th Panzer Division, drove steadily north reaching a position 2 km north of Sevrukovo. The 7th Panzer Division provided security for the east flank along with the 106th Infantry Division in the face of strong Soviet attack by the 25th Guards Rifle Corps that inflicted heavy losses on the Germans. The Soviets had excellent air support provided by elements of the 17th Air Army from the Southwest Front.[29]

To the north, in the 2nd SS Panzer Corps sector, the Germans continued to advance. On the evening of July 6, Manstein had ordered the 4th Panzer Army to drive north about 20 km on July 7 to reach the third Soviet defense line that stretched from just south of Oboyan to Prokorovka. The SS Corps was to move northeast to the Psel River on the road to Prokorovka and then continue without pause to Kursk. The Psel River ran about 40 km southeast from Oboyan before turning a right angle to the northeast, passing about 5 km northwest of Prokorovka. The wedge-shaped parcel of countryside protected by the Psel River would provide a haven for Soviet forces threatening the left flank of the SS Corps drive on Prokorovka. The 48th Panzer Corps to the left, was ordered to reach the Psel River downriver on a line from Schipy to Olchovskii, cross the river, and move on to Oboyan. These were optimistic objectives, but if the operation were to succeed, the German rate of advance had to increase dramatically.[30]

General Hermann Hoth, the 4th Panzer Army commander, committed 700 tanks to the attack on the morning of July 7. To the west on the 2nd SS Panzer Corps front, the Adolf Hitler Division on the left and the Reich Division on the right advanced north of the second line of defense. Moving out at 6 A.M. from the second defense line at Iakovlevo and Prokovka with strong support from the Stukas of the 8th Air Corps, the two divisions moved along the road to Prokovka fighting in open country and driving the weary 51st Guards Rifle Division north. Late in the morning of July 7, elements of the 5th Guards Tank

Corps with from thirty to sixty tanks struck the left flank of the Adolf Hitler Division from northwest of Iakovlevo. At Mikailovka north of Iakovlevo on the Oboyan road, the 1st Guards Tank Brigade was attacked, first by 100 German aircraft, and then by thirty German tanks and an infantry battalion. A few km north of Mikailovka at Prokovka, the 49th Soviet Tank Brigade delayed the Adolf Hitler Division, but by 10 A.M. the division had taken Prokovka. The 31st Soviet Tank Corps, including the 100th Tank Brigade and reinforced by the 29th Tank Destroyer Brigade and 1244th Tank Destroyer Regiment (a total of over eighty antitank guns), tried to hold the Adolf Hitler Division at Ulianovka just east of Prokovka, but were driven north over 10 km to Gresnoie. The 31st Tank Corps then retreated north on the Oboyan road with the 3rd Mechanized Corps. By the evening of July 7, the 52nd Guards Rifle Division had withdrawn 12 km to the north bank of the Psel River at Poleiaevo. The Adolf Hitler Division had reached North Lutschki about 5 km northeast of Ulianov by 3 P.M.[31]

On the right, the Reich Division reached Kalinin from South Lutschki without meeting heavy resistance, and advanced about 8 km from its starting point by 7:35 A.M. on July 7. At 9:20 a very heavy Soviet attack, supported by thirty-five T34s, came from the northwest. Additional heavy tank battles took place between Kalinin and Teterevino including an attack at 10:30 by thirty T34s of the 2nd Soviet Tank Corps which were beaten off by German tanks after a hard battle. The Reich Division advanced over 10 km and reached Teterevino on the Prokorovka road, a major gain, but still over 10 km short of the third line of defense, the day's objective. The Fuhrer Panzer Grenadier Regiment of the Reich Division formed a flank security line from Lutschki to Kalinin while the Reich tanks were driving north. Another attack hit the Reich Division northwest of Teterevino. The Luftwaffe played a major role in beating off the Soviet tank attacks when at 1:45 P.M. on July 7, Stukas destroyed a Soviet tank unit near Iasnaia Poliana northeast of Teterevino. At nightfall the SS Corps halted and formed strong defensive positions on both flanks, as it had moved about 10 km ahead of the adjoining German forces.[32]

The Death Head Division and elements of the 168th Infantry Division were guarding the east flank of the corps in the Schopino area on the Novi Donets River about 5 km east of the first line of defense. Opposite the Death Head Division was the 375th Soviet Rifle Division, holding the west bank of the Novi Donets with the help of the 2nd Guards Tank Corps. At 7 P.M. on July 7, the Death Head Division and the 168th Infantry Division reached the highway west of Schopino and drove the Soviets across the river. The Soviet reacted with heavy air attacks by 178 aircraft and at 11 P.M., a heavy artillery barrage on the infantry of the Death Head Division. By nightfall, the Death Head Division had formed a defensive line on the high ground about 2 km west of the river on a broad front.[33]

On the west sector of the 4th Panzer Army front, the 48th Panzer Corps was still involved in bitter fighting in the second defense line on the morning of July 7, plagued by Soviet tank supported counterattacks. Infantry elements of the 3rd Panzer Division had been providing security for the west flank during the morning, but were relieved in the afternoon by the 332nd Infantry Division and moved north to support the spearhead. The tank regiment of the division attacked the 90th Guards Rifle Division north of Luchanino on the Pena River. To the east, the 3rd Panzer tanks attacked at dawn on July 7 and advanced to a position 3 km northeast of Iakovlevo, pushing the 52nd Guards Rifle Division northward.[34]

The 11th Panzer Division in the center of the corps sector attacked at 3 A.M. on July 7 and took the high ground 1.5 km east of Dubrova, driving back the 67th Guards Rifle Division. The Gross Deutschland broke through the defense line at Dubrova on the Oboyan road and at 2:30 P.M. crossed the Pena River. A half hour later the 11th Panzer Division and the Gross Deutschland encountered the 3rd Soviet Mechanized Corps and the 31st Tank Corps of the 1st Tank Army on the Oboyan road. The series of attacks launched by the Germans lasted for three hours. The 3rd Battery of the 35th Tank Destroyer Regiment attached to the 3rd Mechanized Corps engaged thirty-seven German tanks, including some Tigers, at a range of 200 to 300 meters, putting five Tigers out of action. The 112th Soviet Tank Brigade blocked the Gross Deutschland north of Sirtsevo, destroying or damaging fifteen German tanks including six Tigers at a cost to themselves of fifteen tanks.[35]

The 4th Panzer Army commander had ordered the 48th Panzer Corps to advance 10 km to Verchopenie and to Prokovka 15 km east and 5 km north of the second defense line on July 7. These goals were only halfway to the third defense line, but the corps was far short of the objectives by the evening of July 7. The 48th Panzer Corps could not keep up with the 2nd SS Panzer Corps. Instead the corps was still entangled in the second line of defense. The reason for the delay was that while the SS Corps was pushing back the badly mauled 51st Guards Rifle Division, the 48th Panzer was faced with three rifle divisions (the 90th Guards, the 67th Guards, and 52nd Guards) backed up by three armored corps of the 1st Tank Army (the 6th Tank, 3rd Mechanized, and 31st Tank) that arrived during the day.[36]

Further reinforcements for the 1st Tank Army were arriving on the Oboyan road during July 7, the 309th Rifle Division, three tank destroyer brigades (180 antitank guns), plus mortar, howitzer, and tank regiments from the 38th and 40th Army. The 40th Army, to the west of the 48th Panzer Corps Front, sent the 9th Antiaircraft Division to the 6th Guards Army, a testimonial of the destruction being wrought by the Luftwaffe attacks, and the 86th Tank Brigade to the 1st Tank Army, adding another 60 tanks to the 250 tanks already with that army. The Soviets were concentrating most of their reinforcements on the Oboyan road and placing little in the path of the 2nd SS Panzer Corps on the Prokorovka road, creating a void between the Soviet 6th and 7th Guards Armies. The 183rd Rifle Division was moved to Prokorovka from the 69th Army to fill the gap.[37]

A bright spot for the Germans, in addition to the advance of the SS corps, was the consolidation of the west flank of the 48th Panzer Corps as the Russian attacks were held, and, following Manstein's order, divisions of the 52nd German Corps moved north as far as the Pena River, replacing the 167th Infantry Division and elements of the 3rd Panzer Division. The 255th Division replaced elements of the 3rd Panzer Division at Potschinok north of Korovino blocking the 71st Guards Rifle Division. The 332nd German Division provided security on the left from Bubny to northwest of Korovino. At the same time, the Soviet 40th Army reinforced the troops facing the divisions of the 52nd German Corps, moving the 161st Rifle Division to Dmitrievka and launched a regiment-sized attack on the 255th German Infantry Division at the base of the bulge. The insertion of the 161st Rifle Division allowed the 71st Guards Rifle Division to side-step to the north and keep some pressure on the German 332nd Division. The 52nd German Corps sector was comparatively quiet on July 7, with the Germans experiencing minor attacks. At 2:30 P.M., the 167th German Division that had been relieved by the 52nd German Corps, was ordered to begin moving to the east flank of the 2nd SS Corps to relieve the Death Head Division from its security role around Schopino. The Death Head would then move north between the 48th Panzer Corps and the other two divisions of the SS Corps and add punch to the spearhead. The movements did not begin until the night of July 8 and 9, and even then Manstein hedged on the transfer, and retained one regiment of the 167th Division with the 48th Panzer Corps, which in turn required the Death Head to leave some units with the other two regiments when they took over the flank security.[38]

On the evening of July 7, Manstein, realizing the critical time factor, ordered both the SS Corps and the 48th Panzer Corps to drive north as soon as possible on the next day with all available forces. Unfortunately, the German High Command, concerned about the lack of success in the north by the 9th Army, diverted three groups of aircraft (3rd Fighter Group, 2nd Attack Group, and 3rd Bomber Group), roughly half of the aircraft of the 8th Air Corps, from supporting the 4th Panzer Army to aid the 9th Army. The lack of air support was sorely missed, as the Luftwaffe was a major threat to Soviet armored units moving toward the battle line.[39]

On the evening of July 7, the commander of the 4th Panzer Army learned from aerial reconnaissance of the gathering of Soviet tank units to the north of his troops. In addition to the 2nd Guards Tank Corps, exerting pressure on the right flank against the Death Head Division, two more armored corps were detected by air reconnaissance moving into the area on both sides of the Oboyan road about 5 km north of the second defense line in front of the 48th Panzer Corps. Luftwaffe also reported numerous truck columns moving into the 4th Panzer Army area from the east. Soviet resistance had been very strong during July 7, and the tank supported counterattacks along the Prokorovka and Oboyan roads had been troublesome. The Russian air units were causing difficulty as well.[40]

The severity of the fighting in the open country between the second and third defense lines was indicated by claims of Soviet losses made by the 2nd SS Panzer Corps. The corps claimed 499 prisoners and 121 tanks destroyed or captured, mostly by the Adolf Hitler and Reich Divisions. The Adolf Hitler Division claimed eighty-two tanks, while the Reich claimed only thirty-five, and the Death Head four. These losses reflected the attempts of the Soviet tank units to delay the movement of the SS Corps toward the third line. Only eighteen antitank guns were claimed by the SS Corps, indicating that despite the large number of Soviet antitank guns engaged, they were not overrun by the German panzers.[41]

The weather in the morning of July 8 was almost a repetition of the ideal weather of the previous three days. Although the skies were cloudy, the temperature was warm, and the roads were in excellent condition. There was, however, some rain in the afternoon, but the roads remained passable for vehicles.[42] The advances of July 8 would bring the 4th Panzer Army up to the third defense line, but it would also be the last day of major gains for the Germans. The 4th Panzer Army had received its orders at 8:15 on the previous evening to continue the attacks with the 48th Panzer Corps driving up the Oboyan road and the 2nd SS Panzer Corps driving toward Prokorovka.

On the 48th Panzer Corps Front, most of the Russians were east of Syrzevo on the Pena River 5 km north of Luchanino. The German corps was ordered to break through the elements of the 1st Soviet Tank Army and drive for Oboyan. With strong air support, the 3rd Panzer Division crossed the Pena River after breaking through the Soviet second defense line north of Luchanino. The left flank of the division then took Beresovka about 6 km to the north, driving back the 6th Tank Corps.

The 3rd Panzer Division had a stiff tank battle at Syrzevo at 6 P.M. of July 8. The 40th Soviet Army counterattacked from the left flank of the 90th Guards Rifle Division sector with the 112th Tank Brigade of the 6th Tank Corps and the 1st and 10th Mechanized Brigades of the 3rd Mechanized Corps, a total of over 100 tanks and seven battalions of motorized infantry, stronger than a panzer division.[43]

To the north, Soviets launched another attack 5 km north at Verchopenie with the 3rd Mechanized Brigade and the 49th Tank Brigade of the 3rd Mechanized Corps and the 200th Tank Brigade of the 6th Tank Corps plus some infantry of the 51st Guards and 67th Guards Rifle Division, again, a panzer-division-sized force. The German 3rd Panzer Division had been joined at Verchopenie by elements of the Gross Deutschland and according to Soviet sources had 100 tanks including twenty-eight Tigers. The Germans suffered heavy losses from the Soviet antitank guns. The 48th Panzer Corps had serious fight on its hands, but claimed that ninety-five Soviet tanks wert destroyed.[44]

To the left of the 3rd Panzer Division, the 52nd German Corps was moving north taking over the security of the west flank of the 4th Panzer Army, holding a line as far north of Alexeievka. During July 8, the 52nd Corps experienced hard fighting as the 40th Soviet Army pressed on the west base of the bulge. The 332nd Division destroyed three Soviet tanks during an attack near Korovino by the 71st Guards Rifle Division. The 255th German Division also suffered from battalion-sized attacks at Bubny by the 161st Soviet Rifle Division.[45]

In the center of the corps, the Gross Deutschland advanced north to Verchopenie where it had a stiff tank battle with the 3rd Soviet Mechanized Corps. On the right flank of the 48th Corps sector, the 11th Panzer Division, advancing northeast of the Oboyan road, was hit at noon on July 8 by forty to fifty Soviet tanks from Prokovka, probably the 31st and 5th Guards Tank Corps.[46]

By evening of July 8, the 48th Panzer Corps had gained more than 10 km still far short of the objective set by Manstein for the day. During the rest of the offensive the corps would gain little more than 5 km, as it faced the strongly entrenched 1st Soviet Tank Army and the rifle divisions of the 6th Guards Army. Elements of the Soviet 10th Tank Corps from the Voronezh Front Reserve were arriving in the afternoon of July 8 taking a position opposing the left flank of the 3rd Panzer Division. The road to Oboyan was firmly defended, and the three depleted panzer divisions of the 48th Panzer Corps had no hope of breaking through an enemy that now outnumbered them.[47]

To the east of the 48th Panzer Corps, on the 2nd SS Corps front the Adolf Hitler Division was in the Teterevino area on the evening of July 7, the Reich was on its right between Petrovskii and Kalinin, and the Death Head and the 168th Infantry Division were providing security for the east flank along the Novi Donets.[48] At 9 P.M. of July 7, orders were issued for the following day. The Reich Division was to continue northeast, but the Adolf Hitler was to turn to the northwest against Soviet units south of the Psel River to assist the 11th Panzer Division of the 48th Panzer Corps in its drive for Oboyan. Four of the six panzer divisions in the army were to concentrate on the Oboyan road with the Death Head Division on the way, while only the Reich Division would continue toward Prokorovka.

The Russians were moving reserves during the evening of July 7 and throughout July 8 to the Prokorovka area to block the 2nd SS Panzer Corps. Manstein had ample evidence that both the 69th Soviet Army and the 5th Guards Tank Army were moving to bar the Nazi advance. The Germans had learned the previous evening that Soviet reinforcements (probably elements of the 69th Soviet Army) arrived at Ivanovskii directly in the path of the Reich Division. The Soviet 2nd Tank Corps moved into position south of Prokorovka by the morning of July 8, backing up the third line of defense that ran just in front of Prokorovka.[49]

During the morning of July 8, there were heavy air raids by the Soviet Air Force all along the 4th Panzer Army Front.[50] At 5 A.M., the 1st Battalion of the Adolf Hitler Panzer Regiment launched an attack from Prokovka at the junction of the Oboyan and Prokorovka roads. The Hitler Division encountered nine T34s at 6 A.M. and destroyed one. By 8 A.M. the panzer regiment of the Adolf Hitler passed through Maliie Maiatschki, nearly 15 km north of the second defense line, and drove north toward Gresnoie. The panzers had advanced to a point southwest of Visselyi, 5 km north, where they encountered the 31sth Soviet Tank Brigade, the 192nd Tank Brigade, the 29th Tank Destroyer Brigade, and elements of the 51st Guards Rifle Division at 9:20. A major battle between tanks supported by infantry lasted all day over a 15 km front. The Hitler Division met four T34s at Lutschki at 11:30 and destroyed them, engaged another four T34s at Prokovka at the same time with no success, and destroyed four T34s north of Bol Maiatschki at noon. The Russians were not cleared from Maliie Maiatschki until 2:30 P.M. on July 8.

The Adolf Hitler Division drove back the Soviet units holding Visselyi by 5 P.M., but then withdrew southwest to Lutschki for the night. A probing attack at 6:30 at Visselyi ran into a Soviet antitank gun line, and two Tigers were hit.[51] Although the Adolf Hitler Division had made good progress during July 8, contact with the 48th Panzer Corps was lost as the right flank of the latter corps was held up at Pokrovskii, 5 km west of Maliie Maiatschki on the Oboyan road.[52]

Following the orders of July 7, the Reich Division of the 2nd SS Panzer Corps relieved its panzer and half track units from defensive positions on the right flank and concentrated the panzer regiment, the 3rd Battalion of the Der Fuhrer Regiment (in half tracks) and the 3rd Battalion of the artillery regiment (self-propelled) at Teterevino by 8 A.M. The reconnaissance battalion joined the panzer group at 9 A.M. The group attacked at 8 and, after a brutal tank battle with the Soviet 5th Guards Tank Corps, turned in a northwest direction away from Prokorovka and cut behind the Soviet defenders to reach a hill east of Visselyi at 11 A.M., a 10 km advance. At 1:20 P.M. the Reich panzer group had another hard fight east of Kotschetovka after a farther 3 km advance. The Reich Division was then only 10 km south of the third defense line.[53]

By 6 P.M. of July 8 the infantry of the Reich Division reached Iasnaia-
Poliana, about 15 km southwest of Prokorovka, but ran into strong Soviet
defenses at the railroad just east of the town. By 8 the Reich Division had stabilized its front, but was forced to send its reconnaissance and assault gun battalions to reinforce the Reich infantry on the right flank.[54]

A crisis had emerged on the right flank of the 2nd SS Corps during the
morning hours of July 8. At 9 the infantry of the Adolf Hitler Division
Teterevino on the Prokorovka road was attacked by very strong forces of Soviet
motorized infantry and about 100 tanks of the 5th Guards Tank Army and by
the 10th Tank Corps and the 183rd Rifle Division. The Hitler Division sent its
assault gun battalion to help the infantry and the Luftwaffe attacked the Russian tanks from the air. At 5:30 P.M., the Luftwaffe 8th Corps sent four Stuka
groups, two bomber groups, and an attack group against the 5th Soviet Guards
Tank Army units north of Teterevino. The panzer regiment of the Reich Division was forced to turn and attack the Russian advance from the north. The
Reich tanks were very successful and throughout the evening and night of July
8 continued to destroy more Russian tanks. However, Soviet tanks broke
through the German defenses and nearly overran the supply depot of the Adolf
Hitler Division. The Russians were finally driven back by Hitler Division
infantry.[55]

South of Teterevino, between 11:30 A.M. and 5 P.M. on July 8, the Reich
Division infantry was attacked repeatedly by the 2nd Soviet Tank Corps. Forty
Soviet tanks attacked Teterevino at 3:30 P.M., and another group attacked at 4
in the area of North Lutschki and were stopped by a tank battalion and the
reconnaissance battalion of the Death Head Division that happened to be
passing through on their way north. Twenty Soviet tanks broke through the
German lines and dispersed the divisional artillery. At 11:30 A.M. and again at
1:15 P.M. the 2nd Soviet Guards Tank Corps attacked Kalinin. In the first attack
the Germans destroyed seven Soviet tanks, but five broke through the German
line. At 1:30 P.M. a third attack was made on Kalinin repulsed by the Deutschland Regiment of the Reich Division.

During July 8, the SS infantry was often left on its own to beat off the
Soviet tanks, while the tank regiments were speeding north. During the day,
the infantry destroyed one-third of the Soviet tanks claimed. Even the Luftwaffe was diverted to other areas, while the Soviet air attacks were very strong,
leaving the SS infantry guarding the right flank without much support.[56]

South of Lutschki, the Death Head Division was attacked on the morning
of July 8 by tanks of the 2nd Guards Tank Corps. At 11:45 A.M. forty Soviet
tanks supported by a small infantry component attacked at Visselyie and Ternovka on the Novi Donets River. At 2 that afternoon one battalion of the
Death Head Panzer Regiment and the divisional assault gun battalion were

fighting Russian tanks at Visselyie. At 2:45 another twenty-five Soviet tanks attacked south of Visselyie, and the battle was still in progress at 4:15.

Help was on the way. While one regiment of the 167th Infantry Division was still under 48th Panzer Corps command at Prokovka, about 10 km to the east of Visselyie, the other two regiments moved to Visselyie to relieve the Death Head Division taking over the new sector in the evening. The Death Head Division moved out and marched north on the night of July 8–9, arriving at its new sector west of the Adolf Hitler Division at 2 A.M. on July 9, too late to provide the needed strength to break through to the north on July 8.[57]

The 2nd SS Corps had to use all of its reserves to meet the simultaneous heavy attacks from the northwest, the northeast, and the east. The Reich Division used a battle group consisting of the Reich Engineer Battalion, the 627th Engineer Battalion, and the 3rd Battalion of the 818th Artillery Regiment to replace its reconnaissance battalion holding a defensive position between the Reich and Death Head Divisions.[58]

The first four days had been difficult for the Death Head Division. Beginning with 125 tanks and 39 assault guns on July 4, almost all of which were operational; by the evening of July 8, the division had only 99 tanks and 13 assault guns, and many of these were probably in the division repair shops. Only five of the eleven Tigers remained and twenty-eight of the forty-two modern Pz IVs.[59]

On the other hand, the 2nd SS Corps had its best day so far inflicting losses on the Russians and claimed 183 Soviet tanks destroyed or captured, bringing the total for four days to 401.[60] The total claimed by the 4th Panzer Army on July 8 was 195 Soviet tanks destroyed.[61] The 2nd SS Panzer Corps captured 2,192 prisoners on July 8, one-third of all the prisoners that it would take between July 5 and 15. The Soviets had a hard day under the heavy German assault, but were withdrawing in reasonably good order. Even the 51st Guards Rifle Division, pursued by two panzer divisions for four days, was still in satisfactory condition on July 8 and four days later was holding a 7 km sector on the front line. The SS Corps claimed 111 antitank guns destroyed or captured, equal to over five antitank regiments. The Germans had to destroy large numbers of antitank guns if their tanks were to gain freedom of action to exploit the breakthrough. The success of the Tigers in eliminating the Soviet antitank guns at long range meant that the Russian infantry was left unprotected from the Pz IVs and Pz IIIs.[62]

On the right of the 4th Panzer Army, Army Detachment Kempf was faced with heavy Soviet attacks on the east flank of its drive north on July 8. The 3rd Panzer Corps was striving to close the gap between the Kempf Detachment and the 4th Panzer Army by rolling up the Soviet forces between the two branches of the Donets River north of Belgorod, thereby freeing up the east flank of the 4th Panzer Army. On the morning of July 8, the 168th German Infantry Division was still blocked a few km east of Belgorod, and it attacked the 81st Guards Rifle Division at Staryi Gorod. To the right, the 19th Panzer and 6th Panzer Divisions launched an assault against the 35th Guards Rifle Corps, including the 92nd and 94th Guards Rifle Division. By noon the 6th Panzer had advanced on a wide front, although the 19th Panzer was held up by heavy artillery and rocket fire.

At 11 A.M. of July 8, the 19th Panzer Division advanced east of Blinei Igumenka, 5 km northwest of Staryi Gorod, and hit the 81st Soviet Rifle Division at 4 P.M. with 100 tanks and air attacks. By noon, 250 tanks of the 6th and 7th Panzer Divisions had broken through the Soviet second defense line at Melekovo, driving the 7th Guards Army northward through the second defense line and over 20 km east of the start line on July 5. The 94th Guards retreated eastward, while the 92nd Guards retreated northward. The 19th Panzer turned west and cleared Russian troops from the defensive positions around Danaia Igumenka. The fighting was bitter and both sides suffered heavy losses. By 7 P.M. of July 8 the Germans were in complete control of the Melekovo area.[63]

The 198th and 106th Infantry Divisions of Corps Raus, which were supposed to guard the east flank, could not keep up, and the 7th Panzer Division was obligated to provide security on the east of the corps. The Soviet 94th Guards Rifle Division with tank support launched attacks on the 7th Panzer north of Melekovo. The 92nd Guards Rifle Division also put pressure on the 6th Panzer Division to the north, and late on July 8 the Russians inserted the 305th Rifle Divisions between the two guards divisions, further endangering the flank of the 3rd Panzer Corps.[64]

Despite the potential danger in the east, the Germans persevered. The 198th Infantry Division was ordered to move north using motor transport to free up the 7th Panzer from its security duty. However, the 198th Division did not arrive by the evening of July 8, and the 7th Panzer was still tied down. A gap developed between the 3rd Panzer Corps and Corps Raus to the south, a dangerous situation in view of the strong Soviet forces in the vicinity.

The original mission of the 3rd Panzer Corps to drive east on the road to Korotscha to tie down Soviet reserves and possibly exploit the encirclement at Kursk had to be scrapped. During the evening of July 8, Manstein ordered the 6th and 19th Panzer to turn west on July 9 and cut off the Russian units northeast of Belgorod in the long narrow salient separating the 4th Panzer Army and Kempf Detachment. Lacking reserves of either infantry or tanks, Manstein abandoned one of the objectives of the offensive (Korotscha) and turned the 3rd Panzer Corps to the west and north to help the 2nd SS Corps. The Russians, however, had forestalled Manstein's plans to encircle the units between the two German armies. During the evening of July 8, the 2nd Soviet Tank

Corps had been withdrawn from the salient and moved north to put pressure on the Reich SS Division south of Prokorovka.[65]

On July 8, the Soviet reserves were pouring in to reinforce the embattled defenders against the drives by the 4th Panzer Army and Army Detachment Kempf. The 6th Guards Army received the 111th Guards Artillery Regiment, the 66th Rocket Launcher Regiment, and the 12th Tank Destroyer Regiment from the 40th Army. The 1st Tank Army received the 180th Tank Brigade and 222nd Tank Destroyer Regiment from the 38th Army; the 59th and 60th Tank Regiments and 4th Antitank Regiment from the 40th Army; and the 438th Tank Destroyer Regiment and 38th Rocket Launcher Regiment from the Steppe Front. The reinforcements included over 100 tanks and 60 antitank guns. The tank destroyer regiments were in addition to the 29th Tank Destroyer Brigade and the 869th and 1244th Tank Destroyer Regiments already on the Oboyan road with over 100 antitank guns. Together these regiments formed a formidable obstacle to any attempt to force the Soviet defenses with a tank-led attack.[66]

The 5th Guards Tank Army was moving on July 8 and by the following day was established about 10 km north of Prokorovka after a 360 km trip. The 5th Guards Tank Corps had already arrived on July 8, plus nearly 200 tanks of the 10th Tank Corps. The 5th Guards Army was transferred from the Steppe Front to the Voronezh Front and began a night march on the evening of July 8 to take up a position between the 5th Guards Tank Army at Prokorovka and the 6th Guards Army and 1st Tank Army on the Oboyan road.[67] In addition, the Stavka ordered the 47th Soviet Army to move from Rossoch, 100 km east, to the Korotscha area, about 55 km east of Belgorod, to reinforce the third line of defense behind the 7th Guards Army. The army was not employed before the Germans withdrew later in July, but formed a powerful reserve in the event of some unexpected German move.[68]

In the three days from July 6 to 8, the 4th Panzer Army and the Army Detachment Kempf had broken through the first and second defense lines and were fighting in the 10 km wide zone between the second and third lines. Progress on July 8 was better than in the previous days, but the two German armies were still only about 20 km from their start line, and it was another 100 km to Kursk.

In the four days since the initial attack, the Russians had brought sizable reserves to block the panzers. The Soviets had seven armored corps plus many independent tank brigades and regiments continually attacking all sides of the penetration. Even though the Germans had put about 500 Soviet tanks out of action, there were still about 1,500 more between the German spearheads and Kursk. Hundreds of antitank guns blocked every approach and the advances up the roads to Oboyan and Prokorovka slowed to a crawl in the succeeding days. In four days of hard fighting, the two German armies had advanced only

20 km, a day's march for a rifle company. Although the Germans had broken through two defense lines, there were six more to break before they could enter Kursk.

In order to encircle a large group of Russians in the Kursk bulge, the Germans had to close the pocket in no more than six days. Any longer and the Russians would have time to draw reserves, not only from the Steppe Front, but also the Stavka Reserve. The Germans had to advance about 20 km per day, destroying a defense line every day and preventing the survivors from reinforcing the next line. Instead in the first four days, the Germans had destroyed only two lines and advanced a total of only 20 km. The Soviet reserves were pouring in, and by the evening of July 8, they had outnumbered the Germans in every category, with more reserves on the way. Manstein was not aware of the magnitude of the Russian reserves and clung to the hope that the next day would bring a major breakthrough. Once the Russians had been soundly defeated, Manstein believed that the rate of advance would increase. To achieve the breakthrough, movement was under way to concentrate five of the six panzer divisions on the path to Oboyan.

The warm, sunny days had favored the Germans in the first days, but the clouds on July 8 seemed to portend that the next few days would not be bright for Germany as the Soviet commanders ordered additional armies to the area.

CHAPTER 10

Fighting for the Third Defense Line

The four days from July 9 to July 12 culminated in a wide-ranging battle on a 20 km arc southwest of Prokorovka that marked the high point of the German offensive. In the series of engagements over the next four days, the advance of the three panzer divisions of the 2nd SS Panzer Corps ground to a halt blocked by the 5th Soviet Guards Tank Army, ending any hope of surrounding Russian armies at Kursk.

At 2 P.M. on July 8, orders from 4th Panzer Army headquarters for action on July 9 were issued before the afternoon and evening struggle around Gresnoie and Verchopenie ended. Late in the day, the Hitler Division retired from its advance position at Vesselyi to Lutschki, about 5 km south. The earlier army orders were based on the assumption that the Soviet 1st Tank Army and the 2nd Guards and 5th Guards Tank Corps were all battered units and incapable of offering serious resistance.[1]

The early orders called for the 2nd SS Panzer Corps to halt on the south bank of the Psel River 10 km to the north with the new front extending from Prokorovka to the high ground east of Oboyan, after it had destroyed the Soviet tank units (3rd Mechanized and 31st Tank Corps) between Such Solotina on the west and Gresnoie on the east. The orders anticipated an advance of over 20 km by the Adolf Hitler Division on the left flank of the corps and over 10 km by the Death Head Division in the center, an ambitious goal and far beyond reality, even with the addition of the Death Head Division.[2]

Later on July 8, after learning of the lack of success at Gresnoie and Verchopenie, the 4th Panzer Army changed the mission of the 2nd SS Panzer Corps to defense on July 9, anticipating a drive toward Prokorovka on the following day. Based on the later orders, at 11 P.M. on July 8, 2nd SS Corps headquarters issued orders to its divisions. The Reich Division was to remain on the defensive southwest of Prokorovka, containing the Soviet forces there; the Hitler Division was to reestablish contact with the 11th Panzer Division at Kotschetovka, 10 km west of Koslovka; and the Death Head Division was to destroy the remnants of Soviet units south of the Psel River on a line running from Koslovka, 10 km west of Prokorovka, southeast to Teterevino on the Prokorovka road. One regiment of the 167th Infantry Division was to move between the 48th Panzer and 2nd SS Panzer Corps to restore a link between the two. The other two regiments of the division had relieved the Death Head Division on July 8. The Hitler Tank Regiment was to be withdrawn from the front and given an opportunity to repair and maintain its tanks in preparation for the next stage of the offensive.[3]

The Death Head Division was ordered to create a bridgehead over the Psel near Koslovka on July 9 in preparation for a broad advance to the east to cut off Prokorovka from the north. On the night of July 8–9, the Death Head Division moved some elements from its former position on the east flank of the 2nd SS Corps to a position between the Adolf Hitler and Reich Divisions, adding considerably to the offensive strength of the SS Corps. The Death Head had been involved in defensive actions that were less damaging to its strength than the offensive actions of the other two SS divisions.[4]

On the evening of July 8, both the Soviet commanders and Manstein were faced with difficult decisions. The pace of the battle had slowed, except between the 7th Guards Army and Army Detachment Kempf. Stalin had ordered Vatutin, commander of the Voronezh Front, to halt the German offensives at all costs. The planned Soviet offensives at Orel, on the Mius River, at Kharkov, and elsewhere were all on hold until the Germans were stopped, and there was no further danger of an encirclement at Kursk and a massive breakthrough toward Moscow. The reserves positioned for the other offensives would not be committed until there was no possibility that they might be needed to restore the situation at Kursk. Given this enormous responsibility, Vatutin wanted to play it safe and ordered the 1st Tank Army to dig in its armor, digging pits for each of the tanks so that only the turret was visible in the "hull down" position. Zhukov, the Stavka representative for the Central Front, disagreed and urged that the 1st Tank Army remain flexible and counterattack the Germans, rather than simply defending the Oboyan road. Stalin made the final decision and ordered Vasilevsky, the Stavka representative for the Voronezh Front, to immobilize the 1st Tank Army in defensive positions.[5] This action was obvious to the Germans, and removed any fear that the equivalent of six panzer divisions would overrun the 48th Panzer Corps and plunge into the rear of the 2nd SS Panzer Corps.

The morning of July 9 was cloudy, but warm and dry. There were local thunderstorms later in the day, but the roads were passable. The Hitler Division continued its movement to the northwest and moved through Ryliskii to just south of Such Solotino on the Oboyan road. Elements of the Hitler Division also moved due north and by the evening of July 9 had reached the Psel River 2 km east of Kotschetovka after driving back units of the 31st Soviet Tank Corps.[6]

Despite strong defenses, the Death Head Division cleared the 51st and 52nd Soviet Guards Rifle Divisions from the area northwest of Gresnoie by 10

A.M. on July 9. Panzer grenadiers in half tracks drove west and crossed a branch of the Psel River at Vesselyi, and another group reached high ground 2 km east of Kotschetovka, where it encountered Soviet tanks.[7] A third group drove north about 10 km to reach its objective, Koslovka on the Psel River, and began building a bridge as ordered.[8]

The Reich Division, with a regiment of the 167th Infantry Division attached, held its ground on July 9 on the east flank of the corps. Throughout the day the division was subjected to tank-supported attacks from the north by elements of the 5th Guards Mechanized Corps and the 2nd Tank Corps. Some of the attacks from Prokorovka included eighty to one hundred tanks. As the day wore on, the attacks grew weaker as the Russian units were worn down, despite the absorption of independent tank brigades and regiments by the Soviet tank corps to replace losses. Tanks of the Soviet 5th Guards Tank Army, supported by infantry, attacked the Hitler Division from the Petrovka area northwest of Prokorovka, but were repulsed.[9]

On the right flank of the 2nd SS Panzer Corps on July 9, the 2nd Guards Tank Corps attacked from the east bank of the Novi Donets, hitting the two regiments of the 167th Infantry Division. After some additional company-sized attacks, the remainder of the day was quiet. Overall July 9 was marked by hard fighting by the 2nd SS Panzer Corps, inflicting heavy damage on the stalwart Soviet defenders and absorbing considerable losses.[10]

On the opposite flank of the 4th Panzer Army on July 9, a reinforced Russian regiment attacked the 332nd German Infantry Division north of Beresovka in the 52nd Corps sector during the night of July 8–9 and drove the 332nd Division back. More attacks, some with tank support, were directed at Dmitrievka at the base of the salient against the 255th German Division.[11] Later on July 9, the 332nd Division pushed the 90th Guards Rifle Division west to Savidovka and, with elements of the 3rd Panzer Division, reached Rakovo on the west bank of the Pena River at noon. The Germans identified two rifle divisions and a tank brigade that had been holding sectors versus the German 2nd Army on the western face of the Kursk bulge. To counter the additional Soviet divisions in the 255th and 332nd Division sectors, General Hermann Hoth, the commander of the 4th Panzer Army, ordered the 52nd Corps to thin out the west end of its sector to provide more troops for the east end. Hoth also requested Manstein to order the 2nd German Army to launch attacks to pin the remaining Soviet units on the western end of the Kursk bulge. Manstein refused to issue the order on Hitler's instructions.[12]

In the center of the 4th Panzer Army, Hoth originally ordered the 48th Panzer Corps on July 8 to advance 15 km north to the Psel River at Schipy and to cross if possible.[13] Late in the evening of July 8, the 48th Panzer had achieved almost half of this objective, having advanced over 5 km up the

Oboyan road and taken high ground between Novosselovka on the east and
Kotschetovka on the west, forcing the 3rd Mechanized and 31st Tank Corps to
retreat. Given this success, all limits on the 48th Panzer Corps were removed,
and on July 9, the corps was to continue offensive action.[14]

On July 9, the Soviet 1st Tank Army and the 6th Guards Army facing the
48th Panzer Corps made only minor attacks on the Germans and were forced
to withdraw in some sectors. On the morning of July 9, elements of the 3rd
Soviet Mechanized Corps were still holding a line on the Pena River from
Krasnia Dubrova in the south to Novosselovka on the north with the 67th
Guards Rifle Division opposing the west flank of the 48th Panzer Corps. However, the threat to the German flank had been reduced by the disorganization
of the 6th Tank Corps when it was forced across the Pena River west of Kras-
naia Dubrova by the 3rd Panzer Division. The 3rd Panzer Division made headway at Syrzevo on the east bank of the Pena River, launching twelve attacks
during July 9 in the Syrzevo area with from sixty to one hundred tanks, driving
the 6th Tank Corps west and reaching the Pena River north of Alexeievka.[15]

The Gross Deutschland and 11th Panzer Divisions were ordered to com-
plete the destruction of the 6th Tank Corps and then defend positions on the
Oboyar road at Novosselovka, less than 25 km from Oboyan.[16] The Gross
Deutschland cleared the area east of Verchopenie a few km north of Syrzevo.
The 48th Panzer Corps made progress in the early morning of July 9 up the
Oboyan road with the Gross Deutschland and 11th Panzer Division against the
3rd Mechanized Corps, the 31st Tank Corps, and some elements of the 6th
Tank Corps. The Germans claimed 101 Soviet tanks along the Oboyan road on
July 9, while the Russians claimed to have destroyed 295 German tanks (both
numbers are open to interpretation). The Gross Deutschland Division attacked
Verchopenie on the west between Krasnia Dubrova and Novosselovka with 250
tanks, according to Soviet sources, but a more likely number would have been
about 125. The attack, supported by infantry and heavy air support, began at
11:30 A.M. The 67th Guards Division and the 200th Tank Brigade of the 6th
Tank Corps were heavily bombed, but they put up a stout defense with antitank
guns and tanks, especially the 1st Tank Battalion of the 200th Tank Brigade that
destroyed two Tigers and three medium tanks. Despite inflicting losses on the
Germans, the Soviets were forced to withdraw 6 to 8 km to the north. During
July 9, the 309th Rifle Division arrived on the Oboyan road to reinforce the 3rd
Mechanized Corps and the 67th Guards Division.[17]

On July 9, the 11th Panzer Division attacked the 31st Tank Corps and the
51st Guards Rifle Division defending Orlovka, located about 12 km southwest
of Oboyan with 200 tanks, according to the Russian reports. The number was
probably 100 tanks as other Russian sources place the total of only 500 Ger-

man tanks still operational on July 9 in five panzer divisions. The 309th Division also helped the 51st Guards Division when it arrived later in the day.[18]

On the evening of July 9, the Gross Deutschland reached Novosselovka, driving in a northwest direction to the Pena River, having advancing nearly 10 km. The 11th Panzer Division had moved toward Pokrovskii on the east side of the Oboyan road, parallel with Verchopenie, and advanced 9 km to the north, keeping pace with the Gross Deutschland.[19]

The German 2nd SS Panzer Corps claimed very little destruction of Soviet equipment during July 9. The Adolf Hitler claimed seventeen tanks destroyed or captured, and the other two divisions claimed one. The corps claimed thirty-seven antitank guns, a positive sign that they were continuing to break up the Soviet antitank gun lines. The capture of only sixty-two prisoners indicated that Russian units were holding up well in the face of the panzer attacks.[20]

On July 9, Army Detachment Kempf broke through the Soviet defensive positions. During the night before, Voronezh Front commander Vatutin had ordered the 7th Guards Army to carry out a night attack against the flank of the 3rd Panzer Corps. On July 9, leading the drive north, the 6th Panzer Division with 150 tanks attacked the 92nd Guards Rifle Division, took the high ground north of Melekovo 20 km northeast of Belgorod, and crossed the Belgorod-Korotscha road. The 19th Panzer and 7th Panzer Divisions advanced on either side of the 6th Panzer Division providing flank security. Later in the day the Russians vigorously counterattacked north of Melekovo and forced some elements of the 6th Panzer Division on defense. Other 6th Panzer units crossed the Rasumnoie River east of Olchovatka at the tip of the attack.[21]

To the south, only a few km from Belgorod, the 168th Infantry Division was still trying to overcome the fierce Russian resistance in the well-fortified area around Staryi Gorod. This center of resistance was the anchor for the deep salient that divided the 4th Panzer Army and the 3rd Panzer Corps. The Russians continued to reinforce the units in the salient. Corps Raus continued to provide security for the east flank of the army detachment and there was little activity on the front. Farther south the 42nd Corps had a very quiet day defending its original line.[22]

On July 9, Vatutin, impressed with the enormous importance of the position at Oboyan blocking the road to Kursk, reinforced the 6th Guards Army facing the 48th Panzer Corps. The 10th Tank Corps was already arriving on the Oboyan road, and the 204th and 184th Rifle Divisions, a tank brigade, three tank destroyer regiments, and four rocket launcher regiments were transferred to the Oboyan road sector from the Voronezh Front reserve, including over sixty tanks and sixty antitank guns. Soviet air support was ordered to give the Oboyan road defense priority over other areas on the following day, July 10.[23]

Vatutin also sent reserves to the east flank of the German salient on July 9.

The 69th Soviet Army was inserted north of the 7th Guards Army sector-between the two branches of the Donets River. The 69th Army had been reinforced by two rifle divisions from the Stavka reserve and took command of the units already in the area. The 69th Army then consisted of the 81st Guards, 89th Guards, 92nd Guards, 93rd Guards, 94th Guards, 107th, 183rd, 305th, and 375th Rifle Divisions, 2nd Guards Tank Corps, 148th Tank Regiment, 96th Tank Brigade, 30th Tank Destroyer Brigade, 27th Artillery Brigade, two tank destroyer regiments, and one rocket launcher regiment. The army held the sector opposed to the German 3rd Panzer Corps about midway between the second and third defensive lines.[24]

On the north face of the German penetration, the Stavka sent the 5th Guards Army to the north bank of the Psel River, between the Oboyan road and Prokorovka. The army reached the area northwest of Prokorovka by 1 P.M. of July 9 and by evening had settled into its new sector on the Psel River. At the same time, the Stavka ordered the 27th Army and 4th Guards Tank Corps to the Kursk area and the 53rd Army plus the 1st Mechanized Corps to the south of Kursk. These major movements, however, were not completed until July 13.[25]

Matters were not going as well as expected for the Germans. At noon on July 9, Manstein realized that Soviet resistance was slowing down the offensive and that additional forces would be required. The addition of the Death Head Division to the offensive thrust in the north had helped, but was clearly not enough to break through the ever increasing number of Soviet armored corps. At noon on July 9, Manstein ordered the 1st Panzer Army to send the 24th Panzer Corps with the Viking SS Panzer Grenadier Division and the 23rd Panzer Division to Kharkov to form a reserve for the Battle at Kursk. The corps moved by a night march to Kharkov, arriving on July 10.[26]

Manstein ordered the tank elements of the Adolf Hitler Division to continue in the Oboyan direction on July 10, while the panzer grenadiers of the Hitler Division attacked east toward Vinogradovka, about 7 km southwest of Prokorovka. The panzer grenadiers were to destroy the 2nd Tank Corps and the 183rd Soviet Rifle Division blocking the Prokorovka road and continue to drive up the railroad toward Prokorovka. The Reich Division and the two regiments of 167th Infantry Division were to maintain pressure on the Novi Donets on July 10 to pin the 2nd Guards Tank Corps and the 375th and 81st Guards Rifle Division, while the 3rd Panzer Corps of the Army Detachment Kempf continued its drive north.[27]

The Death Head Division was ordered to seize high ground on both banks of the Psel River northwest of Prokorovka on July 10. The division was to complete the bridge over the Psel River and advance toward Petrovka, northwest of Prokorovka. The 48th Panzer Corps was ordered to destroy the 6th Tank Corps and continue north on the Oboyan road.[28]

Although the pace of the advance was slow, the Germans retained the initiative on July 9. The Russians, on the other hand, continued the methodical buildup of reserves, adding two armies to forces opposing the SS Panzer Corps on July 9. Soviet tanks continued to counterattack and delay the German advance.

On the next day, July 10, nature turned against the Germans. The weather was cloudy with thunderstorms. The roads were muddy and mostly impassable except for horses and cross-country vehicles. The muddy conditions delayed activity on the ground, and the rain reduced the number of planes in the air.[29]

On the left of the 2nd SS Corps, the Death Head Division was scheduled on July 10 to begin a set piece attack against the 51st and 52nd Guards Rifle Divisions early in the morning. On the previous night, the German division had been the victim of a heavy Soviet artillery barrage, and the attack plans were disrupted. Rain in the early morning also upset the SS division preparations and prevented the Luftwaffe from supporting the attack. However the attack did get off at 10 A.M. on July 10 with a panzer grenadier regiment, the Hitler Artillery Regiment, the mortar regiment (less one battalion), the assault gun battalion, and the Tiger company of the Adolf Hitler Division, making this a formidable force. The panzer grenadier regiment moved northeast on the Prokorovka road from a point southwest of Teterevino, while the Death Head Division attacked northeast from the Psel River at Koslovka.

The Death Head units had an easy time, finding light opposition from the 51st and 52nd Guards Rifle Divisions, which had been pounded continuously since the morning of July 5 and had suffered heavy casualties. The Soviet defense line was broken by 4 P.M. at Koslovka and at Kotschetovka, tying in with the 11th Panzer Division. The weather improved at noon and the bridge was completed over the Psel. A second crossing of the Psel was made at Krasnia Octiabr.[30]

The 2nd Adolf Hitler Panzer Grenadier Regiment ran into more serious problems on July 10, though it did advance a few km. The regiment was checked by heavy flanking fire from Vinogradovka on the south and from the north bank of the Psel River. The regiment reached the railroad northeast of Teterevino by 11:30 A.M. and by 2:30 P.M. on July 10 had advanced about 3 km up the railroad toward Prokorovka. The 183rd Soviet Rifle Division was fresh, and the 10th Tank Corps and the 93rd Guards Rifle Division entered the battle during the day. The Russians counterattacked throughout the day, and only after hard fighting did the Adolf Hitler regiment tie in with the Death Head Division to the north and settle down for the night.[31] The tank regiment of the Adolf Hitler was fighting to the east in the Maliie Maiatschki and Gresnoie area in the morning of July 10, and the Germans drove the Russians 5 km north by the end of the day.[32]

During July 10, elements of the Reich Division at Kalinin were relieved by a regiment of the 167th Infantry Division, freeing the SS troops for offensive action to the north, though considerably reducing the pressure on the exposed Soviet flank running along the Novi Donets River. On the evening of July 9, Manstein had redirected the thrust of the 4th Panzer Army and the 3rd Panzer Corps of Army Detachment Kempf to wipe out the Soviet units in the deep salient that separated the two German armies. Elements of the 167th Infantry Division at Schopino, about 10 km north of Belgorod, cooperated with the 3rd Panzer Corps in attacking the 81st Guards Rifle Division and the 375th Rifle Division. The right flank of the Reich Division crossed the Novi Donets from the west at Petrovskii, which was held by the 375th Soviet Rifle Division. This threat led to the withdrawal of Soviet units and eased the advance of the 3rd Panzer Corps north along the east bank of the Novi Donets and released the 7th Panzer Division and the 198th Infantry Division.[33]

To the north on July 10, the Soviets launched a number of tank supported attacks with up to forty tanks on the Reich Division attacking toward Prokorovka. The left flank of the Reich Division finally took the railroad west of Ivanovka 10 km southwest of Prokorovka, but otherwise made little progress.[34]

All three panzer divisions of the 3rd Panzer Corps advanced slowly on July 10 to the north and east against heavy resistance, but there were no Soviet counterattacks on the scale of the previous day. Bad weather reduced the strength of the Russian air attacks in the morning, but with improving weather in the afternoon, the Russians stepped up their air activity.[35]

Soviet reserves arrived in force on July 10. The SS Corps was already beginning to engage units of the 5th Guards Tank Army, including the 10th Mechanized Corps and the 5th Guards Mechanized Corps, on the Prokorovka road by the end of the day. On the north, the Death Head Division discovered that the north bank of the Psel was strongly defended by infantry with artillery and heavy weapons support, the advance elements of the 5th Guards Army.[36]

The reduced level of German operations on July 10 is evident from the low numbers of captured and destroyed equipment. Two SS divisions claimed only two tanks for July 10, compared to seventeen for the previous day. In contrast the Reich Division was heavily engaged, claiming ninety-seven Soviet tanks and twenty-six antitank guns, indicating that some effective work was done on the Soviet antitank defenses. A total of 245 prisoners were taken by the SS Corps, an obvious indication that the Soviet units were holding together, while the single aircraft claim resulted from the very low level of air activity.[37]

To the west on the 48th Panzer Corps Front, the 11th Panzer Division was fighting northwest of Verchopenie astride the Oboyan road at 8 A.M. on July 10, and by evening reached Kotschetovka 5 km to the north and tied in with the Death Head Division to the right. The left flank of the division advanced a few km north to Kalinovka where it tied in with the Gross Deutschland. The fighting during the day was very heavy. On the west side of the Oboyan road, the Gross Deutschland Division made a few km progress, reaching Kalinovka about 5 km north of Verchopenie.[38]

To the left of the Gross Deutschland at 8 A.M. on July 10, the 3rd Panzer Division was defending itself from Soviet counterattacks. Heavy fighting continued until the end of the day. By evening the 3rd Panzer had advanced to a point 3 km northwest of Beresovka south of the Gross Deutschland Panzer Division position.[39]

In the 52nd Corps sector on the morning of July 10, the 332nd Infantry Division had eliminated most of the 6th Soviet Tank Corps and had driven the newly arrived 184th Russian Rifle Division out of Alexeievka on the Pena River. The south side of the Pena River was cleared of Soviet troops. Farther south, the 332nd Division elements northwest of Korovino were defending against attacks by the 71st Guards Rifle Division, while the 255th German Infantry Division repelled two attacks southwest of Bubny by the 100th Soviet Rifle Division of the 40th Army. The day was comparatively quiet. Bad weather had reduced air support for both sides, and the roads were deteriorating.[40]

On the east side of the German advance, Army Detachment Kempf assumed a defensive role on July 10 and was holding off attacks by the Soviet 25th Guards Rifle Corps and the 35th Guards Rifle Corps. To the north, the 3rd Panzer Corps continued to make headway against the Soviet units withdrawing from the salient that separated the Detachment from the 4th Panzer Army. The 7th Panzer Division was still holding a defensive front between Melekovo and Miassoiedovo, 20 km northeast of Belgorod on the Rasumnoie River, facing the 94th Guards Rifle Division. North of Melekovo, the 6th Panzer Division repulsed a Russian counterattack supported by fifty tanks. The 19th Panzer Division was attacked at Dalnaia Igumenka by the 92nd Guards Rifle Division, while the 168th German Infantry Division drove back an attack by the 81st Guards Rifle Division at Staryi Gorod that was still holding out only 2 km from Belgorod. All of the Soviet divisions, including the 81st Guards and 91st Guards Rifle Division, in the path of the 3rd Panzer Corps were now greatly reduced in strength. The Germans claimed to have routed several divisions that fled, leaving behind their equipment.[41]

Since the beginning of the operation on July 5, Army Detachment Kempf claimed to have destroyed 170 Soviet tanks and battered two tank brigades and three tank regiments, in addition to four rifle divisions. The Detachment claimed that two Soviet rifle divisions had been destroyed (probably the 72nd Guards and the 73rd Guards Rifle Divisions). However, the Russians were bringing up reinforcements on the sector held by Corps Raus, including the 270th,

111th, 78th Guards, and 15th Guards Rifle Divisions, all positioned east of the Koren River.[42]

The Germans made very few gains on July 10, and Soviet reserves continued to build up. Oboyan was still Manstein's primary goal in his report to the *Oberkommando des Heeres* (OKH) on July 11.[43] Manstein planned to destroy the newly arrived 69th Soviet Army with the 2nd SS Panzer Corps and the 3rd Panzer Corps, whose cooperation was essential. Corps Raus of Army Detachment Kempf was left with the task of holding off the 7th Guards Army that Manstein believed had been depleted to five or six battered rifle divisions and some tank brigades.

Manstein requested that the 24th Panzer Corps arrive by July 17 to reinforce the east flank of the 4th Panzer Army. The 48th Panzer Corps would take Oboyan and form the inner wall of the pocket, encircling the Soviet forces west of Kursk. Therefore the 24th Panzer Corps would need to move to Kharkov without delay. There might also be need of the 8th and 12th Panzer Divisions at a later date. In addition, infantry reinforcements were needed by the German 2nd Army if it was to roll up the pocket from the west. Currently the 2nd Army was too weak to perform any offensive action.[44]

By the evening of July 10, Manstein had completely abandoned the drive toward Korotscha to strengthen the SS Corps advance north to Prokorovka. Manstein's orders to the 4th Panzer Army for July 11 concentrated on the advance northeast to Prokorovka. However, he realized even that goal was unattainable without the additional panzer divisions that Hitler was reluctant to release in view of the powerful Soviet tank armies poised in front of Army Group Center and Army Group South.

Meanwhile, Manstein ordered the 2nd SS Corps to persevere on July 11, with the Adolf Hitler and Reich Divisions. These two divisions and elements of the Death Head Division were to continue their advance on both sides of the Psel River northwest of Prokorovka, bypassing the strong defenses on the Prokorovka road. The remainder of the Death Head Division was ordered to drive north along the Psel River to Schipy, about 10 km from Oboyan, and outflank the Soviet defenders on the Oboyan road. The third regiment of the 167th Infantry Division was returned to the division and ordered to replace the last elements of the Reich Division at Lutschki to free it to take part in the offensive in the north.[45]

On the extreme left of the 4th Panzer Army, the 52nd Corps was to clear the 90th Guards Rifle Division and other Russians from the Rakovo area north of the Pena River on July 11. Army Detachment Kempf was ordered to provide security for the right flank of the 4th Panzer Army and drive north to threaten the south flank of the Soviet position at Prokorovka.[46] On the evening of July 10, improving weather was expected on the following day and with it the hope for better air support for the ground troops from the Luftwaffe's Stukas. However, July 11 began with heavy rain that turned the roads into seas of mud and made movement impossible except with tracked vehicles. Toward the evening of July 11, the weather did improve, becoming cloudy with strong winds.[47]

The 2nd SS Panzer Corps planned to attack with the Adolf Hitler and Death Head Divisions at 4:15 in the early morning of July 11, with the objective of closing the gap west of Prokorovka that had opened between the two divisions. Overnight and during the early morning of July 11, the Soviet 10th Tank Corps had attacked the Death Head Division bridgehead over the Psel River without success, as the SS division repulsed the Russians. Further hampering the Death Head Division was a tank supported attack on its left flank between Kotschetovka and Koslovka at 4:15 A.M. by the 51st and 52nd Rifle Divisions.[48] At 8:30 another Soviet tank-supported attack struck the bridgehead. The Germans had a difficult time stopping the Russians because the muddy roads immobilized the German munitions trucks creating a shortage of artillery shells.

At 2:20 P.M. on July 11, two more bridges across the Psel River were completed at Bogorodizkoie, including one with sixty-ton capacity capable of handling Tiger tanks, but any advance from the bridgehead was made impossible by the heavy rain. Nothing could move on the ground except tanks, and the Luftwaffe could not fly, but it was essential for the Death Head Division to advance to the northeast to protect the north flank of the Hitler Division. The Death Head was able to advance a few km and cut the road from Prokorovka to Kartaschevka, southeast of Oboyan. The loss of this road made it more difficult to move Soviet troops from the 48th Panzer Corps front to the 2nd SS Corps front.[49]

During the afternoon of July 11, more units of the 5th Guards Army arrived. At 3:30 the 9th Guards Parachute Division arrived at Oktiabriski. Later the 42nd Guards Rifle Division, a tank destroyer brigade, and a howitzer regiment arrived.[50]

Delayed by the weather in the morning of July 11, the Adolf Hitler Division finally attacked northeast along the Prokorovka road and the railroad against stout resistance, including artillery and antitank fire from the 183rd Rifle Division and units of the 5th Guards Tank Army. Hitler Division tanks advanced a few km and reached a hill only 3.5 km southwest of Prokorovka, but hard fighting continued until 8:15 in the evening. At Petrovka, a half km northwest of Prokorovka, a German tank attack was repulsed at 3:30 in the afternoon on July 11. Two batteries of the 233rd Soviet Artillery Regiment were attacked by forty German tanks and even though the regiment put sixteen out of action, it was finally forced to retreat.[51]

Two regiments of the Reich Division, supported by 130 tanks, attacked the 2nd Soviet Tank Corps and elements of the 69th Army at Komsolets, southeast of the railroad about 5 km southwest of Prokorovka at 9:30 in the morning of July 11. The struggle lasted for three hours as the German tanks were picked off by Russian antitank guns. Finally the Russians were forced to withdraw northeast toward Prokorovka.[52] The 2nd Soviet Tank Corps, however, pressed on the south flank of the Adolf Hitler Division at 1 P.M. with a tank-supported attack in the Vinogradovka area about 10 km southwest of Prokorovka, but the attack was held by the 2nd Battalion of the Deutschland Regiment of the Adolf Hitler SS Division.[53]

To the south on the east flank, the 167th Infantry Division relieved the last two regiments of the Reich Division south of Kalinin by 10 A.M. on July 11. However, the Reich Division experienced hard fighting at Ivanovka north of Kalinin as the 2nd Soviet Tank Corps assailed the south flank of the Germans moving toward Prokorovka. The Reich Division was able to advance only 1 km east to Ivanovka. On the right flank of the 167th German Infantry Division, the Soviet 81st Guards Rifle Division and the 375th Rifle Division were withdrawing from south of Schopino.[54]

All across the 2nd SS Panzer Corps sector the Soviets were defending bitterly with excellent artillery support so that little progress was possible for the SS men. The reports for July 11 do not reflect any sign of collapse by the Red Army units. Only 309 prisoners were taken by the 2nd SS Panzer Corps. The SS Corps claimed seventy-two tanks and twenty-two antitank guns, presumably as a result of the bitter fighting against the 2nd Soviet Tank Corps at Komsolets. Only five aircraft were claimed because the bad weather limited air activity.[55]

On July 11, the 3rd Panzer Corps of the Kempf Army Detachment moved forward without sustaining heavy casualties. The Russians were withdrawing, and the Germans had little trouble breaking through their defenses. Although the 6th and 7th Panzer Divisions were still in good condition, the 19th Panzer Division had sustained heavy losses. The 19th Panzer Division, with the 168th Infantry Division on the left flank, drove north toward Kisseliovo, about 20 km northeast of Belgorod on the North Donets River, as the 81st Guards and 92nd Guards Rifle Divisions withdrew. On the west bank of the North Donets, the 168th Infantry Division pressed the flank of the 375th Soviet Rifle Division as it withdrew nearly 15 km north from the salient formed by the North Donets on the east and the Novi Donets on the west.[56] The 19th Panzer continued north on the east side of the North Donets passing through Kisseliovo at noon and ending the day with its north flank over 30 km northeast of Belgorod, an advance of over 15 km for the day, a remarkable achievement for a battle-weary division and an indication that the Soviets were withdrawing voluntarily.[57]

To the east, the 6th Panzer Division had a good day, breaking through the Soviet line at Schachovo and driving the 305th Rifle Division and the 92nd Guards Rifle Division back 15 km to Rshavez. Both of the Soviet divisions had been battered by incessant German attacks.[58] The 7th Panzer Division on the east flank of the 3rd Panzer Corps broke through the Russian line at Schliachovo on the Korotscha road about 25 km northeast of Belgorod, but directed its focus northward protecting the east flank of the 6th Panzer Division in its rapid drive to the north. By the evening of July 11, the 7th Panzer Division sector extended over 20 km from Shena in the south to Kasatschie in the north, generally following the west bank of the Rasumnoie River. The Soviet 94th Guards Rifle Division launched a tank-supported attack at Scheino on the south flank of the 7th Panzer Division during the day.[59]

The 6th Panzer Division was serving as the point with the two other panzer divisions guarding its flanks. The most pressing problem of the 3rd Panzer Corps was dealing with the Soviet reinforcements, notably the 69th Army only 5 km north of the 3rd Panzer Corps spearhead. There was also the possibility that the Soviets would withdraw behind the elaborate fortifications of the third defense line of the 7th Guards Army only 5 km ahead running in a northeast direction from Korotscha to Prokorovka.[60]

The remainder of Army Detachment Kempf was quiet on July 11, as the 7th Guards Army prepared for the next day's attack. The Soviets added the 15th Guards Rifle Division about 20 km due east of Belgorod facing the 106th German Infantry Division of Corps Raus; the 270th Rifle Division was in reserve behind the 15th Guards; and the 111th Rifle Division was in reserve behind the 213th Rifle Division at the southernmost sector of the Army Detachment.[61]

On the other side of the 4th Panzer Army, the 48th Panzer Corps Front was comparatively quiet. The 11th Panzer Division took a hill 2.5 km north of Kotschetovka, and the Soviets counterattacked. Elements of the Gross Deutschland Division were cleaning up in the Pena River valley in the Beresovka area and fighting in Verchopenie. The Soviet 1st Tank Army and 6th Guards Army, no longer aggressive, were content to prevent any further German advance toward Oboyan. The 48th Panzer Corps eventually freed up the Gross Deutschland Division for an attack due north across the Psel River east of Oboyan, and had already withdrawn some elements on July 11.[62]

On the 52nd Corps Front during the previous night of July 10–11, the Soviet 90th Guards and the 184th Rifle Division had attacked the German 332nd Infantry Division at Savidovka, continuing the pressure on the west flank of the 4th Panzer Army. However, on July 11, the 332nd followed the 48th Panzer Corps and crossed the Pena River at Alexeievka in the morning and at Rakovo at noon. During the day, battalion-sized attacks came in the area west of Bubny at the base of the salient in the 255th Infantry Division sector, probably by the 161st Soviet Rifle Division.[63]

By the end of July 11, the 4th Panzer Army claimed over 1,000 Soviet tanks destroyed or captured since July 5. The 48th Panzer Corps took 7,000 prisoners, killed 1,300 Russians, and destroyed or captured 170 Soviet tanks plus large numbers of guns, antitank guns, and 180 mortars.[64] The Germans, cleaning up Russian units south of the Psel River, mistakenly believed that the Russians had no more reserves to reinforce the defense, having used up all their operational reserves in the previous hard fighting.[65] However, the Death Head Division had difficulty crossing the Psel against strong resistance from elements of the 5th Guards Army that had just begun to arrive on the north face behind the 51st and 52nd Guards Rifle Divisions to fill the gap between Oboyan and Prokorovka.

Although the 2nd SS Panzer Corps broke through part of the third defensive line at Prokorovka, the Russians were bringing in more units of the 5th Guards Tank Army to drive back the Germans. Two tank brigades had arrived west of Prokorovka by the evening of July 11, while the 42nd Guards Rifle Division was already in combat.[66]

The Soviet 69th Army in the area northeast of the 3rd Panzer Corps offensive was in a critical position. On July 11, the army committed the 89th Guards Rifle Division to delay the advance of the German 168th Infantry Division advancing north along the railroad east of the Novi Donets River, and the 107th Soviet Rifle Division to the east flank south of Kasatschie to hold back the north flank of the 7th Panzer Division.

Although the Germans had made small gains all along the front on the south shoulder of the Kursk bulge, the table was about to turn. The overall Russian strategy on July 11 was to organize the 5th Guards Tank Army and other units for a massive counterattack at Prokorovka, with all the other armies of the Voronezh Front going on the offensive on July 12 to support the main drive and to pin German forces.[67]

The major battle was fought on July 12, southwest of the town of Prokorovka. It was not a battle with tanks charging on one huge field, but rather a series of attacks and counterattacks across a stretch of countryside ranging in an arc about 20 km wide south and west of Prokorovka, from the village of Ivanovka on the south to the south bank of the Psel River on the north. The weather was cloudy with some heavy rain (so much for the clouds of dust mentioned in several accounts), which made the roads impassable for wheeled vehicles. The inability to move would add to the difficulties of the German forces on this crucial day.

With the Death Head on the north and the Reich and Adolf Hitler SS Divisions in the south, the SS corps drove doggedly northwest on both sides of the road to Prokorovka. The Russians estimated that the three divisions had 500 tanks including 100 Tigers and Ferdinands, but this number is unlikely as the corps began the campaign with only 456 tanks and 137 assault guns, including only 35 Tigers. However, there were forty-five Tigers assigned to the 10th Panzer Brigade, which had been formed on June 23, 1943, just before the

Kursk offensive began. The brigade was apparently a training unit for new Tigers and their crews, rather than a combat unit. The sources do not mention the involvement of the 10th Panzer Brigade in the fighting, but the Tiger battalion of the brigade could have been brought up to the 2nd SS Panzer Corps on July 11, which would have raised its strength to over seventy Tigers. All of the Ferdinands were on the north face with the 9th Army and could not have been involved at Prokorovka. Given the attrition of the previous seven days, the combined strength of the 2nd SS Corps was probably much less than 400 operational tanks and assault guns including 70 Tigers.[68]

The Soviet 5th Guards Tank Army had also planned an offensive for July 12 and launched attacks on a front over 25 km wide from Lutschki on the south to Poleschoiev on the north. The first echelon of the attack was formed by the 18th, 29th, and 2nd Guards Tanks Corps, a total of at least 450 tanks, as the first two corps were seeing their first action and were probably up to strength.[69] The second echelon included the 5th Guards Mechanized Corps and the 2nd Tank Corps with about 300 tanks. The reserve consisted of army troops that were transferred to the 69th Army later in the day.[70]

The Soviet attack was launched at 8:30 A.M. on July 12, preceded by a fifteen-minute artillery barrage and air attacks by the 2nd Air Army. The Germans replied with artillery Pire and their own attack.[71] The SS met fierce resistance every step as they penetrated the third line of defense created originally by the 6th Guards Army, but then manned by the 5th Guards Tank Army with the 5th Guards Army on the west and the 69th Army, the 2nd Guards Tank Corps, and 2nd Tank Corps on the east.

One of the corps of the 5th Guards Tank Army, the 29th Soviet Tank Corps, arrived southwest of Prokorovka at 1:30 P.M. on July 12 with the 32nd Tank Brigade on the north side of the road and the 25th Tank Brigade on the left side of the road. The 31st Tank Brigade and 53rd Motorized Brigade were in reserve. The tank corps was in excellent condition as it entered combat for the first time since being rebuilt during the spring. The replacements were young men, eighteen or nineteen years old, from Gorki and Ivanov, or men returning to their units from hospitals. The replacements were 90 percent Russians and Ukrainians and the remaining 10 percent were Turkestan.[72]

One of the brigades of the 29th Tank Corps, the 31st Tank Brigade, had been formed in Moscow and then moved by rail via Gorki to the Kosterovshie Tank Depot, becoming a school unit to train new crews. The brigade was reorganized in the spring of 1943 at Noginsk, a munitions depot south of Oboyan. All three of the tank brigades were in excellent form and had their full complement of fifty-three tanks. With a total of over 150 tanks in this single corps, the Russians posed a formidable foe to the Germans on the Prokorovka road.[73]

The Adolf Hitler Division sent its tank regiment and panzer grenadiers on the road direct to Prokorovka, breaking into the town on July 12 and then being furiously counterattacked by the newly arrived 29th Tank Corps.[74] The 29th Tank Corps, under pressure from elements of the Death Head and Adolf Hitler Divisions south of the railroad, was reinforced first by the reserve 25th Tank Brigade and then by the 18th Tank Corps in the pitched battle that followed. The 18th Soviet Tank Corps, with T34 tanks in the 181st and 170th Tank Brigades, penetrated to Oktiabriski by 2:30 in the afternoon and met fifteen Tigers that inflicted heavy losses on the Soviet tank brigades.[75] The antitank and artillery regiments played a major role in the Soviet effort, but the Germans drove the Soviet units back through Prokorovka after a series of attacks and counterattacks usually at brigade strength. However, by the evening of July 12, the Adolf Hitler Division had been driven out of Prokorovka.[76] Repeated attacks by groups of thirty-five to seventy tanks from the 2nd Guards Tank Corps and elements of the 69th Army hit the east flank of the Reich Division and the 167th Infantry, securing the right flank of the corps. The 2nd Guards Tank Corps attacked toward Kalinin on July 12, running into the Reich Division, and began a struggle that lasted the whole day.[77]

To the west, the 11th Panzer and the Death Head Divisions attacked the 52nd Guards Rifle Division of the 5th Guards Army with 100 tanks and motorized infantry and air support. The Death Head SS Division, having finally brought its Tigers over Psel across the sixty-ton bridge, struggled to extend the flank of the 2nd SS Panzer Corps. At 8:30 A.M. on July 12, the 5th Guards Army had attacked south toward Gresnoie with 32nd Guards Corps (66th and 13th Guards Rifle Divisions) at Kotschetovka with forty to fifty tanks, and the 33rd Guards Rifle Corps (including the 97th Guards, 95th Guards, 42nd Guards Rifle Divisions, and the 9th Guards Parachute Division). Some of the Soviet units broke through the Death Head Division's defense into the artillery positions of the Adolf Hitler Division to the south. On the other hand, an armored unit of the Death Head Division advanced northeast to 10 km west of Prokorovka at Poleschoiev after overrunning two strong Soviet antitank gun lines and inflicting heavy losses on the Soviets.[78] The struggle lasted all day ending at 8 in the evening of July 12 when the 95th Guards Rifle Division was called from reserve to restore the situation at Poleschoiev. By evening, the 2nd SS Panzer Corps was unable to hold any gains resulting from its attacks toward Prokorovka, and, in fact, was forced to assume a defensive posture by the combined resistance of nine tank and motorized corps, each equal or superior to a panzer division.[79]

To the west of the main battle, the 48th Panzer Corps on the Oboyan road pushed west of Verchopenie with the Gross Deutschland against the 3rd Mechanized Corps and the 67th Guards Rifle Division, broadening the north face of the offensive. However, the 6th Guards Army pressed home attacks from the

west of the bulge with the 204th and 309th Rifle Divisions. By the evening of
July 12, the panzer divisions of the 48th Panzer Corps were on the defensive
from attacks by the 6th Guards Army and the 1st Tank Army on both sides of
the Oboyan road.[80]

West of the Gross Deutschland Division, the 3rd Panzer Division, holding
the west flank of the 48th Panzer Corps, was hit by the 10th Tank Corps and
the 204th and 309th Rifle Divisions of the 23rd Guards Rifle Corps southwest
of Kalinovka.[81] Just west of the Oboyan road and north of Verchopenie, the
3rd Soviet Mechanized Corps and the 31st Tank Corps launched an attack on
the 3rd Panzer Division at 8:30 in the morning on July 12 driving toward
Novoselovski. The 3rd Panzer Division was being pressed by the equivalent of
three panzer divisions and two infantry divisions. Even though all of the Soviet
units were somewhat worn from a week of combat, the 3rd Panzer was also
reduced in strength and did well not to lose ground.[82]

South of the Pena River at Rakovo, the 52nd Corps was attacked on July 12
by tanks and the 22nd Guards Rifle Corps, including the 184th and 219th Rifle
Divisions of the 40th Army. At 11 A.M. the 71st Guards Rifle Division attacked at
Korovino and Pochinok drove in the south flank of the 332nd German Division. At 5 that evening the 219th Rifle Division and the 5th Guards Tank Corps
again attacked the north flank of the 332nd German Division, and the 90th
Guards Rifle Division pressed on the center at Rakovo. Although the 332nd
German Infantry Division held back most of the attacks, the pressure by four
rifle divisions and a tank corps was overwhelming, and the division was hard
pressed to defend its line.[83]

On the other side of the German salient, the panzer divisions of Army
Detachment Kempf were under orders to drive north toward Prokorovka on
July 12 to force the Soviets to withdraw from the territory jutting south that had
separated the two Nazi armies for seven days. The 3rd Panzer Corps received
orders on the evening of July 11 to destroy the opposing 69th Army south of
Prokorovka. The 6th Panzer Division was to cross the North Donets at Rshavez,
while on the west the 19th Panzer Division attacked Kasatschie and drove the
81st Guards and 89th Guards Rifle Divisions north. The 198th German
Infantry Division was to come forward and reinforce the 19th Panzer Division.
Continuing during the night of July 11, the 3rd Panzer Corps with air support
was to attack the rear of the Soviet forces blocking the road to Prokorovka.[84]

In the early morning hours of July 12, the 19th and 6th Panzer Divisions
reached the North Donets River at Rshavez, crossed the river, and created a
bridgehead. The two panzer divisions were in a position to threaten the rear of
the 69th Army facing the east flank of the 2nd SS Panzer Corps. At the tip of
the salient pointed at Belgorod, the German 167th and 168th Infantry Division encircled some Soviet units and formed a pocket, but the 89th Guards

Division was still holding the 168th German Division just north of Gostishevo. The other Soviet units abandoned their positions on the long salient along the Novi Donets and to the west of Dalnaia Igumenka, freeing up the 375th and 81st Guards Rifle Divisions.

On the morning of July 12, the 69th Army had the 92nd Guards Division blocking the German 6th Panzer Division advance at Rshavez, and was assisted after 6 P.M. by the 375th Division from the salient. The 81st Guards Rifle Division was sent to the west bank of the North Donets to delay the 19th Panzer Division.[85]

Voronezh Front commander Vatutin ordered other units of the 69th Army to pressure the 7th Panzer Division. From north to south the 305th, 107th, and 94th Guards Rifle Divisions attacked the extended 7th Panzer Division. To further bolster the attack, Vatutin ordered the 5th Guards Tank Army to transfer to the 69th Army the 26th Guards Tank Brigade, the 1st Motorcycle Regiment, the 53rd Guards Tank Regiment, the 689th Tank Destroyer Regiment, and the 678th Howitzer Regiment to provide the 69th Army with a powerful offensive component. The group included up to 100 tanks, three battalions of motorized infantry, twenty antitank guns, and twelve howitzers, a well-balanced force equal to a German panzer division. The transferred units were in place with the 69th Army by noon of July 12.[86]

In addition the 5th Guards Mechanized Corps, less the 10th Guards Mechanized Brigade and the 29th Tank Brigade, was repositioned to block the advance of the 3rd Panzer Corps. The two remaining mechanized brigades, the 24th Guards Tank Brigade, and the support troops of the corps (the 1447th SU Regiment, 104th Guards Tank Destroyer Regiment, 737th Antitank Battalion, 2nd Guards Motorcycle Battalion, 4th Guards Mechanized Battalion, and more) were far stronger than a German panzer division. The Soviet units had a total of over 120 tanks, 20 self-propelled guns, 12 85mm antitank guns, 20 76mm antitank guns, and 5 battalions of motorized infantry. These two powerful combat groups were poised to strike against the advancing 3rd Panzer Corps on July 12. The removal of these units from the 5th Guards Tank Army made the task of the 2nd SS Corps easier, but not enough to affect the outcome of the battle farther north.[87]

Further support for the 69th Army came from the Voronezh Front reserve. Vatutin sent the 36th Antiaircraft Division, the 10th Tank Destroyer Brigade, and the 27th Artillery Brigade. From the 38th Army came the 441st Rocket Launcher Regiment and from the 40th Army, the 32nd Tank Destroyer Brigade.[88] These artillery units added several hundred guns to the defense, many of which could be used in the antitank role. While the situation on the south flank of the 69th Army was in doubt throughout July 12, by the next day the situation had improved, although the Russians continued to give ground. The 7th Panzer units were compelled to provide security for the east flank of the 3rd Panzer Corps because of the lack of infantry divisions for flank guards.[89]

To the south, Corps Raus held a 20 km frontage, holding back an increasing number of divisions assigned to the 49th Soviet Corps of the 7th Guards Army, including four fresh divisions that had arrived on the previous day. The 7th Guards Army ordered the 73rd Guards, 270th, and 111th Rifle Divisions of the 49th Corps with the support of the 27th Guards Tank Brigade to attack Corps Raus at 9 A.M. on the morning of July 12.[90]

At the end of July 12, Manstein, unaware of the reserves available to the Russian commanders, still thought there was a chance of success. At 9:10 in the evening he ordered the 24th Panzer Corps, including the Viking SS and 23rd Panzer Divisions, both weak divisions with fewer than 100 tanks each, to move from Kharkov to Belgorod on an overnight march.[91] However Hitler refused to release them, and the Battle of Kursk was over.

Both sides had suffered heavy losses. The SS Panzer Corps claimed 249 Soviet tanks destroyed or captured on July 12, 185 by the Hitler Division that drove up the Prokorovka road in the face of the 18th Tank Corps, 61 by the Death Head Division, and only 3 by the Reich Division. The corps took only 968 prisoners and 191 Russians deserted. The destruction of forty-four anti-tank guns again demonstrated their prominent role. The severity of the battle can be judged by the losses of the 18th Tank Corps, 30 percent (45 tanks), while the 29th Tank Corps lost 60 percent (90 tanks). A total of 200 tanks were lost by the 5th Guards Tank Army.[92] General Pavel A. Rotmistrov estimated that each side lost 300 tanks, probably accurate for the Russians and high for the Germans.[93]

July 12 was the climax of the German offensive. The Russians were able to hold the Germans both in the south and in the north, while the first Soviet summer offensive began north of Orel. Only on the 3rd Panzer Corps front were the Germans able to advance, but the gains were meaningless.

CHAPTER 11

Stalemate in the South

Although Manstein still had hopes for the offensive on the morning of July 13, the issue was dead. The Soviets launched a major offensive on the north face of the Orel salient on July 12, and Army Group Center had to pull its panzer divisions from the attack on the Kursk bulge to shore up the defense in the north. There was no possibility of any farther advance south by the 9th Army. Still Manstein believed that committing the 24th Panzer Corps, then in Belgorod, to the attack on the flank of the 4th Panzer Army offered some hope, but given the enormous reserves still available to the Russians, the addition of two under-strength panzer divisions could not alter the balance. The Viking Panzer Grenadier Division had only thirty-one modern tanks, fifteen obsolete tanks, and six assault guns, while the 23rd Panzer Division had only fifty-five modern tanks and eleven obsolete tanks, plus six in repair and transit on July 1, 1943.[1]

The Germans were faced with a serious shortage of infantry as well. They had thinned out their quiet sectors beyond reason to provide the troops for the initial attack. In the 2nd German Army sector at the west end of the Kursk bulge, one weak infantry division was holding a sector 60 km wide, compared to the 50 km held by the entire 4th Panzer Army at the beginning of the offensive.[2]

The weather on July 13 was very bad with heavy rain showers making the roads impassable. The Germans had considerable difficulty in resupplying the combat troops with munitions and rations. The weather hampered efforts of the 2nd SS Panzer Corps to regroup its units for the attack.[3]

The one bright spot for the Germans was the continued advance of the Army Detachment Kempf to the east of the 4th Panzer Army. The 3rd Panzer Corps continued its drive toward Prokorovka. The 19th Panzer Division made progress driving the 81st Guards Rifle Division back toward Schakova. Both the 6th and 7th Panzer Divisions were hit by strong counterattacks as the Soviets brought in new tank and motorized units from the north and east, the 5th Guards Mechanized Corps and the 2nd Guards Tank Corps. The greatest Soviet effort was against the 6th Panzer bridgehead over the North Donets River at Rshavez. The Red Air Force sent massive air strikes against the bridgehead inflicting heavy casualties among the German officers. By the evening of July

13, the Germans had widened the Rshavez bridgehead in a northwest direction with the 7th Panzer Division on the west and the 19th Panzer Division on the east. East of the North Donets River, the 6th Panzer Division provided flank security against encroachment by the 35th Soviet Guards Rifle Corps.[4]

Another pocket was about to be closed to the south as the 7th Panzer Division moved toward Vinogradovka from the south, while the Reich Division moved in from the west.[5] On the south flank of Army Detachment Kempf, Corps Raus beat off Soviet attacks by the 25th Guards Rifle Corps and counterattacked to improve its defensive positions.[6]

Elsewhere there was little good news for the Germans. Late in the evening of July 12, the Death Head Division had been engaged heavily on the Kartaschevka road with units of the 5th Guards Army. Early in the morning of July 13 the Russians attacked the Death Head Division again in regiment force with tank support. The attacks began at dawn and continued until 5 in the afternoon finally breaking through the German defenses, eliminating the narrow salient that had succeeded in reaching the Kartaschevka road the previous day, and driving the Germans back to their position two days before. At 6:15 P.M., however, the Death Head Division launched a counterattack that stabilized the front for the night. The Adolf Hitler Division had been driven out of Prokorovka on the previous afternoon, but experienced very little action on July 13 as Soviet forces west of Prokorovka concentrated on eliminating the salient on the Death Head Division Front. The Reich Division experienced heavy attacks from the Ivanovka area, however.[7]

To the south, the 167th Division, advancing east from Petrovka on the evening of July 12, continued its advance against weak opposition during July 13 on the east bank of the Novi Donets, as the Soviet forces evacuated the triangle formed by the two branches of the Donets River. The 167th Infantry Division, delayed by comparatively weak counterattacks, mainly infantry, took all of the west bank of the Novi Donets River, tying in with the Reich Division to the north and the 168th Infantry Division to the south. The 168th German Division of Army Detachment Kempf was tied in on the east, and both divisions advanced rapidly during the day.[8]

On the 48th Panzer Corps Front, the Soviet 1st Tank Army and 6th Guards Army continued to attack on July 13 after a quiet night. The Russians attacked with sixty to seventy tanks, probably two brigades of a tank corps, with the 11th Panzer Division taking the brunt of the attacks. The Gross Deutschland was fighting to hold high ground 4 km west of Verchopenie against attacks by the 5th Guards Tank Corps and elements of the 10th Tank Corps. The Gross Deutschland attacked the 3rd Soviet Tank Corps at Novosselovka. The 3rd Panzer Division defended itself against massive attacks during the day. The 184th and 219th Soviet Rifle Divisions supported by the 6th Tank Corps broke through the 3rd Panzer Division defense at Beresovka during the afternoon.[9]

The 2nd SS Panzer Corps on July 13, beat off Soviet attacks and made no real advances.[10] The level of combat remained high, however, and the attacks cost the Soviets dearly. The SS Panzer Corps claimed 144 Soviet tanks and nine aircraft shot down. The changing nature of the battle was revealed in that only 297 prisoners were taken and 51 deserters came over to the Germans during the day. Only eighteen antitank guns were claimed, fewer than in previous days.[11]

The weather finally improved on July 14, overcast early but later clear and dry. The sun soon dried out the roads making them usable by all vehicles, an unfortunate turn for the Germans as the weather also improved the mobility of the Soviet armored forces and increased the activity of the Red Air Force.[12]

The 2nd SS Panzer Corps had a quiet night interrupted only by a few Soviet patrols in the Adolf Hitler sector north of the Prokorovka road. At 4 in the morning of July 14, the Reich Division once again attacked to the southeast at Iasnaia Poliana, pushing the 89th Guards Division back and taking the high ground southwest of Pravorot. The Russians resisted violently, and hard fighting persisted from 7 A.M. until noon as the advancing Germans threatened the rear of the 375th Rifle Division trying to halt the advance of the 7th Panzer Division.

At 5 in the afternoon the Reich Panzer Regiment drew artillery fire from the south that escalated into a brisk engagement beginning at 5:15 P.M. in the Ivanovka-Belenikino area that lasted until 6:25 P.M.. The Germans attacked across a minefield and fought house to house in the towns. The Germans continued to advance, forcing the 375th Rifle Division to retreat northeast. The Reich Division continued its efforts into the night attempting to take Pravorot before the Russians could establish a defensive position. However, the attempt was unsuccessful and the Germans were still a few km from the road junction at Pravorot that would have outflanked the 69th Soviet Army to the south and the 5th Guards Tank Army to the north.[13]

The 167th German Infantry Division was on the railroad southwest of Ivanovka on July 14 trying to close a pocket at Schachova from the west while the 7th Panzer Division of the 3rd Panzer Corps was attacking from the west. The Adolf Hitler Division experienced very little activity. The 5th Guards Tank Army was contented to harass the division with heavy mortar and artillery fire.[14]

The Death Head Division also experienced heavy artillery and mortar fire and some patrol activity on the part of the Russians and a battalion-sized attack south of Vessely. The German engineers completed another sixty-ton capacity bridge over the Psel River at 8:40 on the morning of July 14 that would provide the means for the Tigers to cross the river. The 33rd Soviet Guards Rifle Corps reinforced the area southeast of the Vessely River at Prelestnoie and forced the Death Head Division to give up part of the bridgehead.[15]

The very low level of claims made by the 2nd SS Corps for July 14 was evidence of the level of activity for the day. The Russians were applying little pressure on the Germans, as the SS men claimed only three tanks and one aircraft for the day, the lowest since July 5. Only 132 prisoners were taken and 43 deserters came over, again a very low level. The only unusual numbers were the forty-one antitank guns and five guns claimed. Evidently the Germans were reacting to the heavy artillery fire from the Soviets and indulged in counter-battery fire to quiet the Russian guns.[16]

The 48th Panzer Corps had a quiet night. At 4 in the morning of July 14 the Gross Deutschland attacked a hill 5 km northwest of Beresovka, driving back the 219th Soviet Rifle Division, but made little progress otherwise. The 3rd Panzer Division cleared the woods north of Beresovka beginning at 4 A.M. and was counterattacked by twenty Soviet tanks. The 11th Panzer Division fought off strong counterattacks on a broad front. The 332nd Infantry Division on the south of the corps 3 km northwest of Beresovka made a small advance and improved its defensive positions. South of the 332nd Division, the 255th and 57th Infantry Divisions of the 52nd German Corps held off Soviet patrol activity and a company-sized attack. The 48th Panzer Corps claimed sixty-five tanks on July 14, indicating that the Russians were pressing home their attacks.[17] Army Detachment Kempf continued to drive north on the east flank of the 4th Panzer Army on July 14. The 6th and 7th Panzer Divisions drove the Russians out of Alexandrovka south of Prokorovka with heavy losses to the Russians. Soviet counterattacks were repelled and the two panzer divisions converged on Schachovo.[18]

On the nose of the bulge at Kursk, the German 2nd Army was attacked by a two-battalion force at Rylsk, and other attacks took place on the 88th and 82nd German Divisions. In the 35th German Corps area, the 299th and 262nd Divisions were under attack along with the 36th German Division. These attacks marked the first major activity on the 2nd German Army front since the beginning of July, and were deemed as threatening because the Germans were widely stretched compared to the opposing Soviet units. For example, the German 36th Infantry Division was opposed by five Soviet divisions.[19]

The weather the next day, July 15, was mostly cloudy with some heavy rain. The roads were barely useable, and the Germans had difficulty bringing up munitions and supplies. Despite their problems, the change was favorable to the Germans, as the mud created more trouble for the Russians who were trying to push the Germans back and needed to move troops, weapons, and supplies forward. The bad weather also curtailed Soviet air activity.[20]

The Reich Division continued to cooperate with the 3rd Panzer Corps in the drive up the North Donets River. During the night of July 14–15, the Reich Division launched an attack that reached a line east of Vinogradovka and Ivanovka at 5 in the morning, pushing back the 375th Soviet Rifle Division that had been engaged with the Germans since July 5. Heavy rain began at 5 A.M., slowing the German advance. At noon, a regiment of the Reich Division attempted to continue the advance, but the Russian defenses were too strong, particularly the antitank and antiaircraft guns that curtailed German air activity and held back the tanks. The Reich Division claimed to have destroyed twelve Russian antitank guns during the day.[21]

The 7th Panzer Division continued to push ahead on the left flank of the 3rd Panzer Corps and connected with the Reich Division at Mal Iablonovo at 2:20 P.M. on July 15. The gap was closed between the 4th Panzer Army and Army Detachment Kempf, shortening the front and freeing up the 167th German Infantry Division and other elements of the Reich Division. The 167th German Infantry Division had little activity and claimed only three Soviet tanks. Elements of the 167th Division worked with the 168th German Infantry Division to take high ground north of Gostischtschev.[22] The Russians were primarily concerned with delaying the advance of the 3rd Panzer Corps up the North Donets River to the east and pushing back the Death Head Division on the north. The Adolf Hitler Division continued to lay low for the day, stalled at Pravorot, south of Prokorovka, by the Russian 69th Army. The Soviets confined themselves to shelling the Adolf Hitler Division.[23]

The 48th Panzer Corps sector was quiet during the night of July 14–15, but the Russians launched a major assault the next day. The 3rd Panzer Division claimed to have destroyed sixty tanks, probably of the 10th Soviet Tank Corps. The 52nd German Corps to the left of the 48th Panzer Corps had very little activity other than chasing off two Russian patrols. Activity continued on the German 2nd Army front as the Russians attacked at battalion strength on the 82nd German Infantry Division front, losing two T34s.[24]

The continued level of fighting was indicated by the claims of the 2nd SS Corps for July 15. The Germans claimed forty-four Soviet tanks and five aircraft indicating that the Russians were resisting the Germans, especially in the Death Head and Reich Division sectors the location of most of the claims. The corps took 344 prisoners, and 36 deserters came over to the Germans, another indication that the Russians did not have the complete advantage. The Adolf Hitler made practically no claims, confirming the lack of activity in that sector.

A clear indication that the offensive was over was the 4th Panzer Army order of July 15 reprimanding the German troops for not digging defensive positions quickly enough during the past two days. The result had been heavy losses from artillery, mortar, and tank fire. Hoth, the army commander, ordered that once a unit was defending, if only for a single hour, every soldier must immediately dig in. Many soldiers had received head wounds as a result of wearing the *mutze*, a soft cap with a visor that was far more comfortable than a steel helmet during the summer heat. All soldiers were ordered to wear steel helmets at all times. To do otherwise would be considered a lack of discipline and competence.[25]

Another sign of the end was the order issued on the evening of July 14 by the 4th Panzer Army headquarters that henceforth all damaged Soviet tanks and any damaged German tanks that could not be towed were to be blown up immediately to prevent the vehicles from falling into Russian hands. The Germans no longer expected to control the battlefield at the close of each day as had been the case in the previous ten days.[26]

In the days that followed the 4th Panzer Army and Army Detachment Kempf retreated slowly to the original positions held on July 5. The Russians chose not to press the Germans as they retreated, perhaps because the Russians were husbanding their strength for the offensive that was to be launched within a few weeks. German rear guards were past masters at inflicting casualties on advancing opponents who became careless in the belief that the Germans were fleeing. Despite Soviet caution, the Germans continued to inflict losses on the Russians during the retreat. On July 16, two divisions of the 2nd SS Corps claimed 18 Soviet tanks, 29 antitank guns, and 420 Russians killed. The SS divisions also took 1,136 prisoners on that day along with 8 deserters.[27]

For the period from July 5 to July 17, the 2nd SS Corps claimed 1,149 Soviet tanks destroyed and 18 captured, 85 aircraft shot down, 459 antitank guns, 4,262 Russians killed, 6,441 prisoners, and 561 deserters.[28] The 48th Panzer Corps claimed about 500 Soviet tanks destroyed, for a total of over 1,650 tanks, not including tanks lost to Army Detachment Kempf. Many of the tanks claimed as destroyed were only damaged and probably returned to action because the total number of Soviet tanks in the Voronezh Front facing the 4th Panzer Army on July 5 was only 1,657 tanks and 42 SUs. The 5th Guards Tank Army and other tank units from the Steppe Front entered the battle later and suffered far fewer losses. If we accept the Germans' claims of destroyed tanks, there would have been nothing left of the 1st Guards Tank Army and other tank units in the Voronezh Front, and that was obviously not true. On August 7, 1943, the Voronezh and Steppe Fronts had 2,319 tanks compared to 3,173 on July 5. The Russians probably lost about 1,000 tanks during the Kursk battle and more in the two weeks that followed. However, many of the losses were replaced with tanks arriving from the depots.

The preeminent role played by the Tiger tanks was represented by Michael Wittman who commanded the Tiger unit that inflicted heavy losses on the British 7th Armoured Division in Normandy in 1944. At Kursk in July 1943,

Wittman commanded the 1st Company of the SS Corps Heavy Tank Battalion attached to the Adolf Hitler Division. During the Kursk offensive, Wittman claimed twenty-eight T34s and twenty-eight antitank guns, the two most significant targets for the 88mm guns on the Tigers.[29]

The German advance had not been made without cost. By the evening of July 15, the Adolf Hitler Division had suffered considerable losses. Including tanks in repair, the division had only eight Tigers left of the twelve at the beginning of the attack; thirty-two Pz IVs of the seventy-nine; six Pz IIIs of the eleven; and eleven other tanks of thirteen. There were still twenty-eight of the thirty-four assault guns and eighteen self-propelled guns. The division lost 57 tanks of 115, one-half of its strength.[30] Based on this ratio, the nine panzer divisions of the 4th Panzer Army and Army Detachment Kempf probably lost over 600 tanks and 50 assault guns, but by the end of the battle, the nine panzer divisions probably had over 900 tanks and 200 assault guns.

As the Germans withdrew, more and more tanks returned from the repair battalions. On July 23, the 2nd SS Panzer Corps operational tanks included four Pz IIs, seventy-two Pz III (L)s, four Pz IV (S)s, ninety-four Pz IV (L)s, thirty Tigers, seventeen T34s, and seventy-eight assault guns. The corps lacked only five Pz III (L)s, twenty-three Pz IV (L)s, three Tigers, and five assault guns from its authorized strength. After eighteen days of very bitter fighting, the corps was short thirty-six tanks and assault guns, about two tank companies. The losses in other weapons were minor, the loss of 8 percent of its half-tracks being the most serious. The most severe losses were in lives. As of July 16, the 2nd SS Corps had lost 196 officers and 6,232 men and was short of its authorized strength by 1,041 officers and 5,609 men, mostly in the panzer grenadier companies.[31]

Assessing casualties for either side is extremely difficult. Men missing one day would turn up a few days later. Because commanders were concerned with the number of tanks ready and running each morning, the German repair crews were adept at overnight repairs of minor damage that would have stopped a tank during the battle. The Germans usually held the battlefields at the end of each day as the Russians were being forced back by the initial onslaught. The German salvage crews were able to pick up slightly damaged tanks on the field during the night, while the Russians rescued damaged tanks only with great difficulty. After July 15, the positions were reversed, and German tank losses escalated.

German photographs of the first days of the battle show more damaged American Stuart M3 light tanks and Grant M3 medium tanks than Soviet T34s and KVs. Russian tank units engaged in the first few days were independent regiments and brigades that were often equipped with Lend Lease tanks to provide support for the infantry in local counterattacks. These minor counterattacks running head on into the advancing Germans were very costly to the

Russians, but were essential to disrupt the German advance and to give the retreating infantry time to settle in reserve positions. The T34s were reserved for the tank corps and tank armies that were held for the major counterattacks.

In conclusion, the Germans were able to breach the Russian main line of defense on July 5, but many of the Russians withdrew to reinforce the second line. The 4th Panzer Army took three days to break through the second line and close up to the third line. By July 10, the Soviets had gathered reserves at the threatened points and outnumbered the attackers. The Soviet 1st Tank Army dug in its tanks on the road to Oboyan and the Soviet 5th Guards Tank Army threw back the German 2nd SS Panzer Corps in the Prokorovka area on July 12. The Soviets were able to replenish their tank units and move quickly to the offensive.

Even if the 2nd SS Panzer Corps had been able to destroy the 5th Guards Tank Army as Manstein claimed, the 2nd Soviet Tank Army was but a few km to the north, and two more tank armies were within a few days train travel. The 48th Panzer Corps was tied up with the 1st Soviet Tank Army, and the panzer divisions of Army Detachment Kempf had been countered by numerous independent Soviet tank corps. The constant pressure of Soviet tank units on the east and west flank of the 4th Panzer Army penetration continually threatened the 4th Panzer Army and weakened its spearheads. There were insufficient German infantry divisions to create a firm shoulder on either side, a problem the Germans experienced again in the Ardennes in December 1944. As a result, about half of the panzer divisions were held back from the spearhead to bolster the flanks: the 3rd and 11th Panzer Divisions to the west, the SS Death Head for five crucial days on the east, and the panzer divisions of Army Detachment Kempf that struggled with Soviet defenders until finally moving north in a meaningful way after July 10. The weakening of the spearhead and the delays caused by the counterattacks gave the Russians ample time to assemble reserves. As usual, Stalin was reluctant to release more reserves than he thought necessary, but had the 5th Guards Tank Army been driven back, reserves were available. The opening of the Soviet offensives at Orel and on the Mius Front drained off the panzer divisions quickly, and the Germans were hard pressed when the Russians began a third offensive at Belgorod in August.

CHAPTER 12

The North Shoulder

On the north shoulder of the Kursk salient, the main thrust of the German attack was in a sector held by the 13th Soviet Army. The 13th Army had held the line in the middle of the Central Front for some months, and the divisions with only brief periods of combat had few casualties. As a result the rifle companies had far more unit cohesion than the armies in the Voronezh Front that held the southern shoulder of the Kursk bulge. When the companies of the 13th Army divisions withdrew from untenable strong points, the troops withdrew in good order and took their place in the second line, strengthening it enormously. The front line divisions continued to hold sectors in the second line, and reserve divisions filled gaps as the total frontage increased with the German advance.

The German attack was delayed on July 5 by a preemptive Soviet artillery bombardment, but proceeded with a ragged start at 5:30 in the morning by the 41st Panzer Corps and the 23rd Corps. The ground attack was preceded by a German artillery barrage and air attacks beginning at 4:25 A.M. and continuing intermittently until 11 with 50 to 100 aircraft. The 46th Panzer Corps and the 47th Panzer Corps did not strike until 6:30 in the morning.[1] The German 9th Army on the first day made greater use of the infantry divisions supported by assault gun battalions than did the 4th Panzer Army in the south. The progress of the German infantry was slow at first as they infiltrated the strong Russian defenses. On the 41st Panzer Corps sector, the 78th Sturm division sent in the 811th and 813th Panzer Companies of radio controlled miniature tanks carrying explosive charges (Goliaths), which cleared a path through the minefields when exploded.[2]

The Germans met little opposition at first, but by noon on July 5, massive barrages of artillery and mortar fare in addition to heavy air attacks slowed the German advance. On the east flank, the 258th, 31st, and 7th Infantry Divisions of the German 46th Panzer Corps attacked the 280th and 132nd Soviet Rifle Divisions of the 70th Soviet Army at 9:30 A.M. in the Tureika area. The German 258th Division on the west took Obydenki Ismailovo less than 2 km from the start line but was halted by the 280th Soviet Rifle Division as the Soviet division pivoted to the southwest. The German 7th Infantry Division soon occupied

Tureika driving the Soviet 175th Rifle Division south about 4 km, while the German 31st Division took the high ground north of Gnilez, southeast of Tureika, driving the 132nd Soviet Rifle Division south about 6 km.[3]

On the 47th Panzer Corps front, the 20th Panzer and 6th Infantry Divisions attacked with strong tank support including Tigers and assault guns, plus a heavy artillery barrage and air support. The German infantry attacks were supported by one or two tank battalions that broke through the first line of defense. By noon the west flank of the 47th Panzer Corps was in the second defense line, and the fighting was fierce as the Russians stoutly defended their positions.[4]

By 7 in the evening of July 5, the Soviet 132nd and 280th Rifle Divisions were defending the second defense line southwest of Bobrik, 12 km from the start line. One German regiment reached Saborovka, 13 km south of the start line. At 8 P.M. the two Soviet divisions were reinforced by forty 76mm antitank guns of the 167th and 206th Guards Light Artillery Regiments from the 1st Guards Artillery Division and an additional eighty antitank guns of the 3rd Destroyer Brigade and 378th Tank Destroyer Regiment from the 70th Army. Later in the day the Germans attacked again with a battalion of tanks and infantry. In the evening, the Russians counterattacked with infantry and the 27th Guards Tank Regiment near Podsoborovka in the second defense line zone.[5]

At noon on July 5, two additional panzer divisions went into action on the east flank of the 47th Panzer Corps. The 2nd and 9th Panzer Divisions struck the west flank of the 15th Soviet Rifle Division and penetrated the first defense line, driving the Russians south.[6] The east flank of the 15th Soviet Rifle Division in the Archangelsk area was hit by a battalion of sixty tanks supported by infantry of the 292nd German Infantry Division of the 41st Panzer Corps. The 292nd Division penetrated the first line of defense and reached Oserki, about 5 km from the start line. One regiment of the 292nd Division reached Butyrki, an additional 5 km south of Oserki at 10 that night. To the west, the 86th German Division with assault guns in support had great difficulty as they encounter minefields and were subjected to heavy artillery fire from the 5th Soviet Artillery Division. The 86th Division reached Otschki on the road to Maloarchangelsk, nearly 10 km south of the start line, an excellent performance in the face of fierce Soviet resistance. In some instances the Russians fought in their positions until the last man was killed. On the first day, July 5, the 41st Panzer Corps had broken through the first line but advanced only halfway to the second line at Ponyri.[7]

The German 23rd Corps with the 78th Sturm and 216th Infantry Divisions attacked the east flank of the 13th Soviet Army defended by the 8th and 148th Soviet Rifle Divisions. Assisted by good air support, the German 78th Division pierced the first line of defense, advancing 10 km to the road from Protossovo to Maloarchangelsk, and continued south of the road, driving back the Soviet

148th Rifle Division. The German 216th Infantry Division, despite heavy artillery and mortar fire, advanced due east to Ielisaveto, over 10 km from the start line, driving back the 8th Soviet Rifle Division. However, the area between Trossna and Protossovo on the Maloarchangelsk road between the spearheads of the 78th and 216th Divisions was still held by the Russians. During the evening of July 5, a strong tank-supported counterattack by the Russians in the Trossna area created some anxiety for the Germans.[8]

Farther east at 5:30 in the morning of July 5, the 299th and 383rd German Infantry Divisions attacked the 16th Rifle Division of the 48th Army in the area north of Maloarchangelsk. After six hours of heavy fighting, the Germans had made little progress and gave up the attack. The regiment of the 383rd German Infantry Division at Panskaia on the north flank of the division was counterattacked by the 16th Soviet Division with heavy artillery support. The German regimental commander and one of the battalion commanders were killed, which attested to the ferocity of the battle.[9]

The 9th German Army had great difficulty on July 5. Even though the Germans were able to break through the first line of defense everywhere except on the east flank of the attack, the Germans were able to advance only halfway to the second line in most sectors. Nevertheless, this short advance of about 10 km was the most ground taken in any day by the 9th Army and was half the distance covered by the 9th Army during the remaining week of the battle.

The next day, July 6, the Germans had to face a much stronger opponent reinforced by the rapid transfer of Soviet reserves to the second defense line in the critical areas. The Soviet command sent the 16th Tank Corps to Olchovatka versus the 47th German Panzer Corps, the 19th Tank Corps to Molotytschi versus the 20th Panzer Division, the 17th Guards Rifle Corps to Kashara north of Olchovatka versus the 6th German Infantry Division, the 18th Guards Rifle Corps to Maloarchangelsk versus the 78th German Sturm Division, and ordered the 9th Tank Corps to advance into the Central Front. The 60th and 65th Armies on the west face of the Kursk bulge sent the 11th Guards Tank Brigade to the 2nd Tank Army and two other tank regiments. The 48th Army sent the 2nd Artillery Brigade to the 13th Army.[10]

Rokossovsky, the Russian Central Front commander, ordered the 13th Army and the 2nd Tank Army to launch a massive counterattack on the German 9th Army on the morning of July 6 on the entire length of the 13th Army Front. In preparation for the attack, the Russians unleashed a massive artillery barrage by the 4th Soviet Artillery Corps including the 1st Guards Artillery Division and the 5th Artillery Division plus the 21st Mortar Brigade, the 68th Artillery Brigade, and the 37th, 92nd, and 65th Rocket Launcher Regiments.[11] The attacking Russians outnumbered the Germans by about two to one in manpower and committed over 750 tanks and self-propelled guns.

On the west end of the front, the Soviet 19th Tank Corps attacked through the 132nd and 175th Soviet Rifle Divisions hitting the German 46th Panzer Corps including the 7th and 31st Infantry Divisions. The Germans repulsed the attack and counterattacked reaching a line 1 km south of Gnilez, 7 km south of the original start line. Russian artillery fare and air support were heavy, making the advance of the Germans very difficult.[12] The Germans launched another attack due south in the area at 7 in the evening of July 6 and created a bridgehead across the Svapa River 12 km south of the start line, pushing aside the 132nd Soviet Rifle Division. The Germans were heavily counterattacked by Russian T34 tanks, but held the bridgehead.[13]

In the center, the 17th Guards Rifle Corps with the 70th and 75th Guards Rifle Divisions supported by the l6th and 9th Tank Corps struck the 2nd German Panzer Division of the 47th Panzer Corps between Bobrik and Saborovka 10 km south of the start line. In the hard fighting, the 2nd Panzer Division widened the bridgehead over the Svapa River at Saborovka.[14]

On the right, the 18th Guards Rifle Corps supported by the 3rd Tank Corps attacked the 9th Panzer and 6th Infantry Divisions. The 9th Panzer Division had a particularly hard fight, but drove back the 81st Soviet Rifle Division to Beresov Log. The 2nd and 9th Panzer Divisions, attacking with infantry in the first wave and with heavy artillery support, penetrated the Soviet defenses and took high ground on both sides of Olchovatka.[15]

The Soviet 17th Guards Rifle Corps entered the battle between Teploie and Olchovatka, attacking the German 47th Panzer Corps. The 1st Guards Artillery Division plus light artillery and tank destroyer regiments provided the 17th Corps with strong artillery support.[16]

East of Olchovatka, the Soviet 148th, 81st, and 74th Rifle Divisions attacked the 292nd and 86th German Divisions at Ponyri at 3:50 in the morning of July 6 after an artillery barrage by the 12th Artillery Division and air attacks. A fierce battle developed around the largest of the three Ponyri villages as both sides added more units to the struggle, including the German 9th Army reserves, the 12th Panzer and 10th Panzer Grenadier Divisions. The 307th Soviet Division was attacked by elements of the 292nd, 86th, and 78th German Divisions supported by 170 tanks. The 656th German Heavy Panzerjager Regiment with Ferdinand assault guns supported the 86th Sturm Division east of Ponyri. The 107th Soviet Tank Brigade fought a hard battle with a Tiger battalion. The 203rd Rifle Regiment of the 70th Soviet Guards Division destroyed a Tiger with antitank grenades. The 205th Regiment of the same division was attacked by sixty German tanks and destroyed three German Pz IVs with antitank rifles at close range. The 84th Guards Tank Destroyer Battalion of the 75th Guards Division was attacked by Tigers, but managed to destroyed five Pz IVs with 45mm antitank guns. A battery of the 729th Tank

Destroyer Battalion claimed five tanks at Ponyri. The German 41st Corps claimed twenty-eight Soviet tanks, mostly T34s. Although the Russians lost some ground by the evening of July 6, and the German 41st Panzer Corps was fighting in the defense zone on both sides of Ponyri, the Germans were unable to break through the second defense line.[17]

On the German east flank, the 78th Division of the 23rd Corps fought hard to take Protossovo on the road to Maloarchangelsk 10 km from the start line. During the evening of July 6, the 78th Sturm Division repelled a strong Soviet counterattack at Protossovo. After house-to-house fighting, the Germans finally prevailed and by evening had cleared Protossovo and advanced 5 km toward Maloarchangelsk.[18] To the north, the Soviet 15th Rifle Corps with tank support attacked the 216th German Division from the area around Trossna. The Germans held their gains from the previous day with difficulty. The 383rd German Division to the north of the 216th Division was subjected to heavy attacks from the Soviet 48th Army and defended itself in the original defensive positions held on July 5. The German 20th Corps on the west side of the northern attack had no significant activity on July 6.[19]

On the evening of July 6, Rokossovkski ordered the counterattacks to continue the next day. The 3rd Soviet Tank Corps was ordered to attack at Ponyri, and the 18th Guards Rifle Corps was to drive back the German 78th Sturm Division on the Maloarchangelsk road. The 16th and 19th Tank Corps and the 17th Guards Rifle Corps were placed under the command of the 2nd Tank Army to press home the attack against the German 47th Panzer Corps.[20]

Also on the evening of July 6, General Walther Model, commander of the 9th German Army, ordered all five of the 9th Army corps to continue the attack on the following day. The 78th Sturm Division of the 23rd Corps was to push the Soviet 74th Rifle Division toward Luninka 5 km southwest of Maloarchangelsk and establish a defensive position. The 18th Panzer Division of the 41st Panzer Corps was ordered to establish a bridgehead over the Snova River west of Ponyri. The 2nd Panzer Division of the 47th Panzer Corps was to reach the road leading to Fatesh west of Olchovatka. The 4th Panzer Division moved from army reserve to assist the 47th Panzer Corps in its drive south of the Svapa River. The objective of the 46th Panzer Corps was to strengthen the bridgehead over the Svapa River and to take the high ground west of Bobrik. These objectives were very modest, calling for advances of about 5 km. Clearly, the objective of cutting off all of the Russians in a huge pocket could not be achieved before the Soviet reserves arrived. The strong defenses of the 13th Soviet Army and the tank-supported counterattacks had thwarted the German 9th Army.[21]

On July 7, matters did not go well for the German 9th Army. In the 46th Panzer Corps sector on the west flank, elements of the 31st and 7th German

Infantry Divisions fought for high ground west of Gnilez in the Soloschonki area against the 280th Soviet Rifle Division of the 70th Soviet Army. After hard fighting the German 31st Division took a hill and then lost it to a Soviet counterattack supported by tanks, probably from the 19th Tank Corps. The Russians lost only four tanks in the exchange. Both sides reinforced the sector; the Germans added a jager battalion from Group Esebeck to the 31st Division, and the 12th Panzer Division was brought up from army reserve late in the morning of July 7 and introduced in the left flank of the corps sector. The Russians reinforced their position as the 70th Soviet Army moved the 175th Rifle Division to the Fatesh road area and then into the front line between the 280th and 132nd Rifle Divisions. The 175th Division probably contributed to the success of the counterattack in the afternoon, which regained the high ground west of Gnilez. The Germans made little progress in their attempt to widen the base of the attack.[22]

The 9th Army ordered the 47th Panzer Corps to take the high ground south of Bitiug and Kashara about 8 km southeast of Bobrik as quickly as possible. The corps was then to drive south a farther 5 km and take the high ground on either side of Olchovatka. The attack began at 8:30 on the morning of July 7 with a battle group of German light and medium panzers of the 9th Panzer Division and elements of the 6th Infantry Division attempting to break through the second defense line on the 17th Guards Rifle Corps Front. At noon two German infantry regiments of the 6th Infantry Division supported by fifty tank of the 9th Panzer Division struck the 6th Guards Division at Bitiug. At 5 in the afternoon thirty tanks and infantry of the 9th Panzer Division made some gains at Ponyri 2 south of Bitiug, which was held by the 75th Guards Rifle Division and supported by the 3rd Tank Destroyer Brigade from the 70th Army. The Soviets counterattacked with 16th Tank Corps supported by the 2nd Tank Destroyer Brigade. When the Germans reacted with an attack by forty tanks, a battery of the 449th Tank Destroyer Regiment destroyed 15. The Soviet 3rd Destroyer Brigade continued to fight even though the 1st Antitank Battalion lost 70 percent of its men during July 7. For the day, the 17th Soviet Guards Rifle Corps claimed 8,000 Germans killed and 100 German tanks destroyed. The Germans also claimed to have inflicted heavy casualties on the Russians in the bitter fighting.[23]

To the west, the 4th Panzer Division was inserted on the right flank of the 47th Panzer Corps at Teploie, and with its neighbor, the 2nd Panzer Division, attacked late in the day on July 7. The Russians counterattacked with the 43rd and 58th Tank Regiments and units of the Soviet 2nd Tank Army to halt the German advance.[24]

On the 41st Panzer Corps Front the Russians lost ground at Ponyri PC; two battalions of the 10th Panzer Grenadier Division from the army reserve drove back the 4th Guards Parachute Division a short distance at 10 A.M. on July 7 at Polevaia. On the east flank of the 41st Panzer Corps, the 86th German Division attacked at the same time with two infantry battalions supported by tanks, driving back the 307th Soviet Rifle Division. Backed by heavy artillery support provided by the 13th Tank Destroyer Brigade, the 11th Mortar Brigade, and the 2nd Guards Mortar Brigade, the 307th Division counterattacked and destroyed ten Tigers and twelve Pz IVs. The Russian counterattack took a hill in the morning, but the Germans regained it in the afternoon. At 3:30 in the afternoon the German 18th Panzer, 86th, and 292nd Infantry Divisions launched a coordinated attack on both sides of Ponyri PC. The 2nd Battalion of the 159th Guards Artillery Regiment destroyed two Tigers and five other tanks. At 7 in the evening the Germans tried again with a regiment-sized attack supported by sixty tanks on the 307th Rifle Division. The fighting around Ponyri PC surged back and forth. To the left of the 86th German Division, elements of the 36th German Infantry Division reinforced with Ferdinands suffered from heavy artillery fire from the 12th Soviet Artillery Division and attacks by the 148th Soviet Rifle Division. Throughout the day, the Soviets launched powerful counterattacks in response to the German attempts to break through the second defense line.[25]

On the east flank of the 9th Army, the 78th German Infantry Division of the 23rd Corps withstood eleven strong attacks by the Soviet 74th Rifle Division, each of two rifle battalions supported by artillery with the objective of regaining Protossovo on the Maloarchangelsk road. The intense artillery fire came from the Soviet 12th Artillery Division concentrated behind the 74th Rifle Division. The 41st German Corps sent the 78th Division a company of Ferdinands to stiffen the antitank defense.[26]

Despite heroic efforts on the part of the divisions of the 9th German Army, their progress was measured in meters. They could not penetrate the second defense line in the face of the dogged Soviet defenders backed by immense artillery formations. The Soviet antitank guns often outnumbered the attacking German tanks and, despite heavy losses, the antitank batteries took a heavy toll on the Germans. There were few German tank replacements and the strength of the panzer divisions steadily declined. The intensity of the fighting was indicated by a request from 9th Army for 100,000 rounds of tank gun ammunition on July 7 as the three days of attack had reduced the army's stock. With fewer than 500 operational tanks, the request was for 200 rounds for each tank! In three days the 9th Army lost 10,000 men and although 5,000 replacements arrived, the rifle companies were badly depleted. The new replacements probably were held in the divisional replacement battalions rather than introduced into rifle companies in the midst of heavy fighting. Without strong rifle companies to support the panzer forces, German progress was stalled by July 7.[27]

On July 8, the initiative moved to the Red Army. The Soviet retreat halted, and reserves were added to Ponyri PC on the 41st Panzer Corps Front and at Teploie on the 47th Panzer Corps Front. The 70th Soviet Army sent the 140th and 162nd Rifle Divisions to Teploie as reserves against the German main thrust. The 70th Soviet Army also moved the 181st Rifle Division closer to the attack zone and alerted the 229th and 259th Tank Regiments to reinforce the 13th Soviet Army.[28]

The Soviet intention to stage a major counterattack on July 8 was obvious, and all of the German corps commanders were warned to expect attacks during the day. The 9th Army ordered special provisions to improve the fire plans of the artillery and antitank guns to make the guns as effective as possible in combating the Soviet tanks. To counter the expected heavy artillery barrages, the German troops were ordered to dig in and construct weapons pits. German artillery was moved far to the rear to protect it against Soviet counter battery fire.[29]

On the west, the 7th and 31st Infantry Divisions of the 46th Panzer Corps were ordered to defend the flank of the 47th Panzer Corps by attacking in a southwest direction toward the Svapa River. To reinforce the attack, the 12th Panzer Division artillery remained under 46th Panzer Corps command. Battalion-sized attacks by the 175th and 132nd Soviet Rifle Divisions supported by tanks began early in the day. The Germans destroyed two KV1s and two T34s of the 19th Soviet Tank Corps around Teploie.[30]

The 47th Panzer Corps sent in the 4th Panzer Division to relieve the 20th Panzer Division, which was placed in reserve at Bobrik.[31] The German 2nd Panzer, 4th Panzer, and 9th Panzer Divisions with most of the available air support attacked the Soviet 17th Guards Rifle Corps with the objective of reaching a line about 8 km south from Ossinovyi to Leninskii west of the Snova River. The attack was not successful, and even though the Germans made some minor gains at the expense of the 6th Guards Rifle Division west of Ponyri 2, the Germans were unable to cross the road from Ponyri 2 to Olchovatka only a few km from their start line. The Soviet antitank guns, artillery, and tanks of the 16th and 19th Tank Corps supported Soviet counterattacks. The Russian defense was especially strong between Ponyri 2 and Olchovatka. To reinforce the sector, the Russians brought in the 11th Guards Tank Brigade from the 2nd Tank Army and 4th Guards Parachute Division and the 129th Tank Brigade from the Maloarchangelsk area.

The Soviet 3rd Destroyer Brigade once more was heavily engaged. Ranged across the 17th Guards Rifle Corps Front, the brigade engaged 300 German tanks on July 8 beginning at 8:30 in the morning. Typical of the action, the 1st Battery of one Russian artillery regiment opened fire when the Germans drew within 800 m and destroyed one Tiger and three medium tanks. The Germans responded with air attacks and artillery fire on the destroyer brigade, causing more losses to the already battered Soviet brigade.[32]

The German 41st Panzer Corps concentrated on protecting the east flank of the 47th Panzer Corps and keeping contact with the German 23rd Corps on the left. The Russians attacked with fifty tanks and plentiful air support along the railroad east of Ponyri 2. Model ordered the relief of the battle-worn 292nd German Infantry Division at Ponyri PC by the 10th Panzer Grenadier Division. The relief permitted the 292nd Division to absorb some replacements in its battered rifle companies. East of Ponyri PC, two regiments of the Soviet 307th Rifle Division, the 129th and 51st Tank Brigade, and the 27th Guards Tank Regiment attacked the 86th German Infantry Division. The Germans claimed fifty Soviet tanks destroyed or captured.[33]

Farther east on the 23rd German Corps Front, the Soviet 74th Rifle Division began a series of attacks. At 2:30 in the afternoon of July 7, the 12th Artillery Division delivered a heavy artillery barrage on the 78th German Division at Protossovo. The 78th Division was supported with a company of Ferdinands (ten to fifteen vehicles) and two platoons of 150mm Sturmpanzers (six to eight 150mm self-propelled howitzers) that provided a potent antitank force. The Russians suffered heavy losses and gained little ground. The 78th Division was also fighting in Trossna to the north with the 2nd Guards Parachute Division, and the Germans managed to take a hill southeast of the town. To the north, at 6 in the evening, the 383rd German Infantry Division experienced a heavy attack with artillery support from the Soviet 48th Army, again with little change.[34]

The German 9th Army commander called a conference of his corps commanders at 2 in the afternoon of July 8 to review the position. The Soviet minefields and strong defenses had prevented a quick tank-supported breakthrough. Model considered reaching Kursk with a quick tank spearhead impossible. To penetrate the Soviet defense line would take four to five days of slow, grinding attacks. New tactics to overcome the unexpected difficulties presented by the Soviet defenses included attaching more tank battalions to work with the panzer grenadiers and the relief of attacking divisions after a few days to refit and refill with replacements. The new tactics would require a heavy expenditure of men, material, and munitions.[35]

The army group commander, General Guenther von Kluge, was informed of the conclusions of the conference and, at 6 in the evening of July 8, ordered the 10th Panzer Grenadier Division to relieve the 292nd Infantry Division for a few days, and replaced the 10th Panzer Grenadier Division as army reserve with the 36th Infantry Division from the army group reserve. Kluge also moved the 8th Panzer Division from Velize to the 9th Army sector for possible use in the attack. The tank battalions of the 12th Panzer Division were made available for the main thrust of the 47th Panzer Corps.[36]

On the evening of July 8, Model issued orders for the following day: the 47th Panzer Corps was to resume the attack in the early morning of July 9 with the 20th, 4th, 2nd, and 9th Panzer Divisions and the 6th Infantry Division with the objective of breaking through the defense line. The 47th Panzer Corps formed a provisional tank brigade (Panzer Brigade Burmeister) from the 2nd and 4th Panzer Division tank battalions. During the night the German attackers moved up to the Teploie area.[37]

On the morning of July 9, Panzer Brigade Burmeister took a hill south of Samodurovka, but any farther advance was blocked by heavy Soviet antitank fire. On the Olchovatka-Ponyri road, the 2nd and 9th Panzer and the 6th Infantry Division were engaged in heavy fighting. Heavy artillery came from the area between Ossinovyi and Leninskii south of the panzer divisions. The 47th Panzer Corps attacks made no progress, and at 8 in the evening the 9th Panzer Division was attacked west of Olchovatka by the Soviet 6th Guards Rifle Division.[38]

In the 46th Panzer Corps zone, there was some artillery fire from the Soviet 70th Army on the east and a battalion-sized attack on the 20th Panzer Division. At noon on July 9, the 31st Infantry Division and the 20th Panzer Division were combined in Group Esebeck and placed between the 46th and 47th Panzer Corps. At 2 P.M. the group launched an attack, and the 20th Panzer Division made a small breakthrough at Samodurovka but was unable to exploit the gain, and had to settle for defending some high ground south of the town. The remainder of the 46th Panzer Corps continued on the defensive throughout the day under strong Soviet attack.[39]

On the 41st Panzer Corps Front, the 18th Panzer Division and the 292nd Infantry Division launched an attack at 6:30 in the morning of July 9, and after overcoming stout resistance, the Germans breached the defense line on a 500 m front at Ponyri PC. During the heavy fighting that followed, the Germans employed at least one of the Ferdinand battalions. The Russians counterattacked in the afternoon with tank and artillery support but were unable to regain the lost ground. The Luftwaffe played a significant role in the skirmish, which was still in doubt when darkness halted the action.

On the 23rd German Corps Front during July 9, the Soviets sent two companies against the 78th German Division at Trossna and delivered a heavy bombardment on the 78th and 216th Divisions. In the evening the 23rd and 41st Panzer Corps were still under attack; the 47th Panzer Corps was defending its small gain; and the 46th Panzer Corps was on the defensive. Model ordered a pause in the afternoon to rest his troops and to repair tanks with the intention of attacking again on July 10. The poor results achieved on July 9 and the pause in the afternoon indicated that Model had given up any hope of reaching Kursk.[40]

The battle resumed with full force on the morning of July 10. The German objectives set for the day were very modest. The main effort of the German 9th Army on July 10 was concentrated on the 46th and 47th Panzer Corps Fronts. The 47th Panzer Corps with the bulk of the tanks in the 9th Army was assigned the limited task of pushing about 5 km south through Teploie to high ground near Molotytschi. Panzer Brigade Burmeister, then including the 2nd, 4th, and 20th Panzer Divisions less one panzer grenadier regiment, was to remain at Samodurovka north of Teploie in 9th Army Reserve. The Luftwaffe promised to provide all-out support for the 47th Panzer Corps attack.[41]

The 47th Panzer Corps attacked toward Teploie as ordered with the 2nd, 4th, and 20th Panzer Divisions and became involved in intense fighting in difficult terrain. Heavy Soviet artillery and mortar fire plus Soviet air attacks stalled the Germans. By noon of July 10, the Germans gave up and returned to their original positions. The Soviets counterattacked in the afternoon with elements of the 2nd Tank Army, the 19th Tank Corps, the 40th, 70th Guards, and 75th Guards Rifle Divisions supported by the 1st Guards Artillery Division.[42]

The 46th Panzer Corps with the 258th, 7th, and 31st Infantry Divisions was ordered to pressure the east flank of the 70th Soviet Army on July 10. The 258th Division attacked the 280th Soviet Rifle Division but made little progress and was counterattacked twice.[43] The 258th Division took a hill, but was forced to give it up when the 280th Soviet Rifle Division counterattacked. The German 7th Infantry Division advanced a short distance, but the Soviet 175th Rifle Division counterattacked with T34s, forcing the Germans to retreat while losing six T34s. Both corps returned to their original positions by evening. There was no breakthrough and nothing was achieved.[44]

On the east flank the Russians attacked the 78th Division of the 23rd German Corps in the early hours at Protossovo. The Soviet 74th and 148th Rifle Divisions used a regiment of infantry and had strong tank and air support. The Russians lost twelve tanks, but gained some ground. During the day, the 216th and 78th German Infantry Divisions received heavy artillery fire from the Soviet 12th Artillery Division. Elements of the 78th Division with the help of some Ferdinands took a hill near Trossna, and another group took the town at 1 P.M. on July 10, taking 824 prisoners.[45]

In the 41st Panzer Corps sector the 5th Soviet Artillery Division and the Soviet Air Force pounded the 86th and 10th Panzer Grenadier Division positions, followed by tank attacks in the 307th Soviet Rifle Division sector at Ponyri PC, but there were no strong infantry attacks. At 6 in the evening of July 10, six to eight Soviet tanks took a hill near Ponyri PC but were hit by

Stuka attacks and driven off. According to prisoner interrogations, the Russians had suffered heavy losses.[46]

Model had a long conference with the commander of the 47th Panzer Corps concerning the plans for July 11. The divisions of the corps faced with new Soviet units were worn out and battle weary. An attack by the 47th Corps on July 11 was impossible, but the corps was to provide supporting fire. The entire 12th Panzer Division was assigned to the 47th Panzer Corps by Kluge who thought that the addition of two more panzer divisions might improve the situation and planned to move the 5th and 8th Panzer Divisions to the Kursk area.[47]

On July 11, the Russians attacked with a vengeance to hold the German panzer divisions. The heaviest attacks fell on the 41st Panzer Corps at Ponyri PC, but the 46th and 47th Panzer Corps also were heavily engaged. A German attack group tried to hold Trossna in the 23rd Corps sector but was driven back.[48]

In the evening of July 11, Kluge released the 12th Panzer Division and the 36th Infantry Division to the 46th Panzer Corps with the hope of a breakthrough on July 12. A night attack at Olchovatka failed, and the entire 9th Army was in defensive positions during the evening. On the morning of July 12, the Soviet offensive had opened north Orel, and divisions immediately began to flow north to halt the Russian attack. At 8 in the morning of July 12, the 12th Panzer Division and 36th Infantry Division were halted on their way to the 9th Army and turned north. Two battalions of heavy artillery and a company of ten Ferdinands were dispatched also at 8 and two more companies of Ferdinands left at 9. By 11:40 all of the 12th Panzer and 36th Infantry Divisions were under the command of the 2nd Panzer Army defending itself against the new Soviet offensive.[49]

During July 12, the 9th Army was quiet. Later in the day, the 20th Panzer Division was sent to the 2nd Panzer Army, and at 5:45 in the evening Model was given command of both the 9th Army and the 2nd Panzer Army, to coordinate the battle in the Orel salient.[50] During the following days, the Russians launched strong attacks on the 9th Army to prevent the transfer of divisions to the north. Russian and German sources differ on the line on the evening of July 12. German sources showed Trossna, Ponyri PC, Kashara, Teploie, and Obydenki Ismailov, all in German hands on the evening of July 12. To the contrary, Russian maps show all of those towns in Russian hands. The German 9th Army had advanced less than 20 km in the eight days from July 5 to July 12 and had made their best gains on the first two days. Only at Teploie did the Germans make a dent in the Soviet second defense line. The addition of panzer and infantry divisions from the Army Group Center reserve did not change the course of the battle. The Russians had ample reserves to counter any German reinforcements.

The cost to both sides was heavy. The Soviet armies were not able to drive back the Germans easily, even after a number of German divisions had been diverted north. However, while the Russians had ample replacements available for their rifle and tank companies, the Germans had very little in reserve for their divisions. The German Army began its long deadly retreat back to Berlin.

CHAPTER 13

Conclusion

Far more has been published about Stalingrad and the battle of Moscow than about Kursk, even though by most measures, number of men, number of armored vehicles, and casualties suffered per day, Kursk was the biggest battle ever fought. In light of new information released by the Russians, there is justification in another study of the Battle of Kursk. Most Western studies of the battle have been based on German sources, and even Soviet authors frequently quote published German memoirs. Previous studies have related little about the Red Army forces opposing the Germans, certainly not with the same detail regarding the German forces, leaving the impression of a faceless Russian mass of poorly trained cannon fodder. Even many Soviet works provided the division numbers and the commander, with an occasional anecdote about a regiment or battery. However, seldom was enough information provided to give life to the units. With the publication of the comprehensive monthly order of battle of the Red Army, it has been possible to verify and further define the history of each of the Soviet units to the battalion level that took part in battle. Now, the reader can learn more about each unit and better understand how and why Red Army units performed as they did.

The narrative is based on quantitative data such as the number of km advanced, the number of tanks lost, and the villages held plus a limited use of anecdotes from prisoner-of-war interrogations and German and Russian published descriptions. Details in this narrative may be revised when the Russian military archives and files in the Public Record Office are opened to everyone, but the evidence available does support the main thesis, that the Battle of Kursk demonstrated the Red Army could defeat the Germans alone.

The significance of the Battle of Kursk was that after nearly four years of war beginning in September 1939, a staged German offensive was defeated in less than two weeks! In other instances, once the German General Staff had prepared an offensive operation, it had succeeded or had taken months to stop. The campaigns in Poland, France, Norway, and the Balkans had proceeded like clockwork according to the schedules forecast by the German planners.

The initial German attack on Russia in June 1941 continued for nearly six months before the Red Army was able to gather sufficient resources in December 1941 to halt the German army worn down by continuous fighting and running short of supplies. In the summer of 1942, the German offensive in the south moved forward swiftly for hundreds of miles to the shores of the Caspian Sea to be halted after five months by dogged street fighting in Stalingrad. By November 1942 the Germans had occupied all but a few shallow bridgeheads in Stalingrad. Only then was the Red Army able to drive the Germans back, but in the years 1941 and 1942 large areas and thousands of men and machines were lost before the tide turned. Is it any wonder that Hitler was confident that he would be able once again to drive deep into Soviet territory in 1943?

To win at Kursk, the Germans had to crush a defense line in the morning, close up to the next line in the afternoon, and in the evening complete preparations to crush that line the next day. The first day, July 5, went well for the Germans who pierced the first line on both the north and the south shoulders of the Kursk bulge. But even on the first day, the Germans added a note of caution to their reports of the battle going according to plan because too many Russians evaded the attackers and retreated to strengthen the second line.

The Germans were more successful on the south shoulder because of the presence of the powerful 2nd SS Panzer Corps and the Gross Deutschland Panzer Grenadier Division in the 48th Panzer Corps. In all areas except the 2nd SS Panzer Corps sector, the Germans fell behind schedule the first day, giving the Russians ample time to bring in divisions and tank units from the army reserve which delayed the Germans even more on the second day. The Russians were more successful on the north shoulder because the Soviet 13th Army was in better condition than the Russian armies in the south, and there was more artillery support.

The Germans lost the Battle at Kursk by the third day when they had failed to break through the Soviet second defense line. German success depended on their speedy penetration of at least eight successive Soviet defense lines before the Red Army troops in the front line could withdraw to reinforce the next line in the rear, or the Stavka could shift reserves to the threatened points. Rather than cracking the second line on July 6, the Germans were not only stopped in the north but advanced painfully in the south, encountering Russian tank supported counterattacks. The 3rd Panzer Corps of Army Detachment Kempf could not penetrate the strong Russian defenses northeast of Belgorod and failed to match the advance of the 2nd SS Panzer Corps on the right flank of the 4th Panzer Army in the south. This failure forced the 2nd SS Panzer Corps to divert the Death Head SS Panzer Grenadier Division to secure the left flank of the attack because there were no infantry divisions available to the 2nd SS Panzer Corps to perform this task.

On the west flank, the 48th Panzer Corps had infantry divisions to support the right flank of the attack; however, these were sorely pressed by Russian units moving from the 38th and 40th Army. The Gross Deutschland Panzer Grenadier Division soon ran into the 1st Soviet Tank Army (equal to a reinforced German panzer corps) on the road to Oboyan and Kursk. After the initial encounters, the 1st Tank Army dug in their tanks and closed the door to Oboyan. The 2nd SS Panzer Corps continued to advance northeast toward Prokorovka and ran into the Soviet 5th Guards Tank Army. After a series of hard-fought battles, the exhausted Germans withdrew after July 12.

When an army with superior skill attempts to overcome a more numerous foe, a primary objective is to gain local superiority in a vital sector and to use that superiority to break through the enemy's defense, attack adjoining units from the rear, and disrupt enemy communications before the more numerous army can react and bring in reserves. To paraphrase another axiom, in such a situation, the three most important factors are time, time, and time. To win, the Germans had to close the trap at Kursk in four or five days at the most, and given the mobility of the Red Army units provided by American four-wheel drive trucks, even five days may have been too slow.

By the time the Germans broke through the first line and made their way through the rear guards to the second line, the Soviet reserves in the second line, along with the withdrawing Russian divisions and divisions advancing from the third line, had gathered in the second line. Therefore, when the Germans attacked the second line they lacked the power to penetrate the Soviet defenses. The delay cost the Germans time they could not afford, and the Soviet High Command was able to move ample reserves in the path of the German advance.

The Soviet reserves were the determinate factor. The Russians were able to move divisions and tank corps from positions in the rear in a day or less. The Russians were able to put everything on the road within a few hours with the men marching and the supplies and equipment on trucks. On the other hand, the Germans still had to resort to railroad transport to move divisions even short distances. Using the railroad was a cumbersome process for the Germans; assembling trains, finding sidings for simultaneous loading, marching the troops to the loading points, ferrying supplies and equipment by horse-drawn wagons to the sidings, and loading the freight cars. Even if the distance was short enough for the men to march and the vehicles to move on the roads, the Germans lacked sufficient transport to carry the supplies and equipment. The Germans attempted to move an infantry division with trucks to defend the east flank of Army Detachment Kempf, but the movement was unsuccessful, and the division arrived late.

Given the flexibility offered by road mobility, the Russians could safely employ elastic defense, trading ground for German casualties. Although the Germans broke through one of the defensive lines in the north and two in the south, there were still six to go. Even the German penetration of the first line was not a great achievement considering the theory of elastic defense, which encouraged the defender to surrender successive lines of defense while exacting the maximum loss of the attacker's men and material at minimum expense to the defender. Rather than fighting to the last man in the first line, Soviet units withdrew when the Germans had compromised the interlocking network of strong points. The meager bag of prisoners and captured or destroyed weapons accumulated by the 2nd SS Panzer Corps on the first day of the battle, plus the implication of the reports prepared by the corps headquarters, indicated that the Russians pulled out rather than fight to the last man. As the Germans reduced individual strong points, troops in the neighboring Soviet strong points withdrew when deprived of adequate supporting fire from their nearby strong points. As a result, Soviet divisions that held sectors in the first line were still intact ten days later and holding sectors in the third line.

The most serious Soviet losses were incurred in the counterattacks launched to delay the Germans while the next Russian defensive line was reinforced. On the other hand, the Germans suffered most of their losses while breaking through defense lines. Although more Soviet tanks were lost than German, the Germans could not replace losses at the same rate as the Russians. The Soviets were acquiring 2,000 tanks per month from Russian production and Lend Lease arrivals, while German production was less than half that rate. The panzer force could not afford the costly battle of attrition that developed at Kursk. While Hitler had delayed the attack on Kursk a month to give the panzer divisions the benefit of an additional month of production, the Red Army was able to replace losses quickly from tanks and crews in depots. Later in the war, tank armies went into battle with up to a hundred surplus crews already attached to replace battle losses. While Red Army tank units had new T34s and KVs, the Germans still had many Pz IIIs, some armed with 37mm guns that were obsolete in 1942.

Hitler was correct in assuming that the Tiger tanks would have an impact on the battle. Although documentation is scanty, the anecdotes related to awarding the Hero of the Soviet Union medal posthumously to antitank gun crew members testify that the Tigers were accomplishing their primary role of breaking up the Soviet antitank gun line. The Tiger could stand out of range of the Russian 76mm guns and destroy the antitank strong points with fire from their 88mm guns. The German 88mm antiaircraft gun crews on the Western Front in 1944 said that the infantry fought only until the last 88mm gun was destroyed. Once the Soviet antitank gun line was broken, the infantry with no protection from the German medium and light tanks had no option but to withdraw.

Although German tank losses were minimal considering the intensity of the battle, the cost in infantry was high. The three SS divisions lost 20,000 killed, wounded, and missing, mainly in the panzer grenadier companies. There were 120 panzer grenadier companies with about 200 men each in the three divisions for a total strength of about 24,000 men. Given the number of losses, these companies were likely mere shadows by the battle's end on July 12, as the SS infantry was repeatedly left to defend itself from the Soviet tank supported counterattacks. Without the panzer grenadiers, the SS tanks could not hold ground as indicated several times late in the battle when the SS tanks withdrew several km in the evening to a more defensible area for the night, leaving the battlefield to the Russians.

The Kursk battle is interpreted differently by the Russians and Germans. In the eyes of most Russian historians, the battle was of extreme importance as it marked the point at which the initiative on the Eastern Front passed from the Germans to the Soviet Union. After July 1943, the German Army would dance to the tune called by the Red Army, rather than having the Stavka react to the latest plan developed by the German Army High Command.

The Russian interpretation was flawed on several counts, however. The German divisions were not reduced by the Soviet defenses and counterattacks to the extent claimed, and the Germans actually lost fewer tanks. The Russian claims of destroying German tanks were based on tanks hit and out of action, but after minor repairs most of these tanks returned to battle within a few days. Tank tracks and the wheels supporting the tracks were the most vulnerable parts, but both were easy to repair.

Another flaw was that the Russians did not defeat the 4th Panzer Army decisively and merely halted the 9th German Army in the north on July 12. Army Detachment Kempf continued to advance for several days after July 12 and halted of their own accord, not as a result of Soviet action. The Germans on the south shoulder were still a potent force when they retreated, as indicated by the deliberate speed of the withdrawal unhindered by the Russians.

The Russians lost more tanks than the Germans because immobilized Soviet tanks fell into the hands of the advancing Germans even with only minor damage. The German order to blow up these immobilized tanks when the retreat began was revealing. Minor damage to German tanks was quickly repaired because the German repair crews had worked on the German-held battlefield after almost every engagement. When the Germans were driven back by the Soviet offensives that followed, German tank losses escalated rapidly, while Soviet tank losses leveled off.

The German version is quite different. On July 13, Manstein believed that the battle was not lost and that the 24th Panzer Corps was the winning trump card. Although the 4th Panzer Army and Army Detachment Kempf with the help of the 24th Panzer Corps could have continued battering away at the Russians and won tactical victories, the German strategic goal was out of sight well before July 12. The only rational purpose in launching the German offensive was the possibility of cutting off six or more Soviet armies in a pocket that would have equaled the German victories of 1941 and 1942. The pocket had to be closed quickly, and a 200 km gap opened in the Soviet line before the Russians could bring up their reserves. Had the Germans achieved this goal, they might have had the resources to defeat the Russians tank corps and armies piecemeal as they arrived. However, once the 5th Guards Tank Army, the 5th Guards Army, and the 69th Army were in position in the third defense line, there was no chance of breaking through as additional Soviet armies were moving up behind. The addition of two or more panzer divisions from the German Army Group Center reserve had not helped in the north, and there is little reason to believe the addition of two weak panzer divisions would have altered the outcome in the south. Even if the 24th Panzer Corps had been able to break through the first three reserve armies, the other reserve armies had time to occupy the first of the three "front" defensive lines. When Manstein stated that the Soviet reserves were beaten, he was careful to modify the term reserves, first as operational, "*operative*," and later as available, "*greifbaren*."[1]

The Soviet cupboard was far from bare on July 12 as Manstein claimed. Had the Germans defeated the Russians in the tank battle at Prokorovka, additional Soviet tank forces could have been called in. Only three of the five Russian tank armies were involved in the battle, and the one backing up the north shoulder was still fresh. The 3rd and 4th Tank Armies plus numerous independent armored corps, brigades, and regiments were available. The closer the Germans moved to Moscow the better the Soviet communications, and the easier it would have been for the Russians to move in large formations.

In the eyes of many British, German, and American historians, the Battle of Kursk was but one of many dreary occasions on which Hitler intervened at the crucial moment turning victory into defeat by disrupting the carefully laid plans of the professional German officers. Perhaps Hitler had the clearest view of what was happening at Kursk. He knew that the Soviet defenders had suffered heavy losses and that the Tiger tanks had fulfilled his expectations by disabling if not destroying hundreds of Soviet tanks at little cost to the Germans. The elite German infantry in the Gross Deutschland and SS divisions had fought well and had cleaned up behind the tanks, but had suffered serious casualties. These four divisions had driven the 6th Soviet Guards Army and the 1st Tank Army steadily, if slowly, northward for eight days.

Hitler realized that the cost in infantry was high and that by July 13, there was nothing to be gained from continuing to expose German troops in an offensive with an unattainable goal, using troops that would be needed in the immediate future to withstand the onslaught of numerous Soviet offensives up and down the line. The German divisions training in France would have to be sent to Italy to meet Allied threats in the Mediterranean rather than to provide a strategic reserve for Russia, as the divisions from France had saved the Germans in February 1943. Henceforth the Russian Front would have to live on its own resources, and there was no point in squandering German lives for a few more square km of Russian soil.

The interpretation of Manstein's discussion of July 13 with Hitler indicating that Hitler called off the battle because of Sicily is questionable. Although Hitler mentioned Sicily as one reason for the termination of the offensive, Manstein also noted other reasons were given including the threat to the Mius River front and the Soviet attack north of Orel that began on July 12. Hitler did not cancel the offensive at Kursk primarily because of the invasion of Sicily. Only one German division, the 1st Parachute Division from France, was sent to Sicily after the invasion to reinforce the four German divisions being reconstructed from fragments of divisions that had not been able to reach their parent formations in Tunisia and some replacement battalions. Other divisions in France continued to flow to Russia in July and August of 1943.

The failure of Hitler actually to send significant numbers of troops from Russia to Italy and the subsequent transfer of divisions from France to Italy indicated that Hitler knew he could meet the challenge in Italy from resources in France. In fact, only one German SS division left the east, along with the headquarters of the 2nd SS Panzer Corps. As Hitler stated, the SS units were sent to Italy for political purposes, hoping the SS soldiers would infuse some spirit in the Italian Fascists.[2] The Sicily operation did worry Hitler, however, as well as the threat in August of Italian defection, and he ordered the transfer in August of skeleton reforming divisions from France to deceive the Italians that there was a creditable German presence in northern Italy.

Although the Allied invasion of Sicily had little impact on the Battle of Kursk in July, the Allied invasion of Italy in September did have a major impact on the fighting in Russia. The German "Stalingrad" divisions refitting in France in July were sent to Italy beginning in August rather than forming a strategic reserve of twenty divisions that would have been of significance in restoring the situation when the Russians broke through in August 1943.

The Italians may have made their greatest contribution to the Axis cause by opening negotiations for surrender. Given the possibility of a quick, easy occupation of Italy, the British and Americans were compelled to go forward with the Italian invasion in September 1943, rather than concentrating on a second front in France. The Italian campaign turned into a frustrating and costly endeavor for the Allies as the Germans fought a skillful defensive campaign.

A third interpretation of the Battle of Kursk can be considered that supports neither the Russian nor Manstein's version. The Germans failed to win the battle because they did not achieve their objective (they did not close the pocket). The Germans did not lose because the panzer divisions emerged from the battle weakened but still powerful enough to play a major role in delaying the Russian offensives that followed.

The Russians did not lose the battle; they prevented the Germans from closing the pocket. The Russians did not achieve a great victory by destroying the German divisions and driving them from the field of battle. Instead, having suffered heavy losses themselves, the Russians did little to harass the retreating Germans until a new Soviet offensive was launched in August 1943.

Nevertheless, more than any other event, the Battle of Kursk hastened the end of World War II. The Battle of Kursk was the wake-up call that shook the American policymakers into action and made them realize that it was an American responsibility to end the long and bloody war as quickly as possible. The flow of Lend Lease turned into a flood, and Allied plans to invade Europe were finalized and carried through in June of 1944.

About the Author

WALTER S. DUNN, JR. had a 40-year career directing museums, including the Buffalo & Erie County Historical Society and the Iowa Science Center. His books include *The Soviet Economy and the Red Army, 1930–1945* (1995), *Hitler's Nemesis: The Red Army* (1994), and *Second Front Now, 1943* (1981).

Bibliography

Babich, P., and A. G. Baier. *Razvitie Vooruzheniia i Organizatsii Sovetski Suxoputnik Voisk v Godi Velikoi Otechestvennoi Voini.* Moscow: Izdanie Akademii, 1990.

Bartov, Omer. *Hitler's Army Soldiers, Nazis, and War in the Third Reich.* New York: Oxford University Press, 1991.

Beaumont, Joan. *Comrades in Arms: British Aid to Russia, 1941–1945.* London: Davis-Poynter, 1980.

Dunn, Walter S., Jr. *Hitler's Nemesis: The Red Army, 1930–1945.* Westport, CT: Praeger, 1994.

———. *Second Front Now 1943.* University, AL: University of Alabama Press, 1981.

———. *The Soviet Economy and the Red Army, 1930–1945.* Westport, CT: Praeger, 1995.

Erickson, John. *The Road to Berlin.* Boulder, CO: Westview Press, 1983.

Fremde Heer Ost. Captured German Records. Washington, DC: National Archives.

Glantz, David M. *From the Don to the Dnepr: Soviet Offensive Operations, December 1942–August 1943.* London: F. Cass, 1991.

Harrison, Gordon. *Cross Channel Attack: United States Army in World War II.* Washington: Department of the Army, 1951.

Harrison, Mark. *Soviet Planning in Peace and War, 1938–1945.* Cambridge: Cambridge University Press, 1985.

Haupt, Werner von. *Geschichte der 134. Infanterie Division.* Weinsberg: Herausgegeben vom Kamardenkreis der Ehemaligen, 134. Inf.-Division, 1971.

The Illustrated Encyclopedia of 20th Century Weapons and Warfare. 24 vols. New York: Columbia House, 1969.

Keilig, Wolf. *Das Deutsche Heer, 1939–1945.* 3 vols. Bad Nauheim: Podzun, 1956-1972.

Klink, Ernst. *Das Gesetz des Handelns die Operation "Zitadelle,"* 1943. Stuttgart: Deutsche Verlags-Anstalt, 1966.

Koch, Adalbert. *Flak. Die Geschichte der Deutschen Flak-artillerie, 1935–1945.* Bad Nauheim: Podzun, 1965.

Koltunov, G. A. *Kurskaia Bitva.* Moscow: Voenizdat, 1970.

Krivosheev, G. F. *Grif Sekretnosti Snyat. Poteri Vooruzhenikh sil SSSR v Voinakh Voevikh Deistviiakh i Voennikh Konflitakh.* Moscow: Izdatelistvo, 1993.

Losik, O. A. *Stroitelistvo i Boyevoye Primeneniye Sovetskikh Tankovykh Voysk v Gody Velikoy Otechestvennoy Voyne.* Moscow: Voyenizdat, 1979.

Lucas, James. *War on the Eastern Front, 1941–1945: The German Soldier in Russia.* New York: Bonanza Books, 1979.

Manstein, Erich von. *Lost Victories.* Novato, CA: Presidio Press, 1982.

———. *Velorene Seige.* Bonn: Athenaum-Verlag, 1958.

Mehner, Kurt, ed. *Die Geheimentages Berichte der Deutschen Wermachffuhrung im Zweiten Weltkrieg, 1939–1945.* vol. 7. Osnabruck: Biblio Verlag, 1988.

Mitchell, B. R. *European Historical Statistics, 1750–1970.* London: The Macmillan Press, 1978.

Mueller-Hillebrand, Burkhart. *Das Heer, 1933–1945.* 3 vols. Frankfurt am Main: E. S. Mittler & Sohn, 1959–1969.

Murmantseva, V. S. "Ratnii i Trudovoi Podvig Sovetski Jenshin." *Vizh* 5 (May 1985), pp. 73–81.

Parotkin, Ivan, ed. *The Battle of Kursk.* Moscow: Progress Publishers, 1974. Public Record Office. PREM 3 190/3.

Records of German Field Commands, Divisions, Sixty-fifth Division, Captured German Records, Microfilm Series GG 65, T315, Roll 1037.

Sajer, Guy. *The Forgotten Soldier.* New York: Harper & Row, 1971.

Schramm, Percy Ernst. *Kriegstagebuch des Oberkommandos der Wehrmacht.* 4 vols. Frankfurt am Main: Bernard und Graefe, 1961–1965.

Seaton, Albert. *The Russo-German War, 1941–45.* New York: Praeger, 1970.

Stadler, Silvester. Die Offensive Gegen Kursk. Osnabruck: Munion, 1980.

Tessin, Georg. *Verbande und Truppen der Deutschen Wehrmacht und Waffen SS in Zweiten Weltkrieg, 1939–1945.* 14 vols. Osnabruck: Biblio, 1965–1980.

Tiushkevich, Stepan A., ed. *Sovetskie Vooruzhennye Sily.* Moscow: Voenizdat, 1978.

U.S. War Department. *Handbook on German Military Forces. Technical Manual E 30-451.* Washington, DC: GPO, 1945.

Van Tuyll, Hubert P. *Feeding the Bear: American Aid to the Soviet Union, 1941–1945.* Westport, CT: Greenwood Press, 1989.

Zaloga, Steven J., and James Grandsen. *Soviet Tanks and Combat Vehicles of World War Two.* London: Arms and Armour Press, 1984.

Zhukov, Georgi K. *Marshal Zhukov's Greatest Battles.* New York: Harper & Row, 1969.

Ziemke, Earl F. *Stalingrad to Berlin: The German Campaign in Russia, 1942–1945.* New York: Dorset Press, 1968.

Notes

PREFACE
1. Georg Tessin, *Verbande und Truppen der Deutschen Wehrmacht und Waffen SS in Zweiten Weltkrieg, 1939–1945*, 14 vols. (Osnabruck: Biblio, 1965–1980), *passim*.

INTRODUCTION
1. Erich von Manstein, *Verlorene Siege* (Bonn: Athenaum-Verlag, 1958), pp. 488–506.
2. Walter S. Dunn, Jr., *The Soviet Economy and the Red Army, 1930–1945* (Westport, CT: Praeger, 1995), p. 210.
3. Dunn, p. 116.

CHAPTER 1
1. Albert Seaton, *The Russo-German War, 1941–45* (New York: Praeger, 1970), pp. 334-36; Earl F. Ziemke, *Stalingrad to Berlin: The German Campaign in Russia, 1942–1945* (New York: Dorset Press, 1968), p. 79.
2. Burkhart Mueller-Hillebrand, *Das Heer 1933–1945* (Frankfurt am Main: E. S. Mittler & Sohn, 1959–1969), III, Chapter 12, *passim*.
3. John Erickson, *The Road to Berlin* (Boulder, CO: Westview Press, 1983), pp. 45–46.
4. Ibid.
5. Ibid., p. 46.
6. Ibid., p. 47.
7. Ibid., p. 34.
8. Seaton, p. 344.
9. Ivan Parotkin, ed., *The Battle of Kursk* (Moscow: Progress Publishers, 1974), p. 79.
10. Ibid., p. 78.
11. Walter S. Dunn, Jr., *The Soviet Economy and the Red Army, 1930–1945* (Westport, CT: Praeger, 1995), pp. 201–2.
12. Parotkin, p. 79.
13. Ibid., pp. 79–80.
14. Ibid., pp. 80–81.
15. Ibid., p. 81.
16. Georg Tessin, *Verbande und Truppen der Deutschen Wehrmacht und Waffen SS in Zweiten Weltkrieg, 1939–1945* (Osnabruck: Biblio, 1965–1980), I, p. 85.
17. Seaton, p. 346.
18. Erickson, p. 28.
19. Earl F. Ziemke, *Stalingrad to Berlin: The German Campaign in Russia, 1942–1945* (New York: Dorset Press, 1968), p. 84.
20. Erickson, p. 47.

21. David M. Glantz, *From the Don to the Dnepr: Soviet Offensive Operations, December 1942–August 1943* (London: F. Cass, 1991), p. 384.
22. Ziemke, p. 86.

CHAPTER 2

1. S. A. Tiushkevich, ed., *Sovetskie Vooruzhennye Sily* (Moscow: Voenizdat, 1978). p. 329.
2. Georgi K. Zhukov, *Marshal Zhukov's Greatest Battles* (New York: Harper & Row, 1969), p. 491.
3. Walter S. Dunn, Jr., *The Soviet Economy and the Red Army, 1930–1945* (Westport, CT, Praeger, 1995), pp. 37–38.
4. *Fremde Heer Ost*, Captured German Records, National Archives (Washington. DC: General Services Administration, 1982), H 3/1506, Roll 587, Frame 14.
5. *FHO*, CGR, H 3/193, Roll 556, Frame 787.
6. B. R. Mitchell, *European Historical Statistics, 1750–1970* (London: The Macmillan Press, 1978), pp. 7, 31.
7. G. F. Krivosheev, *Grif Sekretnosti Snyat. Poteri Vooruzhenikh sil SSSR v Voinakh Voevikh Deistviiakh i Voennikh Konflitakh* (Moscow: Izdatelistvo, 1993), p. 186.
8. Ibid., p. 152.
9. *FHO*, CGR, H 3/47, Roll 459, Frame 7392.
10. V. S. Murmantseva, "Ratnii i Trudovoi Podvig Sovetski Jenshin," *Vizh 5*, May 1985, p. 74.
11. *FHO*, CGR, H 3/69, Roll 549, Frame 121.
12. Murmantseva, p. 76.
13. *FHO*, CGR, H 3/1508, Roll 587, Frame 24; James Lucas, *War on the Eastern Front, 1941–1945: The German Soldier in Russia* (New York: Bonanza Books, 1979), p. 57.
14. Ivan Parotkin, ed., *The Battle of Kursk* (Moscow: Progress Publishers, 1974), p. 265.
15. Ibid., p. 266.
16. *FHO*, CGR, H 3/1079, Roll 581, Frame 726.
17. Manual of the Red Army, December 1943, *FHO*, CGR, T78, Roll 462, Frame 6441494.
18. *FHO*, CGR, T78, Roll 462, Frame 6441494; H 3/113a, Roll 551, Frame 662.
19. *FHO*, CGR, T78, Roll 460, Frame 6438809-12.
20. *FHO*, CGR, T78, Roll 460, Frame 6438464.
21. Krivosheev, p. 152.
22. P. Babich and A. G. Baier, *Razvitie Vooruzheniia i Organizatsii Sovetski Suxoputnik Voisk v Godi Velikoi Otechestvennoi Voini* (Moscow: Izdanie Akademii, 1990), *passim*. This book is a convenient summary of the changes that occurred in the weapons and organization of the Red Army during the Great Patriotic War.
23. *FHO*, CGR, T78, Roll 460, Frames 6438493 and 6438439.
24. Silvester Stadler, *Die Offensive Gegen Kursk* (Osnabruck: Munion, 1980), p. 130.
25. *FHO*, CGR, H 3/64.2, Roll 460, Frame 6438505.
26. John Erickson, *The Road to Berlin* (Boulder, CO: Westview Press, 1983), p. 67.
27. Dunn, *Soviet Economy*, pp. 169–70.
28. Parotkin, p. 265.
29. Babich and Baier, p. 52.
30. *The Illustrated Encyclopedia of 20th Century Weapons and Warfare*, 24 vols. (New York: Columbia House, 1969), VII, p. 717.
31. Stadler, p. 138.

32. Babich and Baier, p. 160.
33. Ibid, p. 60.
34. Ibid., p. 46.
35. Ibid., p. 43.
36. Ibid, p. 45.
37. Ibid., p. 48.
38. Ibid., pp. 48–49.
39. Ibid., pp. 62–63.
40. Ibid., p. 65.
41. Stadler, pp. 130, 147.
42. Mark Harrison, *Soviet Planning in Peace and War, 1938–1945* (Cambridge: Cambridge University Press, 1985), p. 118.
43. Krivosheev, p. 370.
44. *FHO*, CGR, H 3/104, Roll 551, Frame 251.
45. Krivosheev, pp. 350–51.
46. Ibid, pp. 354–56.
47. Ibid, pp. 357–58.
48. Hubert P. Van Tuyll, *Feeding the Bear: American Aid to the Soviet Union 1941–1945* (Westport, CT: Greenwood Press, 1989), p. 164.
49. Krivosheev, p. 363.
50. Joan Beaumont, *Comrades in Arms: British Aid to Russia, 1941–1945* (London Davis-Poynter, 1980), p. 137.

CHAPTER 3

1. Burkhart Mueller-Hillebrand, *Das Heer, 1933–1945*. III (Frankfurt am Main: E. S. Mittler & Sohn, 1959–1969), p. 111.
2. Ibid., p. 110.
3. Ibid., pp. 98–99.
4. Ibid., p. 99.
5. Ibid., p. 101.
6. Ibid., p. 99; Ernst Klink, *Das Gesetz des Handelns die Operation "Zitadelle," 1943* (Stuttgart: Deutsche Verlags-Anstalt, 1966), p. 82.
7. Percy Ernst Schramm, III2, *Kriegstagebuch des Oberkommandos der Wehrmacht* (Frankfurt am Main: Bernard und Graefe, 1961–65), p. 1573.
8. Ibid., pp. 1572–73; Klink, pp. 35–37.
9. Schramm, I, p. 87E; Mueller-Hillebrand, III, pp. 251–54.
10. Schramm, III1, p. 102.
11. Ibid., p. 224.
12. Klink, pp. 122–24.
13. Mueller-Hillebrand, III, p. 140.
14. Ibid., p. 114.
15. Schramm, III1, p. 75.
16. Ibid., p. 103.
17. Gordon Harrison, *Cross Channel Attack: United States Army in World War II* (Washington: Department of the Army, 1951), pp. 145–46.
18. Klink, pp. 37–38; Schramm, III1, p. 256.
19. Walter S. Dunn, Jr., *Second Front Now, 1943* (University, AL: The University of Alabama Press, 1981), pp. 257–58.
20. Schramm, III1, p. 53.

21. Ibid., p. 45.
22. Adalbert Koch, *Flak. Die Geschiste der Deutschen Flak-artillerie, 1935–1945* (Bad Nauheim: Podzun, 1965), p. 301.
23. Schramm, III1, p. 46.
24. Ibid., p. 71; Klink, p. 34; Koch, pp. 299–300.
25. Mueller-Hillebrand, III, p. 71.
26. Ibid., p. 110.
27. Public Record Office, PREM 3 190/3, CIGS to PM, September 25, 1942.
28. Silvester Stadler, *Die Offensive Gegen Kursk* (Osnabruck: Munion, 1980), p. 132.
29. Georg Tessin, *Verbande und Truppen der Deutschen Wehrmacht und Waffen SS in Zweiten Weltkrieg, 1939–1945*. I, (Osnabruck: Biblio, 1965–1980), p. 125.
30. Schramm, II2, p. 1572.
31. Mueller-Hillebrand, III, pp. 99, 110; Schramm, III2, p. 1481.
32. Walter S. Dunn, Jr., *Second Front Now 1943* (University, AL: University of Alabama Press, 1981), pp. 232–35.
33. Records of German Field Commands, Divisions, Sixty-fifth Division, Captured German Records, Microfilm Series GG 65, T315, Roll 1037, Frame 113.
34. *CGR*, GG65, T315, Roll 1037, Frame 41.
35. *CGR*, GG65, T315, Roll 1037, Frame 97.
36. *CGR*, GG65, T315, Roll 1037, Frames 154, 156.
37. *CGR*, GG65, T315, Roll 1037, Frames 66, 111–12, 728.
38. *CGR*, GG65, T315, Roll 1037, Frames 68–70, 88–92, 725–26, and 761.
39. *CGR*, GG65, T315, Roll 1037, Frame 632.
40. Mueller-Hillebrand, III, p. 111; Schramm, III2, p. 1416.
41. Tessin, I, p. 170.
42. Schramm, III1, pp. 130, 265, and 335; Wolf Keilig, *Das Deutsche Heer 1939–1945*, 3 vols. (Bad Nauheim: Podzun, 1956–1972), 101 44 Division.
43. *CGR*, T78, Roll GG30, Frame 368360; Mueller-Hillebrand, III, p. 117.
44. Klink, p. 37; Tessin, I, pp. 65–66.
45. Mueller-Hillebrand, III, p. 120.
46. Klink, p. 176.
47. Werner von Haupt, *Geschichte der 134. Infanterie Division* (Weinsberg: Herausgegeben vom Kamardenkreis der Ehemaligen, 134. Inf.-Division, 1971), pp. 157–58.
48. Ibid., pp. 161, 164.
49. Ibid., p. 166.
50. Klink, p. 79.
51. Ibid., p. 33.
52. Schramm, III1, p. 57.
53. Haupt, p. 174.

CHAPTER 5
1. G. A. Koltunov, *Kurskaia Bitva* (Moscow: Voenizdat, 1970), p. 75.
2. Ibid.
3. Ibid.
4. Ibid.
5. Ibid.
6. Ibid.
7. Ibid.

8. Ibid.
9. Ibid.
10. The army probably had more than the 22 SUs in the source. Ibid.
11. Ibid.
12. Ibid.
13. Silvester Stadler, *Die Offensive Gegen Kursk* (Osnabruck: Munion, 1980), pp. 80, 114.
14. Koltunov, p. 75.
15. Stadler, p. 146.
16. Ibid., p. 123.
17. Ibid., p. 138.
18. Koltunov, p. 75.
19. Stadler, p. 91.
20. Ibid., p. 30.
21. Ibid., p. 130.
22. Ibid., p. 105.
23. Ibid., p. 123.
24. Ibid., p. 147.
25. Ibid., p. 138.

CHAPTER 6

1. Burkhart Mueller-Hillebrand, *Das Heer, 1933–1945*, vol. In (Frankfurt am Main: E. S. Mittler & Sohn, 1959–1969), pp. 221, 274.
2. Ibid., p. 274.
3. Ernst Klink, *Das Gesetz des Handelns die Operation "Zitadelle," 1943* (Stuttgart: Deutsche Verlags-Anstalt, 1966), pp. 44–45, 142; Mueller-Hillebrand, III, p. 274.
4. Mueller-Hillebrand, III, p. 274; Klink, p. 44.
5. Klink, pp. 163–64.
6. Ibid., pp. 45–46, 241.
7. Mueller-Hillebrand, III, p. 274.
8. Silvester Stadler, *Die Offensive Gegen Kursk* (Osnabruck: Munion, 1980), pp. 30, 34; Mueller-Hillebrand, III, p. 274.
9. Stadler, p. 30.
10. Interview, James Vanderbogert, August 28, 1996.
11. James Lucas, *War on the Eastern Front, 1941–1945: The German Soldier in Russia* (New York: Bonanza Books, 1979), pp. 120–21.
12. Lucas, pp. 120–21.
13. Mueller-Hillebrand, III, p. 274.
14. Ibid.; Klink, p. 142.
15. G. F. Krivosheev, *Grif Sekretnosti Snyat. Poteri Vooruzhenikh sil SSSR v Voinakh Voevikh Deistviiakh i Voennikh Konflitakh* (Moscow: Izdatelistvo, 1993), p. 357.
16. Ivan Parotkin, ed., *The Battle of Kursk* (Moscow: Progress Publishers, 1974), p. 178.
17. Steven J. Zaloga and James Grandsen, *Soviet Tanks and Combat Vehicles of World War Two* (London: Arms and Armour Press, 1984), pp. 140, 225.
18. Zaloga, pp. 140, 225; Krivosheev, p. 357.
19. O. A. Losik, *Stroitelistvo i Boyevoye Premeneniye Sovetskikh Tankovykh Voysk v Gody Velikoy Otechestvennoy Voyne* (Moscow: Voyenizdat, 1979), *passim*.
20. Krivosheev, p. 357.
21. Ibid., p. 357.

22. Walter S. Dunn, Jr., *Hitler's Nemesis: The Red Army, 1930–1945* (Westport, CT: Praeger, 1994), pp. 203–08.
23. Krivosheev, p. 357.
24. Zaloga and Grandsen, p. 165.
25. Dunn, *Hitler's Nemesis*, pp. 158–60; Walter S. Dunn, Jr., *Second Front Now, 1943* (University, AL: University of Alabama Press, 1981), pp. 75–93.
26. Stadler, p. 138.
27. Omer Bartov, *Hitler's Army Soldiers, Nazis, and War in the Third Reich* (New York: Oxford University Press, 1991), p. 191.
28. Ibid., p. 53.
29. Klink, p. 121.
30. Percy Ernst Schranun, *Kriegstagebuch des Oberkommandos der Wehrmacht*, vol. III, no. 1, (Frankfurt am Main: Bernard und Graefe, 1961–1965), p. 686.

CHAPTER 7
1. Ivan Parotkin, ed., *The Battle of Kursk* (Moscow: Progress Publishers, 1974), p. 162.
2. Ibid., p. 177.
3. Ibid., pp. 123–24.
4. Ibid., pp. 36–37.
5. Ibid., pp. 162–63.
6. Ibid., p. 163; G. A. Koltunov, *Kurskaia Bitva* (Moscow: Voenizdat, 1970), p. 60.
7. Koltunov, pp. 60–61.
8. Parotkin, pp. 83–84.
9. Koltunov, p. 68.
10. P. Babich and A. G. Baier, *Razvitie Vooruzheniia i Organizatsii Sovetski Suxoputnik Voisk v Godi Velikoi Otechestvennoi Voini* (Moscow: Izdanie Akademii, 1990), p. 55; Koltunov, pp. 68–69.
11. Parotkin, pp. 40–41.
12. Ibid., p. 41.

CHAPTER 8
1. Guy Sajer, *The Forgotten Soldier* (New York: Harper & Row, 1971), pp. 234–35.
2. Ivan Parotkin, ed., *The Battle of Kursk* (Moscow: Progress Publishers, 1974), p. 45.
3. Silvester Stadler, *Die Offensive Gegen Kursk* (Osnabruck: Munion, 1980), p. 113.
4. U.S. War Department, *Handbook on German Military Forces TM-E 30–451* (Washington, D.C.: GPO, 1945), Section IV, p. ii.
5. Vanderbogert interview, August 28, 1996.
6. Ibid.
7. Stadler, pp. 45, 55.
8. Ibid., p. 45.
9. Ibid., p. 46.
10. Ibid., p. 46.
11. Ibid., p. 31.
12. G. A. Koltunov, *Kurskaia Bitva* (Moscow: Voenizdat, 1970), p. 140.
13. Ernst Klink, *Das Gesetz des Handelns die Operation "Zitadelle," 1943* (Stuttgart: Deutsche Verlags-Anstalt, 1966), p. 211.
14. Ibid., p. 209.
15. Koltunov, p. 135.
16. Ibid., p.139.

17. Klink, p. 241.
18. Koltunov, p. 138.
19. Klink, p. 209; Stadler, p. 48; Koltunov, pp. 140–41.
20. Klink, p. 210; Koltunov, pp. 139–40.
21. Koltunov, p. 141.
22. Stadler, p. 39.
23. Ibid., p. 39.
24. Parotkin, p. 219.
25. Klink, p. 210; Stadler, pp. 44, 55.
26. Klink, p. 241.
27. Burkhart Mueller-Hillebrand, *Das Heer*, 1933–1945 vol. III (Frankfurt am Main: E. S. Mittler & Sohn, 1959–1969), p. 269.
28. Klink p. 211.
29. Stadler, p. 46.
30. Koltunov, p. 136.
31. Klink, p. 213.
32. Koltunov, p. 142.
33. Ibid., p. 142.
34. Klink, pp. 213–14; Koltunov, p. 214.
35. Koltunov, p. 142; Klink, pp. 213–14.
36. Klink, p. 214.
37. Ibid.
38. Ibid.
39. Ibid.

CHAPTER 9

1. Ernst Klink, *Das Gesetz des Handelns die Operation "Zitadelle," 1943* (Stuttgart: Deutsche Verlags-Anstalt, 1966), pp. 217–18; G. A. Koltunov, *Kurskaia Bitva* (Moscow: Voenizdat, 1970), pp. 143–44.
2. Klink, p. 219; Koltunov, p. 144.
3. Klink, p. 219.
4. Silvester Stadler, *Die Offensive Gegen Kursk* (Osnabruck: Munion, 1980), p. 72; Klink, p. 217; Koltunov, p. 143.
5. Stadler, p. 72.
6. Stadler, p. 72; Klink, p. 217; Koltunov, pp. 143–44.
7. Stadler, pp. 49–50, 56.
8. Koltunov, pp. 146–47; Kurt Mehner, ed., *Die Geheimentages Berichte der Deutschen Wermachfführung im Zweiten Weltkrieg, 1939–1945*, vol. 7 (Osnabruck: Biblio Verlag, 1988), p. 96; Stadler, p. 50.
9. Stadler, p. 56.
10. Koltunov, pp. 147–48; Klink, pp. 211, 218; Mehner, p. 96; Stadler, p. 54.
11. Stadler, p. 55.
12. Ibid., pp. 51–52, 55.
13. Stadler, p. 51; Koltunov, p. 149.
14. Mehner, p. 96; Klink, p. 218.
15. Stadler, p. 51; Koltunov, p. 149.
16. Koltunov, pp. 148–49; Klink, pp. 211, 218; Stadler, pp. 49, 52, 55, 57.
17. Stadler, p. 64.
18. Koltunov, p. 151; Stadler, p. 49.

19. Klink, p. 215.
20. Koltunov, p. 144.
21. Ibid., p. 145.
22. Ibid.
23. Koltunov, p. 150; Klink, p. 215.
24. Mehner, p. 96.
25. Klink, p. 215.
26. Koltunov, p. 152.
27. Klink, p. 227; Stadler, p. 60.
28. Koltunov, p. 155.
29. Klink, pp. 227–28, 231; Koltunov, pp. 154–55.
30. Klink, pp. 219–22.
31. Koltunov, pp. 152, 154.
32. Stadler, pp. 57–60; Klink, p. 220.
33. Stadler, pp. 57, 60.
34. Koltunov, p. 154.
35. Ibid., pp. 152–53.
36. Klink, p. 220.
37. Stadler, p. 59; Klink, p. 230; Koltunov, p. 154.
38. Stadler, p. 59; Klink, pp. 220–21, 231.
39. Klink, p. 221.
40. Stadler, pp. 61–62.
41. Ibid., p. 73.
42. Ibid., p. 74.
43. Koltunov, p. 156.
44. Koltunov, p. 156; Klink, p. 221; Stadler, pp. 57, 60–61, 73.
45. Stadler, pp. 70, 73–74; Koltunov, p. 157.
46. Klink, p. 222; Stadler, p. 74.
47. Klink, pp. 222, 231; Koltunov, p. 157.
48. Stadler, p. 61.
49. Klink, pp. 223, 231; Stadler, p. 61.
50. Stadler, p. 66.
51. Koltunov, p. 156; Klink, p. 222; Stadler, p. 69.
52. Stadler, pp. 65–68.
53. Ibid., p. 69.
54. Ibid., pp. 59, 69.
55. Stadler, pp. 65–66; Klink, pp. 222, 231; Koltunov, p. 157.
56. Stadler, p. 69.
57. Ibid., pp. 57–58.
58. Ibid., p. 66.
59. Ibid., pp. 66–68.
60. Ibid., pp. 65, 67, 73, 81.
61. Mehner, p. 102.
62. Stadler, p. 73.
63. Koltunov, pp. 159–60.
64. Klink, pp. 228, 231; Mehner, p. 102.
65. Klink, pp. 228, 229.
66. Koltunov, p. 158.
67. Klink, p. 232.

68. Koltunov, pp. 156, 158.

CHAPTER 10
1. Silvester Stadler, *Die Offensive Gegen Kursk* (Osnabruck: Munion, 1980), p. 69.
2. Ibid., p. 65.
3. Ibid., pp. 69, 65, 71.
4. Ibid., pp. 71, 65.
5. Ernest Klink, *Das Gesetz des Handelns die Operation "Zitadelle," 1943* (Stuttgart: Deutsche Verlags-Anstalt, 1966), pp. 218–19.
6. Ibid., p. 224; Kurt Mehner, ed., *Die Geheimentages Berichte der Deutschen Wermachfuhrung im Zweiten Weltkrieg, 1939–1945*, Vol. 7 (Osnabruck: Biblio Verlag, 1988), p. 106.
7. Mehner, p. 106; G. A. Koltunov, *Kurskaia Bitva* (Moscow: Voenizdat, 1970), p. 160.
8. Klink, p. 224.
9. Stadler, pp. 75, 79–82; Klink, pp. 224, 231.
10. Stadler, p. 82; Klink, p. 224.
11. Stadler, p. 82.
12. Mehner, p. 106; Stadler, pp. 79, 82; Klink, pp. 224–25.
13. Stadler, p. 67.
14. Klink, p. 223.
15. Koltunov, pp. 158–59; Klink, pp. 224, 232.
16. Stadler, p. 70.
17. Koltunov, pp. 159–60.
18. Ibid., pp. 158–59.
19. Klink, pp. 224, 232.
20. Stadler, p. 91.
21. Mehner, p. 106; Koltunov, p. 160.
22. Klink, pp. 229–31.
23. Ibid., p. 232.
24. Koltunov, p. 162; Klink, pp. 232–33.
25. Koltunov, p. 162; Klink p. 233.
26. Klink, p. 225.
27. Klink, p. 225; Stadler, p. 75; Koltunov, p. 163.
28. Klink, p. 225; Stadler, p. 75.
29. Mehner, p. 110; Stadler, p. 84.
30. Stadler, pp. 84, 87, 89; Mehner, p. 110; Koltunov, p. 164.
31. Stadler, pp. 84, 87, 89; Klink, p. 233.
32. Koltunov, p. 164.
33. Klink, p. 229.
34. Stadler, pp. 84, 89–90; Klink, p. 226; Mehner, p. 110.
35. Stadler, pp. 88, 90.
36. Stadler, pp. 89–90; Koltunov, p. 164.
37. Stadler, p. 99.
38. Ibid., pp. 86, 90.
39. Stadler, p. 86; Klink, p. 225.
40. Stadler, pp. 89, 86, 90; Klink p. 233.
41. Mehner, p. 110; Klink, p. 230.
42. Mehner, p. 110; Klink, p. 230.
43. Klink, p. 235.

44. Ibid., pp. 235–36.
45. Ibid., pp. 226, 234.
46. Ibid., pp. 227, 234.
47. Stadler, pp. 89, 93.
48. Ibid., pp. 89, 95.
49. Ibid., pp. 93–95, 97.
50. Koltunov, p. 165.
51. Stadler, pp. 93, 95; Koltunov, p. 165.
52. Koltunov, p. 165.
53. Stadler, p. 95; Mehner, p. 114.
54. Stadler, pp. 94–95, 97; Mehner, p. 114.
55. Stadler, pp. 93, 106.
56. Klink, pp. 234, 237.
57. Klink, p. 237; Mehner, p. 114.
58. Klink, p. 237; Mehner, p. 114.
59. Klink, p. 237; Mehner, p. 114.
60. Klink, pp. 234, 237.
61. Ibid., p. 243.
62. Stadler, p. 94; Klink, pp. 236, 234; Mehner, p. 114.
63. Stadler, pp. 94, 97; Klink, p. 236; Koltunov, p. 165.
64. Stadler, p. 97; Klink, p. 236.
65. Klink, p. 237.
66. Ibid., p. 243.
67. Ibid.
68. Koltunov, p. 167; Ivan Parotkin, ed., *The Battle of Kursk* (Moscow: Progress Publishers, 1974), p. 104; Stadler, p. 34; Burkhart Mueller-Hillebrand, *Das Heer. 1933–1945* vol. III (Frankfurt am Main: E. S. Mittler & Sohn, 1959–1969), p. 221.
69. Koltunov, p. 166.
70. Parotkin, p. 74; Koltunov, pp. 166–67.
71. Koltunov, p. 167.
72. Stadler, p. 105.
73. Ibid., pp. 105, 114.
74. Ibid., p. 107.
75. Klink, p. 243; Koltunov, p. 168; Parotkin, pp. 103–04.
76. Koltunov, p. 169.
77. Koltunov, p. 169; Stadler, pp. 100, 102.
78. Stadler, p. 100; Klink, p. 233; Koltunov, p. 172.
79. Koltunov, pp. 170, 172; Stadler, p. 107.
80. Koltunov, p. 164; Klink, pp. 238–39.
81. Koltunov, pp. 171–72.
82. Koltunov, p. 172; Mehner, p. 118.
83. Klink, p. 239; Koltunov, pp. 164, 171.
84. Klink, pp. 233, 238.
85. Mehner, p. 118; Koltunov, p. 171: Klink, pp. 243–44.
86. Klink, p. 243; Koltunov, pp. 167, 171, 174.
87. Klink, p. 243; Koltunov, p. 170.
88. Klink, p. 244.
89. Ibid., pp. 239, 243–44.
90. Klink, p. 239; Koltunov, p. 173.

91. Stadler, p. 104.
92. Koltunov, p. 176.
93. Mehner, p. 118; Klink, pp. 233, 238; Parotkin, pp. 74, 104, 172; Stadler, p. 115.

CHAPTER 11
1. Burkhart Mueller-Hillebrand, *Das Heer, 1933–1945* vol. III (Frankfurt am Main E. S. Mittler & Sohn, 1959–1969), p. 274.
2. Ernst Klink, *Das Gesetz des Handelns die Operation "Zitadelle," 1943* (Stuttgart Deutsche Verlags-Anstalt, 1966), p. 240.
3. Silvester Stadler, *Die Offensive Gegen Kursk*(Osnabruck: Munion, 1980), p. 109.
4. Klink, pp. 240–41.
5. Ibid., p. 240.
6. Ibid., p. 241.
7. Klink, p. 240; Stadler, p. 109.
8. Stadler, pp. 109, 116.
9. Stadler, pp. 109–10, 116; Klink, pp. 239–40.
10. Stadler, p. 113; Kurt Mehner, ed., *Die Geheimentages Berichte der Deutschen Wermacht-fuhrung im Zweiten Weltkrieg, 1939–1945* vol. 7 (Osnabruck: Biblio Verlag. 1988), p. 122.
11. Stadler, p. 124.
12. Stadler, p. 118; Mehner, p. 126.
13. Stadler, pp. 118, 121, 125.
14. Mehner, p. 126.
15. Stadler, pp. 118–19; Mehner, p. 126.
16. Stadler, p. 131.
17. Mehner, p. 126; Stadler, pp. 119, 125.
18. Mehner, p. 126.
19. Ibid.
20. Stadler, p. 126; Mehner, p. 130.
21. Stadler, p. 126; Mehner, p. 130.
22. Stadler, pp. 126, 128–29; Mehner, p. 130.
23. Stadler, pp. 126, 139.
24. Mehner, p. 130; Stadler, p. 126.
25. Stadler, pp. 132–33.
26. Ibid., p. 125.
27. Ibid., p. 148.
28. Ibid., p. 154.
29. Ibid., p. 127.
30. Ibid., pp. 129, 139.
31. Ibid., p. 165.

CHAPTER 12
1. Ernst Klink, *Das Gesetz des Handelns die Operation "Zitadelle," 1943* (Stuttgart: Deutsche Verlags-Anstalt, 1966), p. 246.
2. Klink, p. 246; G. A. Koltunov, *Kurskaia Bitva* (Moscow: Voenizdat, 1970), p. 106; Ivan Parotkin, ed., *The Battle of Kursk* (Moscow: Progress Publishers, 1974), p. 44.
3. Klink, pp. 246, 247.
4. Ibid., p. 247.
5. Kurt Mehner, ed., *Die Geheimentages Berichte der Deutschen Wermachtfuhrung im Zweiten Weltkrieg, 1939–1945.* vol. 7 (Osnabruck: Biblio Verlag, 1988), p. 93; Koltunov, pp. 107–9, 112.

6. Klink, p. 247.
7. Mehner, p. 93; Koltunov, p. 109; Klink, p. 247.
8. Mehner, p. 93; Klink, pp. 246–47.
9. Mehner, p. 94; Koltunov, p. 110.
10. Klink, pp. 255, 256; Koltunov, p. 114.
11. Koltunov, pp. 115–16.
12. Klink, p. 248.
13. Klink, pp. 247–48; Mehner, pp. 96–97.
14. Klink, p. 247.
15. Klink, pp. 247–48; Mehner, p. 97.
16. Klink, p. 256.
17. Mehner, p. 97; Koltunov, pp. 116–21; Klink, pp. 247–48.
18. Klink, p. 247.
19. Mehner, p. 97.
20. Klink, p. 255.
21. Ibid., pp. 248–50.
22. Mehner, p. 99; Klink, pp. 248, 251.
23. Klink, p. 249.
24. Koltunov, pp. 121, 124–25; Mehner, p. 99; Klink, pp. 250–51, 256.
25. Mehner, p. 99; Koltunov, pp. 122–23; Klink, pp. 248, 250, 256.
26. Klink, p. 251; Mehner, p. 99.
27. Klink, pp. 251, 256.
28. Ibid., p. 257.
29. Ibid., p. 252.
30. Mehner, p. 103; Klink, pp. 252–53.
31. Klink, p. 252.
32. Mehner, p. 103; Koltunov, pp. 126–27; Klink, pp. 252–54, 257.
33. Mehner, p. 103; Koltunov, p. 129.
34. Mehner, p. 103; Klink, pp. 251–53.
35. Klink, p. 258.
36. Ibid., p. 259.
37. Ibid., p. 257.
38. Ibid., p. 253.
39. Ibid.
40. Klink, p. 253; Mehner, p. 107.
41. Klink, p. 259.
42. Mehner, pp. 111, 115.
43. Klink, p. 259; Mehner, p. 115.
44. Klink, p. 259; Mehner, p. 111.
45. Klink, p. 260; Mehner, pp. 111, 115.
46. Klink, pp. 259–60; Mehner, p. 111.
47. Klink, p. 260.
48. Ibid., p. 260.
49. Ibid., p. 262.
50. Ibid., p. 263.

CHAPTER 13
1. Erich von Manstein, *Velorene Seige* (Bonn: Athenaum-Verlag, 1958), pp. 500–501.
2. Ibid., pp. 501–502.

Index

Adolf Hitler Division, 58
Antiaircraft Divisions, Soviet
   5th, 71
   8th, 73
   10th, 68
   12th, 66
   16th, 66
   23rd, 75
   26th, 70
Antiaircraft Militia, 38–39
Antiaircraft Regiments, Soviet
   82nd, 71
   1695th, 74
Antitank Battalions, Soviet
   747th, 77
   752nd, 78
Army Detachment Hoth, 56
Army Detachment Kempf, 12, 50, 59
Artillery Brigades, Soviet
   27th, 69
   33rd, 69
   68th, 68
Artillery Divisions, Soviet
   5th, 64
   12th, 64
Assault Gun Battalion, German, 202nd, 56

Casablanca Conference, xiii
Caucasus, 17
Corps Raus, 60

Das Reich Division, 58
Death Head Division, 58–59
Destroyer Division, Soviet, 2nd, 66
Don Front, moving Soviet forces from, 8–9

11th Army, 79

fanal, x
1st Guards Army, 13
1st Panzer Army, 14
1st Tank Army, divisions of, 72–73
4th Panzer Army, 15, 50, 61
   divisions of, 56–59
4th Tank Corps, 4
5th Guards Army, divisions of, 76
5th Guards Tank Army, xi
5th Shock Army, 15
5th Tank Army, 15
40th Army
   divisions of, 71–72
   rifle divisions of, 5–6
40th Tank Army, 4
42nd Corps, divisions of, 60
47th Army, 76
48th Army, divisions of, 65–66
52nd Army, 79
53rd Army, divisions of, 75–76

Gehlen, Reinhard, viii, xiii
German Armies
   Army Detachment Kempf, 12, 50, 59
   18th Panzer Division, 51
   87th Infantry Regiment, 50
   1st Panzer Army, 14
   4th Panzer Army, 15, 50, 56–59, 61
   15th SS Panzer Grenadier, 45–46
   41st Panzer Corps, 51–52
   42nd Corps, 60
   46th Panzer Corps, 53
   47th Panzer Corps, 52–53
   48th Panzer Corps, 57–58
   interpretation of battle, 189–90
   9th Army, 50, 54–55
   9th SS Panzer Grenadier, 45
   90th SS Panzer Grenadier, 45–46
   134th Infantry Division, 46–47

209

212

losses, 119–20, 130, 137, 141, 149, 152,
153, 156, 157–58, 163, 166, 167,
168, 169, 170, 177, 178, 180
most serious Soviet losses incurred
during, 188
overview of, x–xv
primary reasons for, xv
Prokorovka battle, xii, 158–60
reasons Germans lost, 186–88
Rzhev, 6
significance of, 185
Southwest Front, 15
Soviet strategy, 1–2
Voronezh Front, 4–6, 10–11
see also Kursk salient, north shoulder
of; Kursk salient, south shoulder of
Kursk salient, 112–13
Kursk salient, north shoulder of
July 5th activity in, 172–74
July 6th activity in, 174–76
July 7th activity in, 176–78
July 8th activity in, 179–81
July 9th activity in, 181–82
July 10th activity in, 182–83
July 11th activity in, 183
July 12th activity in, 183
Kursk salient, south shoulder of, 164–71
July 12th activity in, 164–65
July 13th activity in, 165–66
July 14th activity in, 166–67
July 15th activity in, 167–69

Lost Victories (Manstein), xi

Mainstein's Miracle, 17
Manstein, Erich von, xi, xiii
Mechanized Battalion, Soviet, 38th, 77
Mechanized Brigade, Soviet, 58th, 74, 80
Mechanized Corps, Soviet
1st, 78
2nd, 78–79
3rd, 73
5th, 80
7th, 80
8th, 80
9th, 80
Model, Walther, 176
Mortar Brigade, Soviet, 21st, 68

Mortar Regiments, Soviet
264th, 78
271st, 77
273rd, 74
290th, 71
479th, 66
480th, 75
Motorcycle Battalions, Soviet
51st, 67
75th, 77
76th, 78
83rd, 74

9th Army, 50
divisions of, 54–55
23rd Corps, 50, 51

129th Brigade, 25
Operation Citadel, xi

Panzer Battalion, German, 52nd, 58
Panzer Brigade, German, 10th, 58
Panzer Corps, German
3rd, 59–60
41st, 51–52, 54–55
46th, 53–55
47th, 52–53
48th, divisions of, 57–58
Panzer Divisions, German
2nd, 52–53
3rd, 58
4th, 54
6th, 59
7th, 59
9th, 52
11th, 57–58
12th, 54
18th, 51
19th, 59
20th, 52
106th, 60
320th, 60
Panzer Genadier Division, German,
10th, 54
Parachute Division, German, 2nd, 45
Paulus, Friedrich von, 1
Poltava, 16
Prokorovka, major battle at, xii, 158–60

Stackpole Military History Series

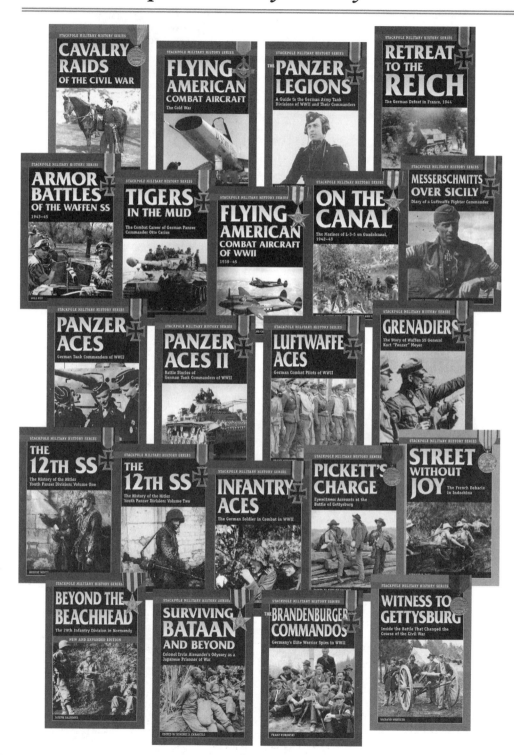

Real battles. Real soldiers. Real stories.

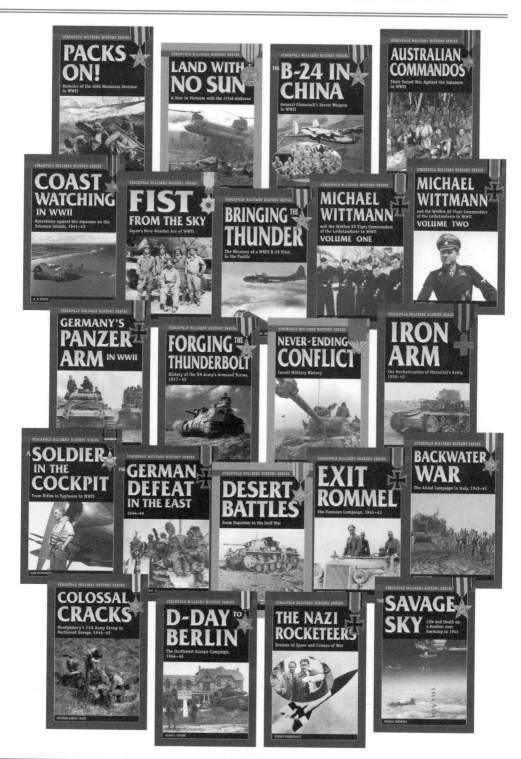

Stackpole Military History Series

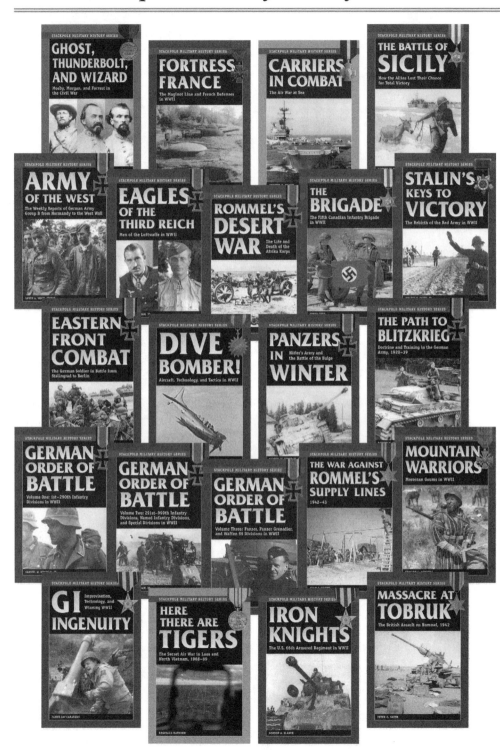

Real battles. Real soldiers. Real stories.

Stackpole Military History Series

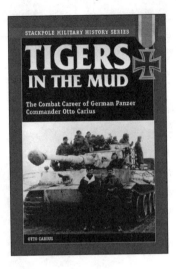

TIGERS IN THE MUD
THE COMBAT CAREER OF GERMAN PANZER COMMANDER OTTO CARIUS

Otto Carius,
translated by Robert J. Edwards

World War II began with a metallic roar as the
German Blitzkrieg raced across Europe, spearheaded
by the most dreadful weapon of the twentieth century:
the Panzer. Tank commander Otto Carius thrusts the
reader into the thick of battle, replete with the
blood, smoke, mud, and gunpowder so common
to the elite German fighting units.

$19.95 • Paperback • 6 x 9 • 368 pages
51 photos • 48 illustrations • 3 maps

Stackpole Military History Series

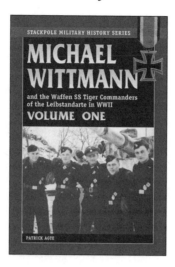

MICHAEL WITTMANN AND THE WAFFEN SS TIGER COMMANDERS OF THE LEIBSTANDARTE IN WORLD WAR II
VOLUME ONE
Patrick Agte

By far the most famous tank commander on any side in
World War II, German Tiger ace Michael Wittmann destroyed 138
enemy tanks and 132 anti-tank guns in a career that embodies the
panzer legend: meticulous in planning, lethal in execution, and
always cool under fire. Most of those kills came in the snow and mud
of the Eastern Front, where Wittmann and the Leibstandarte's
armored company spent more than a year in 1943–44 battling the
Soviets at places like Kharkov, Kursk, and the Cherkassy Pocket.

$19.95 • Paperback • 6 x 9 • 432 pages • 383 photos • 19 maps • 10 charts

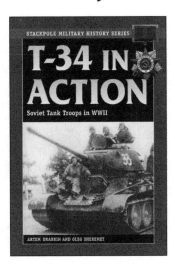

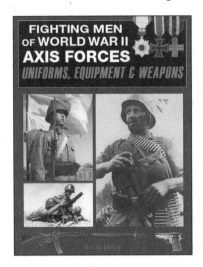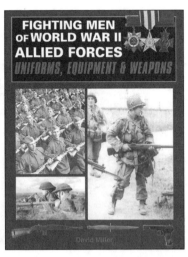